Anonymous

The Proceedings of the Linnean Society of New South Wales

Vol. 3

Anonymous

The Proceedings of the Linnean Society of New South Wales
Vol. 3

ISBN/EAN: 9783337331535

Printed in Europe, USA, Canada, Australia, Japan

Cover: Foto ©Suzi / pixelio.de

More available books at **www.hansebooks.com**

THE PROCEEDINGS

OF THE

LINNEAN SOCIETY

OF

NEW SOUTH WALES

FOR THE YEAR

1912

Vol. XXXVII.

PLATES.

SYDNEY:
PRINTED AND PUBLISHED FOR THE SOCIETY
BY
W. A. PEPPERDAY & CO., 119A PITT STREET
AND
SOLD BY THE SOCIETY

1913.

W. A. PEPPERDAY AND CO.,
GENERAL PRINTERS,
119a PITT STREET, SYDNEY.

CONTENTS OF PROCEEDINGS, 1912.

PART I. (No. 145).

(Issued August 26th, 1912.)

	PAGES
Presidential Address delivered at the Thirty-seventh Annual General Meeting, March 27th, 1912, by W. W. FROGGATT, F.L.S.	1-43
The Constitution of the Gastropod Protoconch: its value as a Taxonomic Feature, and the Significance of some of its Forms. By H. LEIGHTON KESTEVEN, D.Sc., Lecturer in Physiology and Biochemistry, Technical College, Sydney. (*Communicated by Dr. H. G. Chapman.*) (Plate i.)	49-82
Revision of the Amycterides. Part ii. *Talaurinus*. By EUSTACE W. FERGUSON, M.B., Ch.M. (Plates ii.-iii.)	83-135
The Chemistry of *Doryphora sassafras*. By JAMES M. PETRIE, D.Sc., F.I.C., Linnean Macleay Fellow of the Society in Biochemistry	139-156
Supplementary List of the Marine Algæ of Australia. By A. H. S. LUCAS, M.A., B.Sc.	157-171
On a Collection of Parasitic Hymenoptera (chiefly bred), made by Mr. Walter W. Froggatt, F.L.S., in New South Wales, with Descriptions of new Genera and Species. By P. CAMERON. (*Communicated by W. W. Froggatt*)	172-216
Descriptions of two new Species of *Ichneumonidæ* from the Island of Aru. By P. CAMERON. (*Communicated by W. W. Froggatt*)	217-219
Hydrocyanic Acid in Plants. Part i. Its Distribution in the Australian Flora. By JAMES M. PETRIE, D.Sc., F.I.C., Linnean Macleay Fellow of the Society in Biochemistry	220-234
Hon. Treasurer's Financial Statement, Balance Sheet, etc.	43-47
Elections and Announcements	136
Notes and Exhibits	48, 136

PART II. (No. 142).

(Issued 13th December, 1912).

Contributions to our Knowledge of Soil-Fertility. No. v., The Action of Fat-Solvents upon Sewage-sick Soils. By R. GREIG-SMITH, D.Sc., Macleay Bacteriologist to the Society	238-243
Notes from the Botanic Gardens, Sydney. No. 17. By J. H. MAIDEN and E. BETCHE	244-252

CONTENTS.

PART II. *(Continued).*

	PAGES
On some Land-Shells collected in Queensland by SIDNEY W. JACKSON. By C. HEDLEY, F.L.S. (Plates iv.-x.)	253-270
The *Polyplacophora* of Lord Howe and Norfolk Islands. By C. HEDLEY and A. F. BASSET HULL. (Plates xi.-xiii.)	271-281
On some Trematode Parasites of Australian Frogs. By S. J. JOHNSTON, B.A., D.Sc., Demonstrator in Biology, University of Sydney. (Plates xiv.-xliii., and Key Plates)	285-362
The Mosses of the Yarrangobilly Caves District, N.S.W. By DR. V. F. BROTHERUS and REV. W. WALTER WATTS. (Communicated by J. H. Maiden)	363-382
The Sphagna of Australia and Tasmania. By REV. W. W. WATTS. (Communicated by J. H. Maiden)	383-389
Elections and Announcements	235, 282, 390
Notes and Exhibits	235-237, 283-284, 390-394

PART III. (No. 143).

(Issued 19th March, 1913).

The Ferns of Lord Howe Island. By the Rev. W. WALTER WATTS	395-403
On some new and rare Australian *Agrionidæ* [NEUROPTERA: Odonata]. By R. J. TILLYARD, M.A., F.E.S. (Plates xliv.-xlix.)	404-479
Descriptions of some new Species of Coleoptera. By H. J. CARTER, B.A., F.E.S. (Plates l.-li.)	480-491
Notes on the Genus *Stigmodera*, with Descriptions of eleven new Species, and of other *Buprestidæ* [COLEOPTERA]. By H. J. CARTER, B.A., F.E.S. (Plate lii.)	497-511
Plankton of the Sydney Water-Supply. By G. I. PLAYFAIR. (Plates liii.-lvii.)	512-552
A Description and Figures of three Specimens of *Molacanthus* from the Central Pacific Ocean. By ALLAN R. McCULLOCH, Zoologist, Australian Museum. (Plates lviii.-lix.)	553-555
Elections and Announcements	492, 556
Notes and Exhibits	492-496, 556-558

PART IV. (No. 144).

(Issued 22nd July, 1913).

	PAGES
The Eucalypts of Parramatta, with Description of a new Species. By CUTHBERT HALL, M.D., Ch.M. (Plates lx.-lxi.)	561-571
On some Australian *Anisoptera*, with Descriptions of new Species. By R. J. TILLYARD, M.A., F.E.S. (Plate lxii.)	572-584
On two unrecorded Myrtaceous Plants from New South Wales. By R. T. BAKER, F.L.S. (Plates lxiii.-lxiv.)	585-589
Australian Bees. i. A new *Crocisa*, with a List of the Australian Species of the Genus. By T. D. A. COCKERELL.	594-595
A small Collection of Bees from Tasmania. By T. D. A. COCKERELL	596-599
Synonymical Notes on some recently described Australian *Cicadidæ*. By W. L. DISTANT	600-601
Revision of the Australian *Curculionidæ* belonging to the Subfamily *Cryptorhynchides*. Part xi. By ARTHUR M. LEA, F.E.S.	602-616
Notes on the Native Flora of New South Wales. Supplementary Lists to Part viii., Camden to Burragorang and Mount Werong. By R. H. CAMBAGE, F.L.S. (Plate lxv.)	617-621
Notes on the Native Flora of New South Wales. Part ix., Barraba to Nandewar Mountains and Boggabri. By R. H. CAMBAGE, F.L.S. (Plates lxvi.-lxvii.)	622-654
Contributions to our Knowledge of Soil-Fertility. vi. The Inactivity of Soil-Protozoa. By R. GREIG-SMITH, D.Sc., Macleay Bacteriologist to the Society	655-672
A new Endoparasitic Copepod: Morphology and Development. By H. LEIGHTON KESTEVEN, D.Sc., Lecturer in Physiology, Technical College, Sydney. (Plates lxviii.-lxx.)	673-688
The Fibrovascular System of the Quince Fruit compared with that of the Apple and Pear. By D. MCALPINE, Corresponding Member. (Plates lxxi.-lxxii.)	689-697
Notes on Australian *Lycænidæ*. Part v. By G. A. WATERHOUSE, B.Sc., B.E., F.E.S.	698-702
Note on the Relation of the Devonian and Carboniferous Formations west of Tamworth, N.S.W. By L. A. COTTON, B.A., B.Sc., Assistant Lecturer and Demonstrator in Geology, University of Sydney, and A. B. WALKOM, B.Sc., Linnean Macleay Fellow of the Society in Geology	703-708

PART IV. *(Continued).*

	PAGES
A new Species of *Eriochloa* from the Hawkesbury River. By A. A. HAMILTON	709-711
Description and Life-history of a new Species of *Nannophlebia*. By R. J. TILLYARD, M.A., F.E.S. (Plate lxxiv.)	712-726
On some Trematode Parasites of Marsupials and of a Monotreme. By S. J. JOHNSTON, B.A., D.Sc., Demonstrator in Biology, University of Sydney. (Plates lxxv.-lxxvii.)	727-740
Elections and Announcements	590, 652
Notes and Exhibits	559-560, 590-593, 652-654
Special Meetings	741, 742
List of Donations and Exchanges	743-766
Title-page	i.
Contents	iii.
List of Plates	vii.
Corrigenda	vi.
List of new Generic Names	vi.
Index	i.-xl.

CORRIGENDA.

Page 67, line 20—for *Cerithiopsis cacuminatus*, read *Cerithiopsis acuminatus*.

Page 90, line 16—for *Sclerorrhinella geniculatus*, read *Sclerorrhinella geniculata*.

Page 99, line 24—for *Psaldirua*, read *Psalidura*.

Page 123, line 33—for *Talaurinus sculpularis*, read *Talaurinus scapularis*.

Page 152, line 6—for *Laurelia Novæ-Zealandeæ*, read *Laurelia Novæ-Zealandiæ*.

Page 232, line 23—for *Heliocharis*, read *Heleocharis*.

Page 353, line 35—for *Diplodiscus temporatus*, read *Diplodiscus temperatus*.

Page 449, line 29—for *Prosagrion*[nomen nudum, R.J.T.], read *Ischnura pruinescens* Tillyard.

Page 453, lines 6 and 13—for *Prosagrion pruinescens*, read *Ischnura pruinescens*.

Page 497, line 3—for BURRESTIDÆ, read BUPRESTIDÆ.

Page 534, after line 28, a sentence has been inadvertently omitted. It should read—With the growth of the frustule, this columella gradually broadens, and divides longitudinally into two parts.

Page 631, line 22—for *Lomaria capense*, read *Lomaria capensis*.

LIST OF PLATES

PROCEEDINGS, 1912.

Plate I.—*Cymatium* spp.
Plate II.—*Talaurinus* spp.; *Peritalaurinus* sp.; *Sclerorrhinella* sp.
Plate III.—*Talaurinus* spp.
Plates IV.-X.—Queensland Land-Shells.
Plates XI.-XIII.—*Polyplacophora* of Lord Howe and Norfolk Islands.
Plates XIV.-XLIII. (with Key-Plates XXII.-XLIII.)—Trematodes of Australian Frogs.
Plates XLIV.-XLIX.—Australian *Agrionidæ*.
Plates L.-LI.—*Scelocantha gigas*, n.sp.; and *Tillyardia mirabilis*, n.sp.
Plate LII.—*Stigmodera* spp.; and *Neocuris ornata*, n.sp.
Plates LIII.-LVII.—Plankton of the Sydney Water-Supply.
Plates LVIII.-LIX.—*Molacanthus* sp.
Plate LX.—*Eucalyptus Parramattensis*, n.sp.
Plate LXI.—Map of Parramatta District, showing Distribution of the Eucalypts.
Plate LXII.—Australian *Anisoptera*.
Plate LXIII.—*Eucalyptus Laseroni*, n.sp.
Plate LXIV.—*Melaleuca Irbyiana*, n.sp.
Plate LXV.—*Quintinia Sieberi* growing in conjunction with *Alsophila australis*.
Plate LXVI.—Taugúlda or Barber's Pinnacle, Boggabri, N.S.W.
Plate LXVII.—Groups of *Melaleuca bracteata* F.v.M., and Permo-Carboniferous(?) sandstone cliffs, Maule's Creek, N.S.W.
Plates LXVIII.-LXX.—*Ubius hilli*, gen. et sp.n.: morphology and development.
Plates LXXI.-LXXIII.—Fibrovascular System of Quince, Apple, and Pear fruits.
Plate LXXIV.—*Nannophlebia risi*, n.sp., and *N. eludens*.
Plates LXXV.-LXXVII.—Trematode Parasites of Marsupials and of a Monotreme.

LIST OF NEW GENERIC NAMES PROPOSED IN THIS VOLUME (1912).

	Page		Page
Brachysaccus [Trematoda]	316	*Lisseurytoma* [Hymenoptera]	282
Cluthaira [Hymenoptera]	211	*Mehlisia* [Trematoda]	732
Cratodicatoma [Hymenoptera]	205	*Philogalleria* [Hymenoptera]	190
Dolichosaccus [Trematoda]	308	*Ubius* [Crustacea]	673

each forewing, measuring 5 × 2 mm. (Sydney; September), and 2 × 1 mm.(Sydney; October). (2) A gynandromorphous specimen of *Troides priamus pronomous*(C. York; February), in which the body and the right wings are female, and the left wings male and female. (3) A gynandromorphous specimen of *Papilio aegeus ormenus*(Darnley Island; June), in which the wings, both above and beneath, show irregular development of the male and female pattern. (4) *Euryeus cressida*(Kuranda; June), in which veins 5 and 7 of the left hindwing, instead of being $2\frac{1}{2}$ mm. apart, as in the right hindwing, approach one another and fuse for about 1 mm., and then separate. (5) Two abnormal neurations in *Belenois java teutonia*; a male(Sydney; December), in which, on both forewings, veins 9 and 11 join one another, and run together to the apex; and a female(Sydney; December), in which vein 11 of the forewings fails to reach vein 2, as is usual. (6) *Euplœa sylvester*, male(Cape York; April), veins 9 and 10 in the right forewing, instead of being independent, are fused together for the greater part of their length, and only separate just before reaching the costa : in the left forewing, these same veins arise independently, but, at about half their length, fuse for about 2 mm. (7) *Junonia vellida* (Lord Howe Island; February), in which, though the right side is normal, the cell of the left forewing is closed by a stout vein, and beyond this a second smaller closed cell has been formed.

Mr. Fred Turner exhibited a specimen of *Glyceria fordeana* F.v.M., collected near Blacktown, but the circumstance was regarded as quite accidental, the seed no doubt having been brought from the western country, in railway trucks that conveyed sheep to the Riverstone meat-works. This western grass has been found by Mr. Turner near Lake Urana, but it does not seem to grow naturally nearer the coast. It is fairly common on Pevensey Station, west of Hay, on the Lower Murrumbidgee, also on the Lachlan, and common on land liable to inundation in the Darling River country. Mrs. H. Forde discovered this grass on the Lower Darling in 1865, and Baron von Mueller graciously named the species after that estimable lady who, under very great difficulties, executed beautiful coloured drawings of some of the typical plants of that region. Mr. Turner figured and described *Glyceria fordeana* in the Government "Agricultural Gazette," Vol.iv., p.413.

Mr. Froggatt exhibited a number of dipterous larvæ taken from the windpipes of kangaroos. Mr. Theo. R. Broughton, of Moramana, Walgett, N.S.W., who forwarded the specimens, reports that nearly every kangaroo killed, and examined by him, in the Walgett district during the last two months, was infested with the larvæ. Though very different from the larvæ of the sheep nasal fly(*Oestrus ovis*), they evidently represent a species of the same genus. Efforts are now being made to breed out and determine the fly.

THE EUCALYPTS OF PARRAMATTA, WITH DESCRIPTION OF A NEW SPECIES.

By Cuthbert Hall, M.D., Ch.M.

(Plates lx.-lxi.)

In no genus of plants does the distribution of the species appear to depend more on physical factors than is the case with the Eucalypts. The natural barrier of the dry, hot, barren region of Central Australia divides the genus into two main groups, the Eastern and Western, very few species being common to both; while the Main Dividing Range breaks up the Eastern group into three subgroups, the coastal, the highland, and the inland. Those that we are concerned with, belong to the coastal, though several of them are also found on the highlands and inland.

The Parramatta District embraces an area 14 × 18 miles, and in this no less than twenty-four Eucalypts occur, and possibly there may be an odd tree or two of several other species, which are to be found in places just outside this area. But these twenty-four species are not regularly and evenly scattered around, but follow definite lines of distribution, depending mainly on soil-formation, but also other physical factors, such as prevailing winds, elevation, humidity of atmosphere, drainage, proximity to a stream, and distance from the sea-coast. Certain species are found over the whole area, notably *E. eugenioides* and *E. resinifera*, while others are strictly localised. The seeds of these must be constantly being carried on to adjacent localities, yet they do not even seem to germinate, or, if seedlings spring up, they perish at an early age, or are crowded out by other species. For instance, I have never found *E. longifolia* growing in the northeastern quadrant of this area, yet it is very common on the deep clay of the southern side. Again, it is very common to find certain species, which are not at all closely related botanically, to be constantly associated with one another. Thus *E. hemiphloia*, *E. crebra*, and *E. tereticornis* very commonly occur together, as also do *E. saligna*, *E. punctata*, *E. acmenioides*, *E. paniculata*, and *E. pilularis*. In addition, *E. corymbosa* and *E. hæmastoma* are generally met in company. The physical conditions suiting one member of the group, suit the others.

The Parramatta District may be briefly described as a huge natural amphitheatre, with the town lying rather low in the centre, at a level of 50 to 100 feet above the sea; and the Parramatta River running west to east, dividing it into a northern and southern half. The latter is covered by a deep, heavy Wianamatta clay-shale formation, much of it rather low-lying and fairly level, but gradually rising to a height of about 150 feet. This country has a fair rainfall, but the soil is not very fertile, in places being almost barren, though, with careful cultivation, grapes and peaches grow well. It is also suited to rose-growing, but citrus fruits do badly. To the west of the town, we still have the Wianamatta clay, but the atmosphere is much drier, the rainfall less, it gets less of the sea-breezes, and is exposed to the hot dry westerlies in summer, and to very severe frosts in winter. On the northern side, the land rises to a much greater height, 500-550 feet at Galston, and is mainly composed of Hawkesbury sandstone or a thin stratum of Wianamatta clay-shale overlying this, while deep gullies erode it, and give free drainage. This part is the home of citrus fruit, the growing of which has always been the main Parramatta industry. Through the district are also a number of volcanic dykes and necks, the best known of which are those at Dundas and Prospect. The soil overlying these is richer in quality, but is not deep enough nor extensive enough to have any influence on the character of the flora.

Let us now consider, in detail, the various Eucalypts and their distribution. In the rather flat, deep-clay country around Rookwood, Granville, and Auburn, in the south-eastern quadrant, where there is much ironstone-gravel in the clay, we mostly find *E. siderophloia*(Broad-leaved Ironbark), *E. longifolia*(Woollybutt), and *E. resinifera*(Red Mahogany); while, on the higher ground, one meets a good proportion of *E. tereticornis* (Red Gum), *E. eugenioides*(White Stringybark), and *E. hemiphloia*(Yellow Box).

The most shapely of the above Eucalypts will almost invariably be found to be *E. resinifera*. Growing on the deep clay, this tree is of slower growth, and good spreading habit; and, with its fairly broad dark green leaves, it throws a most agreeable shade. As it is very hardy, and will grow in almost any soil, clayey and sandy alike, it is a pity it is not more extensively planted for ornamental purposes and as a breakwind. The timber is also of value commercially. Near Rookwood, a few *E. hæmastoma*(Scribbly Gum) may be seen on poor clay soil, which probably is not very deep. As one proceeds westwards along the deep clay-formation, the proportion of *E. tereticornis* and *E. hemiphloia* increases, and this is the well-known type-locality of the latter. More *E. eugenioides*, too, is seen, and around Fairfield, Westmead, and Merrylands, *E. crebra*(Narrow-leaved Ironbark) makes its appearance, the atmosphere here, on account of the absence of sea-breezes, being drier and hotter in summer. At Fairfield and Cabramatta, a few specimens of *E. paniculata* (White Ironbark) occur, while *E. siderophloia* is very plentiful. Dr. Woolls has recorded *E. sideroxylon*(Red-flowering Ironbark) as growing in this neighbourhood, but it seems to be very scarce, having been almost cut out by timber-getters. The most remarkable instance of localisation of a species is that of *E. maculata* (Spotted Gum). This, one comes on quite suddenly at Smithfield, extending in a westerly and southerly direction, where it forms the bulk of the forest vegetation, being associated mainly with *E. eugenioides* and *E. siderophloia*. Moreover, the soil on which it occurs, does not seem to differ materially from that around, being a stiff clay with much ironstone therein. Mr. R. H. Cambage has recorded *E. maculata* between Camden and Burragorang, and it also occurs at Gosford, Clyde River, and other parts of the coast of New South Wales, apparently in the same patchy way. There must be some particular conditions of environment that are always requisite for its growth, but exactly what these are, it is hard to say. Around Cabramatta, Woolls has recorded *E. Bosistoana*, and Mr. J. H. Maiden has recently described *E. Boormani* as occurring. With regard to *E. capitellata*(Brown Stringybark), which Woolls has recorded for Parramatta, I have failed to find it here. As it grows on the Hawkesbury sandstone around Sydney, and at Cronulla and National Park, he may have found it on some of the sandstone-formations hereabout, or he may have classified some of the larger-fruited forms of *E. eugenioides* as *E. capitellata*. Leaving Fairfield, and working in a north-westerly direction to Prospect, Blacktown, and Seven Hills, the three commonest Eucalypts are still *E. hemiphloia*, *E. tereticornis*, and *E. crebra*, with a proportion of *E. eugenioides*, *E. longifolia*, and *E. siderophloia*. At Blacktown, I found a tree of *E. Bosistoana* (Ribbon or Bastard Box) growing alongside a creek.

Coming now to the northern side of the Parramatta River, the home of the citrus fruit-growing industry of Australia, one cannot fail to be struck with the immediate change in the varieties of Eucalypts growing there. Instead of the deep clay of the southern part, we have outcrops of Hawkesbury sandstone, and, even where the clay exists, it is mostly a thin layer, through which the roots penetrate to the sandstone. Around Rydalmere and Dundas, where the sandstone is bare, we find mostly *E. resinifera*, *E. corymbosa* (Bloodwood), and *E. hæmastoma*. *E. pilularis* (Blackbutt) also grows to magnificent proportions, except on the tops of the ridges. Where the sandstone is overlaid by the clay-shale, we find the following species:— *E. pilularis*, *E. punctata* (Grey Gum), *E. acmenioides* (White Mahogany), *E. resinifera*, *E. paniculata* (White Ironbark), and *E. saligna* (Sydney Blue Gum). Throughout Ermington, Dundas, Eastwood, Pennant Hills, Carlingford, and Dural, these are the prevailing trees. Where the clay is a little deeper, *E. eugenioides* and *E. siderophloia* appear; and where it is deeper still, as along the Carlingford Road, *E. tereticornis* also is in evidence, but without its usual companion, *E. hemiphloia*. At North Rocks, on the sandstone ridge, the Sydney Peppermint, *E. piperita*, is frequent, while along the creek near the Rydalmere Asylum dairy, a clump of *E. robusta* (Swamp Mahogany) is growing. At Eastwood, Mr. Baker has recorded *E. umbra* (Bastard White Mahogany). On the highest hills about Dural and Galston, at an elevation of 400-600 feet, I have frequently come across *E. eximia* (Yellow Bloodwood). This is a Blue Mountain species, and I do not think it is generally known that it comes so close to the coast.

Finally, when we come to the north-western quadrant, around Baulkham Hills and Kellyville, the sandstone gives place to the deep clay-shale formation, and we have a corresponding change in the Eucalypts; and we find *E. hemiphloia, E. tereticornis, E. crebra*, with a lesser proportion of *E. eugenioides* and *E. siderophloia*.

I should like to add a few words on the flowering periods of the Eucalypts above considered. This is a subject which merits greater consideration than it has so far received. Many Eucalypts flower regularly at the same period every year, others bloom irregularly; and when rain follows a dry spell, they make fresh growth, which soon forms buds, which later on come into flower. Such is the case with *E. eugenioides*, different specimens of which may be seen in bloom over the greater part of the year, though the main body of bloom comes out in May. With other species again, if the season is dry and unfavourable, the flowering may be slight or missed altogether, or it may be a month or two late. Again, a profuse blossoming after a good season or after a rest, is usually followed by a scanty one the next season. *E. tereticornis* and *E. paniculata* are winter and spring bloomers, and flower regularly from June to October, coming in earlier in some years than others. *E. robusta* is very regular, and lasts from June to the end of July. *E. Bosistoana* comes in August, while *E. crebra* corresponds to *E. paniculata*, viz., June to October. The species which bloom in midsummer are *E. resinifera* (December), *E. siderophloia* (January), and *E. saligna, E. piperita, E. acmenioides*, and *E. pilularis* in January and February. In the autumn, *E. hæmastoma, E. punctata*, and *E. hemiphloia* flower in February and March, while *E. longifolia* and *E. corymbosa* come out in March and April. *E. globulus*, cultivated, flowers generally in June and July, and *E. citriodora*, cultivated, in June. The latter grows exceedingly well, better than about Sydney, though the frosts may cut it up when young.

Though the Eucalypts, what with one species and another, may be found in flower every month of the year, yet their near relatives, the Angophoras, all bloom in the summer about the same time. *A. lanceolata* leads off early in December, then come *A. intermedia* and *A. subvelutina* in the middle of that month, and lastly *A. cordifolia* early in January.

In considering the question of hybridisation between Eucalypts, full consideration should always be given to the time of the year at which they flower. Thus, crossing of *E. robusta*, which blooms in winter, with *E. hemiphloia*, which is out in summer, would be impossible, though there is a chance of such crossing occurring between *E. tereticornis* and *E. paniculata*, or *E. saligna* and *E. acmenioides*. But the mere fact of two species growing together and flowering at the same time, yet maintaining constant and specific characteristics over a great range, points to the conclusion that hybridisation is most unlikely or impossible between them. In fact, I think the law may be laid down, that natural hybridisation is unlikely to occur between two species growing freely together and flowering at the same time. The mere fact of these species keeping pure, favours this view. Experience with the Acacias bears out this. These, in the majority of instances, flower in the early spring, and mostly at the same time; yet the species keep distinct. The most reliable instances of hybridisation of Acacias, so far recorded, are those between *A. Baileyana* and *A. decurrens*, *A. dealbata* and *A. podalyriæfolia*, and *A. pycnantha* and *A. podalyriæfolia*, the parents in each case occurring in widely separated localities. If I were attempting to hybridise Eucalypts, I should expect greater chances of success from two species growing widely apart, as say from Western and Eastern Australia, than from two growing together and blooming simultaneously.

In addition to the Eucalypts already mentioned, there are several other species growing in adjacent localities, and which may occur in the Parramatta area, but I have so far failed to come across them. Such are *E. squamosa* (Ironwood) found at Cabramatta, Wahroonga, and Richmond, and so almost sure to be also in the area under review; and others possibly present, are *E. nigra* R. T. Baker, *E. patentinervis* R. T. Baker, and *E. Fletcheri* R. T. Baker.*

CLASSIFICATION.

Eucalypts growing mainly on sandstone (Hawkesbury).

  E. corymbosa.   E. hæmastoma.
  E. eximia.   E. squamosa.
            E. piperita.

Eucalypts growing mainly on deep clay (Wianamatta).

  E. crebra.   E. maculata.
  E. sideroxylon.   E. longifolia.
  E. siderophloia.   E. Boormani.
  E. hemiphloia.   E. tereticornis.
  E. Bosistoana.   E. Parramattensis, sp.nov.

Eucalypts mainly growing on clay (thin layer) overlying sandstone.

  E. paniculata.   E. acmenioides.
  E. umbra.   E. saligna.
  E. pilularis.   E. punctata.

Eucalypts occurring on all formations.

  E. eugenioides.   E. resinifera.

Eucalypt growing in swampy ground.

  E. robusta.

---

* Mr. Fletcher informs me that, some years ago, a few trees of *E. Baueri* (to which species Mr. Maiden refers the specimens recorded, under the name of *E. polyanthemos*, in the Fl. Austr., as collected at George's River, by Robert Brown) were to be found on the north bank of the creek, a little west of Lansdown Bridge on the Liverpool Road.

Eucalyptus Parramattensis, sp.nov.

Arbor mediocris, lævis, 15-30 ped., ramulis angulatis, teretibusve pendulis; foliis heterophyllaceis, primis vel juvenilibus in petiolum contractis, alternis, 7"-9" longis, 1½" latis, lanceolatis, falcatis; secundis vel maturis alternis, petiolatis, lanceolatis, nonnunquam falcatis, 5"-6" longis, concoloribus, subcoriaceis, nonnunquam nitidulis; venis prominulis, vena media pallida, venis lateralibus nonnihil obliquis, patule ascendentibus, reticulatis, ante marginem unitis, vena peripherica a margine nonnihil remota; glandulis oleosis numerosis; pedunculis axillaribus, 4'''-6''' longis, 4-7 floris; floribus pedicellatis, operculo hemisphærico, nonnunquam breviter acuminato, 3'''-4''' longo, calycis tubo circa 2''' longo; fructu hemisphærico, 3''' lato, margine rotundo, valvis exsertis.

A medium-sized tree, 15-30 feet high, as far as seen; branchlets angled or round, drooping, giving the tree a light graceful appearance; stem 2-2½ feet in diameter. Found growing in a flat low-lying situation, on poor clay soil, in company with *E. hæmastoma*.

Hab.—Fairfield, Cabramatta, Auburn (C. Hall), Milton (R. T. Baker), all in New South Wales.

Bark smooth, whitish or greyish, stripping off in flakes in the autumn, intermediate between the barks of *E. hæmastoma* and *E. punctata*, but without the insect-markings of the former.

Leaves heterophyllaceous.

Seedling leaves.—Cotyledons very small, obtusely triangular, sometimes slightly emarginate; first pairs of leaves linear or narrow-lanceolate, obtuse, opposite, decussate, petiolate.

Primary or juvenile leaves large, up to 7 or 9 inches long and over an inch broad, petiolate, lanceolate, falcate. Secondary or mature leaves lanceolate, sometimes falcate, but smaller than the primary leaves, a uniform dark green colour on both sides, subcoriaceous sometimes shining; venation moderately well-marked, the reticulations giving a roughish surface; lateral veins oblique, fairly distant, and having a looping arrangement with the marginal vein, which is clearly defined and fairly removed from the edge; oil-glands numerous.

Peduncles axillary, 4-6 lines long, bearing few flowers, 4-7.

Buds on a short pedicel, 1½-2 lines long; calyx-tube 1½''' long; operculum hemispherical and domed or conical and shortly acuminate, much longer than calyx-tube.

Fruit hemispherical, 3 lines in diameter, rim rounded to the dome of the ovary or base of valves, which are free from the rim and often recurved.

Timber.—A pale pink-coloured wood, of little economic value, as far as seen; it is soft, seasons badly, and is attacked by borers in the young trees, so far as known. Perhaps now that the species is differentiated, more favourable specimens may be discovered.

Oil.—Mr. H. G. Smith reports that the yield of oil from this species was 0·57 per cent., steam-distilled from material collected as for commercial oil-distillation. The crude oil was but little coloured, and had an odour resembling that of the better crude oils of the Eucalyptol-pinene class. The oil consisted principally of Eucalyptol; the terpene was dextro-rotatory pinene and phellandrene was quite absent. The specific gravity at 15°C. was 0·9223; rotation $a_D + 2·7°$; refractive index at $18°C. = 1·46291$. It was soluble in 1·2 volumes 70 per cent. alcohol. The saponification number for the free acid and ester was 4·6, representing only a small amount of ester. The usual volatile aldehydes occurring in these oils were detected. The amount of Eucalyptol in the crude oil, determined by the resorcinol method, was 78 per cent. The essential oil from this Eucalypt is one of the best of the Eucalyptol class, but, unfortunately, the yield is too small to allow the species to be worked commercially.

Remarks.—This species has evidently been confused with *E. tereticornis*, a tree common in the neighbourhood in which it grows. The fruits of this tree are quite distinct from those of *E. tereticornis* and its varieties, for the rim, instead of being domed, is rounded like the edge of a pudding-basin, a feature that characterises it from any other species (*vide* Plate lx., fig.5). The hemispherical fruits might suggest *E. resinifera*, but the bark is smooth, and the timber quite distinct from that of this species, as is also the oil.

The buds are not unlike those of *E. squamosa* Deane and Maiden, but that is the only resemblance to this species.

From var. *lanceolata* R. T. Baker and H. G. Smith, of *E. tereticornis* (syn. *E. Seeana* Maiden), it differs in the shape of the fruits, timber, and primary leaves.

From *E. dealbata*, it differs in having the secondary or mature leaves much darker in colour, and the intramarginal vein closer to the edge: the pedicels are longer, and the rim of the fruit rounded instead of truncate; the primary or juvenile leaves, too, are quite different from the glaucous ovate-lanceolate ones of *E. dealbata*, the timber of which is also more open in the grain, and of even less value.

With regard to the classification of the leaves, I have preferred to describe them under three headings, viz., *seedling leaves*, including the cotyledons and the first 8 or 10 pairs following them; *primary or juvenile leaves*, including those we usually find in the young tree, on true suckers springing from the roots and base of the stem, on shoots springing from the butt of the trunk or branch when the tree has been cut down or a branch has been lopped, and on adventitious shoots springing from the trunk and larger branches; and lastly, *secondary or mature leaves*, those which occur on the mature tree. In this way, we can best characterise the heterophylly which is so typical of the Eucalypts. The terms primary or juvenile seem, to me, preferable to horizontal, sucker, or abnormal as applied to the "young state" foliage. Horizontal, used much by continental writers, especially in describing *E. globulus*, is quite wrong, because, when the young leaves are petiolated, they, in most cases, very early tend to assume the vertical position. The term abnormal, too, is scarcely suitable. The milk dentition of children is, in some respects, comparable, and one would hardly call this the abnormal dentition. The term "sucker," too, applies to one condition in which these leaves occur, but omits the others.

In conclusion, I have to record my grateful thanks to Mr. R. T. Baker for his excellent drawing delineating this species, and his valuable help to me in differentiating and describing it; also to Mr. H. G. Smith, for his report on the oil.

EXPLANATION OF PLATES LX.-LXI.

Plate lx.

Eucalyptus Parramattensis, n.sp.

Fig.1.—Seedling.
Fig.2.—Primary or juvenile leaves.
Fig.3.—Twig in bud and secondary or mature leaves.
Fig.4.—Twig, with fruit.
Fig.5.—Section of fruit [enlarged].

Plate lxi.

Map of Parramatta District, showing distribution of the Eucalypts.

ON SOME AUSTRALIAN ANISOPTERA, WITH DESCRIPTIONS OF NEW SPECIES.

By R. J. Tillyard, M.A., F.E.S.

(Plate lxii.)

The following species are dealt with in this paper:—

Synthemis spiniger, n.sp.
Metathemis brevistyla subjuncta, n.subsp.
Metathemis guttata aurolineata, n.subsp.
Austrogomphus doddi Tillyard.
Austrogomphus manifestus Tillyard.
Austrogomphus armiger, n.sp.
Austroeschna parvistigma Selys.
Austroeschna multipunctata Martin.
Austroeschna forcipata Tillyard.
Petalura pulcherrima, n.sp.

Subfamily CORDULIINÆ.

1. SYNTHEMIS SPINIGER, n.sp.

♂ (unique). Total length 53, abdomen 40, forewing 32·5, hindwing 31·5 mm.

Wings: *neuration* black, bases of wings touched with deep black bordered by saffron; *a distinct round creamy spot at extreme base of costa on all four wings*. Pterostigma 2·7 mm.; black. One basilar, four submedian, and one hypertrigonal crossveins; *triangles* free normally (right hindwing triangle once crossed); *post-trigonals* of forewing, one double followed by 6-7 single rows. *Nodal Indicator* $\begin{vmatrix} 13, & 7\text{-}8 \\ 9\text{-}11, & 9\text{-}11 \end{vmatrix}$ Head: *vertex* black, hairy; *front* hairy, deeply and widely cleft in middle, black at base and in cleft, with sides and lower parts glaucous dirty yellowish-grey; *clypeus* and upper part of *labrum* dirty greyish-brown; rest of *labrum* dull ochreous; *labium* ochreous. Thorax: *prothorax* black. *Meso-* and *metathorax* black above, shading to dark brown on shoulders; a fine yellow line along dorsal ridge, and a pair of round yellow humeral spots close up to prothorax; sides with a straight ochreous band bordered above by steely black; a small round yellowish spot and an elongate yellowish patch very low down; *notum* black, scutella yellow. *Legs* black. A b d o m e n very slender, 1-2 swollen, 3 very slender, then widening from 4 to 6, 6 to 8 tapering, 9-10 narrow. Colour black, with yellowish spots as follows:—2, a pair of very small round central spots; *auricles* yellowish-brown: 3, a pair of triangular basal spots, and two small central spots touching dorsally: 4, a pair of very small basal spots, and a pair of central spots touching dorsally, larger than in 3: 5, a trace of basal spots, a pair of round dorsal spots two-fifths from base, larger than in 4; 6-8, a pair of round dorsal spots near centre, decreasing in size from 6 to 8; all central spots crossed by the fine transverse black line of the supplementary carinæ: 9-10 black, 10 swollen basally into a rounded dorsal tubercle. A p p e n d a g e s: *superior* 3·8 mm., black, slender, first three-fourths straight, converging, last quarter turned slightly inwards; tips rather blunt. *Inferior* 2 mm., semitransparent brown edged with black; narrow subtriangular, upcurved. The superior carry a large inferior spine at bases (Plate lxii., figs.15, 16).

Hab.—Waroona, W.A., taken by Mr. G. F. Berthoud; January 27th, 1912.

T y p e : ♂, Coll. Tillyard.

This is the most interesting *Synthemid* yet discovered, for it combines in itself characteristics of the two genera *Synthemis* and *Metathemis*, and probably represents, fairly closely, what the immediate ancestors of our East-Australian *Metathemis* were like, before they evolved to their present condition. The known species of *Metathemis* are very closely allied, and, at a not very remote period, were probably represented by only one form, which may have been the same in Eastern and Western Australia. After the great desert barrier arose, the Western form seems to have barely held its own, and is now only represented by this single rare species; while, on the other hand, the Eastern form spread far and wide, and altered considerably in the process. Though *Synthemis spiniger* is generically a true *Synthemis*, possessing the peculiar shape of the abdomen and the long appendages of that genus, yet it is remarkable in possessing the two characters that are most prominently developed in *Metathemis*, viz., the four bright basal wing-spots, and the basal spine of the superior appendages. It is clearly very closely allied to *S. leachi* Selys, which was taken in company with it by Mr. Berthoud; but it can be at once distinguished from this latter species by its smaller size, by possessing only two dorsal thoracic spots instead of four, by the more slender and less spotted abdomen, and by the straighter appendages and the prominent basal spine. In general appearance, it resembles *Metathemis nigra* Tillyard, closely, but this latter species has short appendages and no dorsal thoracic spots. It would be of great interest to find the female of this species, to see to what stage of development the ovipositor has reached.

2. METATHEMIS BREVISTYLA SUBJUNCTA, n.subsp.

Total length, ♂♀ 41; *abdomen* ♂♀ 30; *forewing* ♂ 28·5, ♀ 31; *hindwing* ♂ 27·5, ♀ 30·5 mm.

It differs from the type as follows:—(1) Smaller, more compact build. (2) Much shorter *pterostigma*, ♂ 2, ♀ 2·5 mm., covering just two cellules. (3) Smaller spots on abdomen. (4) The two spots forming the upper lateral band of the thorax are *just joined, instead of being quite separate* (Plate lxii., compare fig.1*a* type-form, fig.1*b*, *M. subjuncta*). This difference is very distinctive and quite constant. (5) Wings of both sexes quite transparent, instead of being tinged with brown as in the type-form, especially the female. (6) Ground colour almost black, much darker than in type-form.

Hab.—Dorrigo and Ebor, N.S.W. December, 1911, and January, 1912.

Types: ♂♀, Coll. Tillyard.

This subspecies is very distinct from the type while on the wing, as it flies more swiftly and keeps very close to the surface of the water. The type-form has a slow soaring flight, and prefers to fly high up round bushes and trees. The two forms could be easily named while flying, but in spite of their very distinctive difference of appearance, they cannot be claimed as distinct species.

3. METATHEMIS GUTTATA AUROLINEATA, n.subsp.

Total length, ♂ 43, ♀ 44·5; *abdomen* ♂ 32·5, ♀ 33; *forewing* ♂ 30, ♀ 33; *hindwing* ♂ 30, ♀ 33.

It differs from the type as follows:—(1) Shorter *pterostigma*, ♂ 2, ♀ 2·5 mm., that of ♂ covering 1½-2 cellules only. (2) Frontal yellow spots comparatively close, 0·5 mm. apart in ♂ and 1 mm. in ♀. (3) Colouration black or very dark brown with gold or yellow markings; the colouration of the type-form is brown with creamy markings. (4) *A pair of distinct antehumeral lines or rays on thorax*, gold or yellow, from 1·5 to 2·5 mm. in length. These are not present in the type-form.

Hab.—Dorrigo and Ebor, N.S.W. December, 1911, and January, 1912.

Types : ♂♀, Coll. Tillyard.

Very distinct from the type-form, but, in my opinion, not above subspecific rank. Some of the females which I took at Ebor, approach the type-form in size and colouration. It is of interest to note that, on the Dorrigo Plateau, two of the species of *Metathemis* are replaced by new subspecific forms, while the third species, *M. virgula* Selys, is exactly like the type-form. *Synthemis eustalacta* Burm., and *S. macrostigma orientalis* Tillyard, also occur on this plateau, and are of typical form.

Subfamily GOMPHINÆ.

4. AUSTROGOMPHUS DODDI Tillyard.

A single male taken by Mr. F. P. Dodd at Kuranda, N.Q., November, 1906, was described by me in these Proceedings (xxxiv., p.249), and the male appendages figured. At Pallal, N.S.W., in December, 1910, I found this species quite common along the Horton River. The males resemble the type very closely, but are somewhat more brightly coloured, and of slightly stouter build.

♀. *Total length* 45, *abdomen* 32, *forewing* 28, *hindwing* 27 mm.

Wings very slightly touched with brown in mature specimens; *pterostigma* 3·7 mm., black with yellowish centre. *Nodal Indicator* |14-15, 8-10| Colouration of head and thorax as in male; *occiput* | 9-11, 9-10| yellow carrying two dark brown spurs, flat subtriangular, downy, placed close up to eyes (Plate lxii., fig. 2). Abdomen fairly stout, cylindrical, 1-2 enlarged, 7-9 slightly enlarged. *Colour*: 1, yellow; 2, very dark brown with a thick yellow sub-oval dorsal mark, and two large lateral yellow spots; 3-6, black, with two large semioval basal yellow spots; 7, basal half yellow, with irregular black lines, apical half black; 8, black, with two large yellow spots; 9, black, with two small yellow spots; 10, black. *Appendages* 0·7 mm., slightly pointed, yellow. *Vulvar scale* with two pointed short branches.

Hab.—Kuranda, N.Q., and Pallal, North-western New South Wales. November to December.

Types: ♂♀, Coll. Tillyard.

5. AUSTROGOMPHUS MANIFESTUS Tillyard.

A unique female of this rare species was described by me (*loc. cit.*, p. 248) in 1909, from Kamerunga, N.Q. At Pallal, N.S.W., I took four males and three females, two in the act of emergence.

♂. *Total length* 49, *abdomen* 37, *forewing* 26, *hindwing* 25 mm.

Wings: *pterostigma* black, 2·8 mm. *Nodal Indicator* $\begin{vmatrix} 12 & 7\text{-}8 \\ 8 & 8 \end{vmatrix}$ Head and thorax as in female. Abdomen long and slender, 1-2 much enlarged, 3-6 and part of 7 very slender, rest of 7 and whole of 8 much swollen, 9 long and tapering, 10 tapering. Breadth: across 1, 3 mm.; across 3-6, 1 mm.; across 8, 2·5 mm.; across end of 10, 1·5 mm.; length of 9, 2·7 mm.: of 10, 1·6 mm. *Colour* black marked with yellow as follows: 1, a broad dorsal mark, and sides yellow; 2, a rather irregular dorsal mark, sides and auricles yellow; 3-6, a basal band and a suspicion of a dorsal line along 2 and part of 3; 7, basal two-fifths yellow; 8, a pair of medium basal lateral spots and a pair of small apical lateral spots; 9-10, black with yellow lines in sutures: sides of 8 and 9 enlarged downwards into leaf-like folds or sheaths, larger in 8 than in 9. Appendages: *superior* 1 mm., yellow, sharply pointed and much upturned, carrying an elongate, downcurved, black tubercle beneath. *Inferior* 0·6 mm., black, upcurved, bifurcated, downy, tips rounded (Plate lxii., figs. 3, 4).

♀. A correction is necessary in the description already published. The *occiput* is black, hairy, with a large central yellow patch, from the border of which project *two finely pointed yellow spikes* (Plate lxii., fig.5).

Hab.—Pallal, N.S.W.; Kamerunga and Mackay, N.Q. December.

Types: ♂♀, Coll. Tillyard.

Now that the male is known, I am able to place this species as being most closely allied to *A. arenarius* Tillyard, from N. Queensland. It resembles this species in the elongation of segments 9 and 10 of abdomen, in the lateral sheaths of 8 and 9, in the slender abdomen strongly swollen at 8, and in the peculiar form of the appendages. It differs from it, however, very completely in the whole colour-scheme.

6. AUSTROGOMPHUS ARMIGER, n.sp.

♂. *Total length* 41-43, *abdomen* 30-32, *forewing* 24-26, *hindwing* 22-24 mm.

W i n g s : *neuration* black, fine; *pterostigma* 3·5 mm., reddish-brown between the nervures. *Triangle* of hindwing very much wider than that of forewing. *Hindwing* strongly angulated, anal triangle 3-celled. *Nodal Indicator* ‖9, 6-7|. H e a d : *eyes* black, bordered beneath with yellow; |8, 7-8| *occiput* yellow; *vertex* black with a large round yellow spot close up to occiput; *front, clypeus,* and *labrum* bright yellow; *labium* yellow, paler on sides. T h o r a x : *prothorax* nearly 4 mm. wide, hairy, black, with two geminate yellow dorsal points, and a large oval yellow spot on each side. *Meso-* and *metathorax* black, marked with yellow as follows :—a fine collar in front, interrupted dorsally; a suspicion of a line on the dorsal ridge; two large antehumeral stripes or patches, subrectangular and slightly excavated on outer margin; sides completely yellow; *scuta* and *scutella* yellow. *Legs* black, basal parts of femora yellow. [*Note.*—In the specimens received by me, the markings of head, thorax, and abdomen are coloured a peculiar pinkish-brown. This colour is obtained by killing any species of *Austrogomphus* in excess of chloroform or ammonia, or even in a *damp* cyanide bottle; hence I do not hesitate to describe the markings as *yellow*. Possibly the pterostigma is also yellow. Specimens of *A. collaris* received at the same time are coloured pinkish-brown; this species is marked with yellow when alive.] A b d o m e n : 1-2 swollen, 3-7 slender, 8-10 slightly enlarged. *Colour* black, marked with yellow as follows :—1, downy, a dorsal patch and large lateral spots; 2, downy, a dorsal mark shaped like a Roman torch; sides yellow, *auricles* small, yellow touched with black; 3, two large basal blotches nearly meeting dorsally; two lateral spots towards apex; 4-7, two large basal spots nearly meeting dorsally; 8-9, two small basal spots; 10, black, *carrying, at extreme outer apical edge, a pair of small black projecting spurs about 0·5 mm. long*; in profile, the spur is rather broad and rounded, and hollowed out on the outer surface (Plate lxii., figs.6, 7a). A p p e n d a g e s : *superior* 1·5 mm., yellow, subforcipate, meeting at tips, which are slender and pointed inwards; with a fine yellow spur projecting outwards near base, parallel to, but not quite as long as the spur on 10. *Inferior* 0·5 mm., broad, bifurcated, upcurved, yellow (Plate lxii., figs.6, 7, *s.i,b*).

♀.*Total length* 39-42, *abdomen* 28-30, *forewing* 27-28, *hindwing* 25-26 mm.

Pterostigma 4 mm. *Occiput* with a projecting yellow ridge carrying long hairs, but without tubercles (Plate lxii., fig.8). Similar to male, but with thicker cylindrical abdomen carrying pairs of large oval spots both basal and central on 3-7; 8-9 with large spots low down on sides; 10, yellow on sides. *Vulvar scale* with two exceedingly short pointed slender contiguous branches. *Appendages* 0·5 mm., black, pointed.

Hab.—Waroona, W.A. Taken by Mr. G. F. Berthoud; November, 1910 and 1911; three males and nine females.

T y p e s : ♂♀, Coll. Tillyard.

This very rare insect differs so much from the other members of the genus, that it will probably form the type of a new genus. The remarkable development of parallel spurs on segment 10 and the superior appendages seems to be a contrivance to enable the male to clasp the occipital ridge of the female, which, in this species, is not furnished with the usual tubercular processes by which this object is accomplished.

Subfamily ÆSCHNINÆ.

7. AUSTROÆSCHNA PARVISTIGMA Selys.
8. AUSTROÆSCHNA MULTIPUNCTATA Martin.

These two forms have, so far, been regarded as distinct races or varieties of one species, each inhabiting its own geographical region. The type-form, *A. parvistigma* Selys, occurs commonly on mountain-streams throughout Tasmania, and on the Mount Lofty Ranges, near Adelaide. In Victoria, it is replaced by *A. multipunctata* Martin, which extends through Gippsland to the Kosciusko district of New South Wales, and right up to the Blue Mountains, descending to the coastal hills around Sydney. Further north, at Dorrigo, I found *A. multipunctata* last year as early as October. Later on, in December, at an elevation of 4,000 to 5,000 feet, at Ebor (Guy Fawkes), N.S.W., I found both forms flying together, and was enabled to study them on the spot. As a result, I have now no doubt as to the specific distinctness of the two forms, which can be separated even in the larval stage. In the imagines, besides the differences noted by Martin in the size of the pterostigma and form of appendages, there is a well-marked and constant difference, both of colouration and colour-pattern on head, thorax and abdomen. So distinct are they, that I was able to distinguish both sexes on the wing. The following are the chief differences:—

A. parvistigma Selys.

Pterostigma 2-2·3 mm.; *membranule* 2 mm., triangular, grey.

Colouration very dark brown or black, with creamy markings in the mature insect.

Head: a thin whitish band along *front* bordering the clypeus, and separated from it by a dark line in the suture.

A. multipunctata Martin.

Pterostigma 2·7-3 mm.; *membranule* slightly shorter and wider, outer edge convex.

Colouration rich dark brown, with pale blue-grey markings in the mature insect (creamy only in immature females and very immature males).

Head: *front* continuously dark brown right down to clypeus.

Thorax: dorsal bands scarcely more than mere lines, short, curved, whitish, each followed by three spots behind, one each side of interalar ridge, close up to dorsal ridge: and one, larger and more rounded, above interalar ridge and lying further away from dorsal ridge. Humero-lateral band consisting of three separate creamy-white spots, the first two waved, the third round; lower lateral surface with four creamy spots.

♂. *Abdomen* very much spotted—1, a large spot low down on each side: 2, two basal spots, two central transverse lines, two apical spots, a large spot on each auricle, a large creamy band on each side of genitalia: 3-4, two basal, two central, and two apical spots: 5, ditto, central spots placed one-third from base, apical spots very small: 4-7, a conspicuous comma-shaped spot low down on each side: 6-7, apical spots absent or obsolescent, central spots close up to basal spots, isolating a black cross-mark: 8, basal and central spots conjoined with two large basal spots; a suspicion of two lateral apical spots; two small basal lateral spots: 9-10, two lateral apical spots: 10 only slightly raised dorsally into an obtuse tubercle.

Thorax: dorsal bands more conspicuous, longer, waved, pale bluish-green, each followed by a single spot just above interalar ridge; humero-lateral band with the first two waved spots enlarged to form curved bands of pale bluish-green; third spot as in *A. parvistigma* but bluish-green; lower lateral surface with four creamy spots touched with blue or green

♂. *Abdomen* much *less spotted* (the name *multipunctata* is unfortunate, from this point of view)—1, as in *A. parvistigma*: 2, a cross formed of four separate bluish dorsal lines; on each side, a curved apical spot: a creamy spot on auricles, and large band bordering genitalia: 3, more pointed than in *A. parvistigma*; basal, central, and apical spots bluish, much smaller than in *A. parvistigma*: 4-5, a pair of central bluish spots very close together; on each side a lateral apical spot: 4-7, with comma spot as in *A. parvistigma*: 6-7, a pair of small slanting spots close together one-third from base: 8, two large bluish basal spots: 9-10, with lateral apical spots: 10, raised dorsally into a large, sharply-pointed tubercle.

♀.*Abdomen*: basal spots very large on 3-7, central spots flat and narrow, apical spots very small or absent; 8, with two basal dorsal spots, and two large apical lateral spots; 9, with large, apical, lateral spots.

♂.*Appendages*: *superior* 4 mm., *inferior* 1·4 mm.

♀.*Abdomen*: basal spots absent except in 3; central spots fairly large, brownish, crossed by black line of carina in 3-4; 8, with small, basal spots; 8-9, with medium, brown, lateral, apical spots.

♂.*Appendages*: *superior* 3·7 mm., *inferior* 1·2 mm.; tips of superior thicker and more rounded; tip of inferior more truncate than in *A. parvistigma*.

For comparison of colour-pattern of segments 2-4 of abdomen of males, see Plate lxii., figs.9, 10.

9. AUSTROÆSCHNA FORCIPATA Tillyard.

Planæschna(?) *forcipata* Tillyard, These Proceedings, 1906, xxxi., p.726.

Austroæschna forcipata Tillyard, Martin, Coll. Zool. de Selys-Longchamps, Fasc. xix., Aeschnines, p.102, No.14, 1909.

Austroæschna severini Foërster, Ann. Soc. Ent. Belge, 52, p.191, 1908; Martin, *loc. cit.*, p.103, No.15.

The male only of this species has been described. Foërster's *A. severini* is clearly synonymous, the appendages as figured by Martin being exactly like those of my type-male of *A. forcipata*. This figure is more correct in detail than the sketch sent by me to M. Martin and my own figure, but is sketched with the appendages slightly tipped down, making the inferior appear shorter. The colouration of Foërster's specimen shows it to be a faded immature male.

♀.*Total length* 65-71, *abdomen* 49-54, *forewing* 47-51, *hindwing* 46-50 mm.

Wings slightly clouded all over with brown. *Pterostigma* 2·5-3 mm., black. *Membranule* nearly 2 mm., brown. *Nodal Indicator* ‖20-22, 15-16‖. *Head* and *thorax* as in male. Abdomen ‖14-16, 15-18‖ stouter, thicker, and more cylindrical than in ♂: 1-2, swollen; 3-7, narrower; 8-10, slightly swollen.

Colour dark chocolate-brown to black, marked as follows with green—1, green with two basal brown spots; 2, a fine dorsal cross made of four separate parts, of which the basal upright is subtriangular, the rest being lines; an apical transverse band; sides largely green; 3-6, black, with a pair of large apical spots nearly meeting dorsally; 7, similar but with smaller spots; 8-10 black. *Appendages* 1 mm., pointed, black. *Ovipositor* ending in a semicircular cutting edge armed with about fourteen serrated spines, and projecting slightly beyond end of abdomen.

Hab.—Kuranda, Cairns, Cooktown, Herberton, and Atherton, N.Q. December to January.

Types: ♂♀, Coll. Tillyard(♂, Kuranda, January, 1905, taken by myself; ♀, Kuranda, January, 1908, taken by Mr. F. P. Dodd).

The series of six males and three females in my collection, shows considerable variation in size.

Subfamily PETALURINÆ.

10. PETALURA PULCHERRIMA, n.sp.

♂. *Total length* 104, *abdomen* 77, *forewing* 58, *hindwing* 57, *expanse of wings* 122 mm.

Wings: *neuration* black, strong; *pterostigma* narrow, black, forewing 11, hindwing 12 mm. Head: *eyes* nearly black, 2mm. apart across occiput; *ocelli* conspicuous; *antennæ* 4 mm., slender, black; *vertex* and base of *front* black; *front* yellow, with a large flat triangular black patch next clypeus; *postclypeus* very dark brown, with a yellow patch on each side; *anteclypeus* very dark brown; *labrum* bright yellow, bordered with black along mouth; *genæ* yellow; *labium* yellowish (Plate lxii., fig.13). Thorax: *prothorax* very narrow, hairy, black, with a conspicuous narrow yellow collar behind. *Meso-* and *metathorax* dark brown, with a pair of subtriangular curved yellowish dorsal bands close up to dorsal ridge (Plate lxii., fig.14); sides brown, with two broad parallel straight yellow bands. *Legs* black, large, strong; measurements of femur, tibia and tarsus: fore, 9, 9, 4·5; middle, 12, 9, 5; hind, 16, 11, 5·5 mm. respectively. Abdomen slender; breadth at 1-2,

5 mm.; at 5-6, 2 mm.; at 8-10, 3·5 mm. *Colour* black and yellow, as follows: 1, blackish, hairy, a faint yellowish dorsal line, and a patch of yellow on sides; 2, black with a fine dorsal line, a fine transverse basal line, a slightly wider transverse apical band, and most of sides, yellow; *auricles* flat, inconspicuous, yellow; 3-4, black, broader basal and apical bands of yellow, joined by a broad sublateral band crossed by the black line of the carinæ; conspicuous black bands along all sutures; 5-7, black, with irregular yellow basal and apical bands of yellow diminishing in width from 5 to 7; 8, black with a fine basal yellow line and a conspicuous apical yellow band; 9, basal three-fifths black, apical two-fifths irregularly yellow; 10, black, a touch of yellow basally and on the curved apical borders(Plate lxii., fig.11). A p p e n d - a g e s : *superior* 7 mm. long, by 5·5 mm. broad, black, leaf-like, shaped as in *P. ingentissima* Tillyard, but much smaller. *Inferior* black touched with brown, 2 mm. long, by 3 mm. wide, trapezoidal, curved, a slight projecting median point underneath; shape intermediate between that of *P. ingentissima* and *P. gigantea* (Plate lxii., fig.12).

♀.Unique. *Total length* 95, *abdomen* 69, *forewing* 62, *hindwing* 61, *expanse* 130 mm.

Differs from male in its shorter and more cylindrical abdomen; breadth at 1-2, 5 mm.; at 3-4, 4·5 mm.; at 5-9, 4 mm.; 10, slightly narrower. Yellow markings all broader and more conspicuous. *Appendages* 1 mm., short, straight, black, tips rather blunt, with two stiff hairs projecting from each. *Ovipositor* reaching just to end of abdomen, upcurved, carrying two filaments, and, on the keel between and below them, a row of sharp bristles set close together.

Hab.—Cooktown, N.Q., six males taken by myself; January, 1908. Kuranda, N.Q., one female taken by Mr. F. P. Dodd; December, 1907.

T y p e s : ♂♀, Coll. Tillyard.

This very beautiful insect is intermediate in size between *P. ingentissima* Tillyard, and *P. gigantea* Leach, but resembles the former in its slenderness of build. It may be easily distinguished from both by the conspicuous black and yellow colour-pattern, recalling that of *Uropetala caroori* White (from New Zealand) in general effect; and also by the relatively small size of the superior appendages of the male, and by the intermediate form of the inferior appendage. The colouration of the frontal parts of the head is very distinct also, and is much more yellow than in *P. ingentissima*.

Note on Synonymy.—*Austroæschna aspersa* Martin, *loc. cit.*, p.96, No.7(1909), is synonymous with my *A. anacantha*, These Proceedings, 1907, xxxii., p 732. *Telephlebia Racleayi* (printer's error for *Macleayi*) Martin, *loc. cit.*, p.142(1909) is synonymous with *Austroæschna costalis* Tillyard, These Proceedings, xxxi., p.724. *Macromia viridescens* Tillyard (unique ♀) is the female of *M. terpsichore* Foërster.

EXPLANATION OF PLATE LXII.

Fig.1.—Upper lateral thoracic band, *a* in *Metathemis brevistyla brevistyla* Selys; *b* in *M. brevistyla subjuncta*, n.subsp.

Fig.2.—*Austrogomphus doddi* Tillyard, ♀, occiput.

Fig 3.—*Austrogomphus manifestus* Tillyard, ♂, appendages, dorsal view.

Fig.4.—*Austrogomphus manifestus* Tillyard, ♂, appendages, lateral view.

Fig.5.—*Austrogomphus manifestus* Tillyard, ♀, occiput.

Fig.6.—*Austrogomphus armiger*, n.sp., ♂, appendages, dorsal view, of right side.

Fig.7.—*Austrogomphus armiger*, n.sp. ♂, appendages, lateral view.

Fig.8.—*Austrogomphus armiger*, n.sp., ♀, occiput.
  a, spur of segment 10; *b*, spur of superior appendage; *s*, superior appendage; *i*, inferior appendage.

Fig.9.—*Austroæschna parvistigma* Selys, ♂, colour-pattern of segments 2 to 4 of abdomen.

Fig.10.—*Austroæschna multipunctata* Martin, ♂, colour-pattern of segments 2 to 4 of abdomen.

Fig.11.—*Petalura pulcherrima*, n.sp., ♂, colour-pattern of abdomen(× 1·5).

Fig.12.—*Petalura pulcherrima*, n.sp., ♂, inferior appendage from below (× 1·5).

Fig.13.—*Petalura pulcherrima*, n.sp., ♂, colour-pattern of head from in front (× 1·5).

Fig.14.—*Petalura pulcherrima*, n.sp. ♂, colour-pattern of thorax from above (× 1 5).

Fig.15.—*Synthemis spiniger*, n.sp., ♂, appendages, dorsal view.

Fig.16.—*Synthemis spiniger*, n.sp., ♂, appendages, lateral view.

ON TWO UNRECORDED MYRTACEOUS PLANTS FROM NEW SOUTH WALES.

By R. T. Baker, F.L.S.

(Plates lxiii.-lxiv.)

Eucalyptus Laseroni, sp.nov.

A small tree under 40 feet high, and about 1 foot in diameter, with a fibrous but hard stringy bark, in the general acceptation of the latter term.

Abnormal leaves ovate, lanceolate, slightly falcate in some instances, petiolate, attenuate, varying in size up to 5 inches long, and up to 2 inches broad. Normal leaves lanceolate, alternate, subcoriaceous, average leaves under 4 inches long, and 1 inch wide, occasionally shining. Venation distinctly marked, the basal lateral veins sometimes running the whole length of the leaf, and well removed from the edge; the other lateral veins not so oblique, more transverse.

Buds in clusters, on axillary peduncles about $\frac{1}{4}$ inch long. Operculum sharply conical.

Fruits hemispherical, capitular, rim domed, valves scarcely or not exserted, $\frac{1}{4}$ inch in diameter, pedicel varying in length up to 2 lines long.

Arbuscula usque ad 35' alta. Cortex fibrosus, tam in ramis quam in trunco persistens, viridis, et hinc "Bastard Stringybark." Folia 3-5" longa, fere 1-2" lata, lanceolata, ovata, alternata, subcoriacea, concoloria; venis patentibus, peripherica a margine remota, venulis obliquatis. Pedunculi $\frac{1}{4}$" longi, axillares, solitarii, 10-15-flori. Fructus $\frac{1}{4}$" longi, pilulares; margine convexo, valvis non exsertis.

Remarks.—This tree, so far, is known only from the Black Mountain district, where Mr. Laseron obtained material in July, 1907. He states in his field-notes that it is regarded locally as a cross between "Silver-Top Stringybark," *E. laevopinea*, and "Sally," *E. stellulata*. A few trees are to be found on a rough, rocky basalt hillock, about half a mile south of Black Mountain railway station.

It is a small tree, 35 feet high, and 1 foot in diameter, as far as seen. The fibrous bark covers the trunk, and decorticates in long strips from the main branches, which are otherwise smooth, but darker than in *E. stellulata*. The timber is yellowish-brown, and tough to cut, but brittle.

The small stellate clusters of buds are larger than those of *E. stellulata*, but the colour of the upper branches, though fainter, is also suggestive of that species. The leaves are more inclined to lanceolate than ovate in shape, as obtains in *E. stellulata*, whilst the venation is distinct. The midrib is stronger, and the venation not so parallel as in *E. stellulata*. The bark, timber, and especially the fruits are also different. The venation seems to be intermediate between that of the typical Stringybarks and the Peppermint group, but more approaching that of *E. dives*. One or two trees were noticed in another locality, associated with *E. stellulata*, from which it is easily distinguished in the field. The venation somewhat resembles that of *E. coriacea*, but the fruits are different, and especially the buds and bark.

The fruits fairly well match those of *E. capitellata*, but this is the only resemblance to that species amongst Stringybarks.

In a botanical sequence, it might be placed between the Stringybarks and the Gums or Smoothbarks, such as *E. stellulata* or *E. coriacea*.

Timber.—From the specimens seen, this is not a good timber. It is fairly close-grained, of a pale colour, but the presence of gum-veins will militate against its general utilisation by the commercial world.

Oil. Mr. H. G. Smith, F.C.S., reports as follows on this economic:—The material was collected at Black Mountain, New England District, August, 1907. The oil distilled from the leaves and branchlets, in the ordinary way, was equal to 0·368 per cent. The crude oil was dark-coloured, but could be easily cleared to an olive-brown tint. The oil of this species contains a rather large amount of lævo-rotatory pinene (not less than 30 or 40 per cent.) with some phellandrene, and less than 5 per cent. of eucalyptol. Esters were present, the saponification number being 13·4. A considerable amount of the oil boiled at a high temperature, and consisted largely of the sesquiterpene usually found in this class of Eucalyptus oils. The specific gravity at $15°C = 0·9095$; rotation $a_D = -8·1°$; refractive index at $18°C = 1·4799$; and required 6 volumes 80 per cent alcohol to form a clear solution. On rectification, 54 per cent. came over below 175°C.(corr.); 7 per cent. between 175-225°; and 32 per cent. between 225-270°, the greater portion above 260°. The specific gravity of the first fraction at $15° = 0·8705$; of the second $= 0·9006$; of the third $= 0·9428$. The rotation of the first fraction $a_D = -15·9°$; of the second $= -13·6$. The refractive index at 18°C. of the first fraction $= 1·4662$; of the second $= 1·4722$; of the third $= 1·4967$. On again distilling the first fraction 20 per cent. came over below 157°C. This had sp.gr. at $15° = 0·8665$; rotation $a_D = -19·1°$; refractive index at $19° = 1·4644$. The nitrosochloride was easily prepared with this, and melted at the usual temperature.

The oil of this species differs considerably from that of *E. stellulata*, in the presence of such a large amount of pinene, in a deficiency in phellandrene, and consequently a much less lævo-rotation, in the large amount of high boiling constituents, and in an increased ester-content.

MELALEUCA IRBYIANA, sp.nov.

A small glabrous tree or shrub, found growing in or near swamps, with very slender filiform branchlets. Leaves very small, alternate, ovate, lanceolate, acute or obtuse, concave and broad above the base, erect or slightly spreading in the upper portion, imbricate almost appressed in the new growth, striate, mostly one line long. Flowers in compact or loose cylindrical spikes, mostly about one inch long, the axis growing out before the flowering is over, the floral leaves persistent. Calyx-tube cylindrical, about one line long, glabrous; lobes short, broad, striate, shorter than the tube, with a pinkish tinge. Petals twice as long as the calyx, lobes persistent, staminal bundles about 2 lines long, the claw scarcely exceeding the petals, each with numerous filaments.

Fruiting-calyx globular, contracted, and mostly entire; only occasionally do the minute calyx-lobes crown it.

Frutex glaber, erectus, ramis gracilibus, ramulis junioribus filiformibus; foliis minimis, alternis, ovatis, mucronatis vel elliptico-lanceolatis, 1-2′″ longis, striatis, paucinerviis, sessilibus; floribus spicatis, brevibus, rhachidibusque glabris; capsulis compactis, pilularibus.

Remarks.— This Melaleuca was discovered by Mr. L. G. Irby, Museum Collector, when collecting on the Lawrence Road at Casino, where it is not common, in the swamps in that locality.

It is a shrub or small tree, and is differentiated in the field by its delicate filiform branchlets, and very small leaves. In this latter respect it stands quite alone among Melaleucas. The most suitable specific name for it has already been appropriated for a Western Australian species. The leaves, however, are not unlike those of some Epacrids, and so a derivative of this name would also be specially applicable; they are numerous, imbricate, sometimes appressed, especially in the extremely slender branchlets. Although acuminate, they are not pungent-pointed, but rather obtuse; the striations are few and not nearly so well marked as in *M. styphelioides*, its nearest ally. Another feature that may be mentioned is, that the leaves are deciduous in herbarium material, in contrast to the persistent leaves of *M. styphelioides*. It also resembles this species in that it has little or no oil in its leaves. It differs from *M. styphelioides* in the smallness of its leaves, and in the venation, glabrous character, calyx-lobes, and fruits, and the same remarks apply to other species of the genus.

In a systematic classification it would be placed in Series v. of Bentham's subdivision of the genus (Flora Australiensis, Vol.iii., p.125):—"Leaves alternate or opposite. Flowers either solitary or few and distinct, or in more or less interrupted oblong-cylindrical or elongated spikes, sometimes at first terminal but the axis usually growing out before the flowering is over, rarely in dense lateral cylindrical spikes. Rhachis glabrous, pubescent or villous." Under this heading is a section :—" Leaves mostly alternate, Flowers usually numerous," which includes *M. leucadendron*, *M. lasiandra*, *M. genistifolia*, *M. styphelioides* and *M. Hueyelii*; and it is between these last two, that it is now placed.

EXPLANATION OF PLATES LXIII.-LXIV.

Plate lxiii.

Eucalyptus Laseroni.

Fig. 1.—Twig with normal leaves and buds.
Fig. 2.—Individual abnormal leaf.
Fig. 3.—Fruits.
All natural size.

Plate lxiv.

Melaleuca Irbyiana.

Fig. 1.—Twig with flowers and buds.
Fig. 2.—Twig with fruits.
Fig. 3.—Individual leaf.
Fig. 4.—Bud.
Fig. 5.—Flowers.
Nos. 3, 4 and 5, enlarged.

ORDINARY MONTHLY MEETING.

October 30th, 1912.

Mr. W. W. Froggatt, F.L.S., President, in the Chair.

The President announced :—

(1) That the Council was prepared to receive applications for three Linnean Macleay Fellowships, tenable for one year from April 1st, 1913, from qualified Candidates. Applications should be in the hands of the Secretary, who will afford all necessary information to intending Candidates, on or before 30th November, 1912.

(2). That a Special General Meeting would be held on Wednesday evening, 27th November, 1912 (after the Ordinary Monthly Meeting at 7.30 p.m. on the same date). *Business:* To consider certain proposed amendments in the Rules, submitted by the Council.

The Donations and Exchanges received since the previous Monthly Meeting (25th September, 1912), amounting to 25 Vols., 79 Parts or Nos., 8 Bulletins, 5 Pamphlets, and 4 Reports, received from 64 Societies and 3 Individuals, were laid upon the table.

NOTES AND EXHIBITS.

Dr. Kesteven reported that, on several days in last week, when the weather conditions were favourable, he had noticed remarkable mirage-effects in Hyde Park, looking towards Liverpool-street.

Mr. Tillyard exhibited the larval skin and freshly-emerged male imago of the very rare dragonfly, *Austrocordulia refracta* Tillyard, together with the type male and female for comparison. The latter were taken at Cooktown in January, 1907, and only one other specimen is known. The larva was taken in February,

1911, at Heathcote, N.S.W., and has attained a considerable scientific interest in already published papers as the "unknown larva X," which is the only form yet discovered for the Group *Idocordulina* (Subdivision of the *Cordulinæ*). One of the larvæ was first found in 1907, at Heathcote, but died in the act of emerging three years later; so that it has taken five years to discover to what species it really belonged. No imagines have ever been seen or taken at Heathcote. Two other larvæ are now practically full-fed in Mr. Tillyard's aquarium, and may be expected to emerge shortly.

Dr. J. B. Cleland showed portion of a bull's hide, from the Hawkesbury River, showing small, scattered nodules due to the distension of sebaceous glands with numerous specimens of the acarid, *Demodex folliculorum*, var. *boris*. These massed acarids formed small yellowish caseous areas. Also leaves of a species of *Lomatia* now exported in bundles to Germany, for decorative purposes, when dried.

Mr. A. G. Hamilton exhibited a rather striking life-size photograph of one of the largest specimens of the green frog (*Hyla cærulea*) taken near Sydney.

Mr. A. A. Hamilton exhibited, and offered notes on, three interesting plants from the National Herbarium, Sydney — (1) *Medicago hispida* Gartn., var. *inermis* Urb., from the Domain, Sydney(J. H. Camfield), the University grounds(W. M. Carne), and other Sydney localities, not previously recorded from New South Wales. — (2) *Acacia obtusata* Sieb., from Bell, N.S.W.(A. A. Hamilton; September, 1912), a species well-established on the Southern Tableland, but rare on the Blue Mountains. — (3) *Cotula reptans* Benth., from Ballina, N.S.W.(W. Bauerlen; March, 1893), recorded as from Manly southwards, and by Mr. F. M. Bailey from Queensland.

Mr. E. Cheel exhibited, and communicated notes on, a series of botanical specimens comprising (1) Sweetbriar (*Rosa rubiginosa* L.) collected at Colo viâ Hill Top, badly infested with Rose-Rust [*Phragmidium subcorticinum* (Schrank) Winter], believed to be unrecorded previously for New South Wales, though known in some of the other States.—(2) A grass which appeared to be *Lolium rigidum* Gaud., var. *rottbœllioides* Heldr., from Centennial Park(E. Cheel; September, 1899), and Bungarra, S.A.(S. Browne; December, 1906), infested with the teleuto-stage of Puccinia; and from Hunter's Hill(W. M. Carne; September, 1912), infested with the uredospore stage of a Rust; examples of other species of *Lolium* were shown for comparison. –(3) A grass, *Festuca duriuscula* L., var.(?) from the Hawkesbury Agricultural College, Richmond (C. T. Musson), and from the Botanic Gardens, Sydney, exhibiting a similar abnormal growth to that described by Sinclair in "Hortus Gramineus Woburnensis" (p.260; 1825) as a "Viviparous Fescue Grass."—(4) Additional specimens of the common Kangaroo Grass showing two distinct forms, one glabrous, the other with tubercle-based bristles.

Mr. E. Mackinnon showed, and communicated notes on, a series of interesting parasitic fungi, comprising—(1) *Graphiola phœnicis* Fr., attacking the fronds of the Date Palm (*Phœnix dactylifera* L., from Wollongbar Experimental Farm(Dr. J. B. Cleland); a new record for New South Wales, and probably for Australia.—(2) *Uromyces orchidearum* Cke. & Mass., on an orchid, *Chiloglottis diphylla* R.Br., from the Kurrajong.—(3) *Cytospora leucostoma* Aderhold, on an Appletree branch, from Home Rule, N.S.W.—(4) *Septoria tritici* Desm., on Federation Wheat, from Harden, N.S.W.—(5) *Peronospora trifoliorum* de Bary, on Lucerne, from the Hawkesbury Agricultural College, Richmond.—(6) *Sclerotinia sclerotiorum* Mass., showing the sclerotial stage on French Beans, and also the rarer apothecial stage grown in a sugar-solution from sclerotia from Cow Peas, from the Hawkesbury Agricultural College.

Mr. Froggatt exhibited a named collection of typical Australian and Tasmanian Bees in illustration of Prof. Cockerell's papers. Also, for Mr. W. B. Gurney, specimens of a large Lecanid Scale, *Lecanium berberis*, a European scale of the grape vine, recorded some years ago in Victoria, but only noticed within the last year in the vineyards of New South Wales. As it is a most prolific species, it may become a very serious pest, if neglected.

Before concluding the business of the Meeting, the President reminded the Members of the death of Dr. James C. Cox, formerly a very active Member and Office-bearer of the Society, on 29th September. It was accordingly resolved that an expression of sympathy should be tendered to Mrs. Cox and family.

AUSTRALIAN BEES. i. A NEW CROCISA, WITH A LIST OF THE AUSTRALIAN SPECIES OF THE GENUS.

By T. D. A. Cockerell.

(Communicated by W. W. Froggatt, F.L.S.)

Crocisa waroonensis, sp.nov.

♂. Length 9 mm., expanse a little over 20. Markings (due to hair) chalk-white; face, occiput and greater part of cheeks covered with white hair, lower part of cheeks and underside of head with black hair; labrum gibbous at sides; ocelli in a straight line; vertex shining, very sparsely punctured; flagellum obscurely brownish beneath; mesothorax shining strongly, unevenly, not densely punctured; anterior third, sides narrowly, and posterior corners of mesothorax covered with long loose white hair; scutellum with sparse small punctures, its posterior margin 〜〜-like, the posterior middle occupied by a quadrate patch of white hair, twice as broad as long, white hair also extending from beneath the margin; sides of metathorax with long white hair; pleura with the upper half densely covered with white hair, the under side of thorax with scanty black hair; tegulæ black, with very fine punctures, and a patch of white hair in front; wings with the basal half clear hyaline, the apical dark fuscous, clouded or spotted with paler in the region of the cells; third submarginal cell very narrow, but strongly bulging outwardly; anterior and middle tibiæ covered with white hair on outer and posterior side except at apex; hind tibiæ with the apical half free from white hair except posteriorly; middle and hind basitarsi with a little white hair; hind basitarsi flattened and curved; abdomen rather closely punctured, as follows: two transversely placed large hour-glass-shaped ones on first segment; four spots or patches each on second and third, the inner round, the outer (especially on second) large patches; two large patches each on fourth and fifth; venter with lateral spots of white hair. There is no basal spot on first abdominal segment.

Hab.—Warooma, Western Australia, April 4, 1908 (G. F. Berthoud). Froggatt, No.210.

This may be compared with *C. quadrimaculata* Rads., which it resembles in the colour of the wings, but *C. quadrimaculata* has the thorax above with nine white spots, and the maculation of the first abdominal segment is different. It is very much smaller than *C. lugubris* Smith.

I give a list of the known Australian species of *Crocisa*.

i. Blue-spotted Species. For a table, see Entomological News, February 1907, p.46.

C. lamprosoma Boisduval. Queensland.

C. turneri Friese. Queensland and New South Wales.

C. quartinæ Gribodo. Confused with *C. cærulæifrons* W. F. Kirby, which is quite distinct.

C. darwini Cockerell. Port Darwin. Blue markings, shining.

C. tincta Cockerell. Toowoomba, Queensland. Markings of abdomen pale blue.

C. beatissima Cockerell. Adelaide. Markings of abdomen bright blue, but not shining.

ii. White-spotted Species. For tables, see Bull. Amer. Mus. Nat. Hist., xxiii.(1907), p.232; and Entomologist, August, 1910, p.217.

C. albopicta Cockerell. Mackay, Queensland.

C. waroonensis Cockerell. Western Australia.

C. rotundata Friese (*albomaculata* Smith, preoccupied). Mackay, Queensland.

C. lugubris Smith.

C. macleayi Cockerell. New South Wales.

C. quadrimaculata Radoszkowski. New South Wales.

Excluded Species.

The following two blue-spotted species have been considered to be Australian. I have seen them only from Amboina, and do not believe they occur in Australia.

C. novæ-hollandiæ Lepeletier. "New Holland."

C. nitidula Fabricius.

A SMALL COLLECTION OF BEES FROM TASMANIA.

By T. D. A. Cockerell.

(Communicated by W. W. Froggatt, F.L.S.)

Comparatively little is known of the bees of Tasmania, so it may be worth while to report on a small collection sent by Mr. W. W. Froggatt, obtained by the well-known entomologist, Mr. Arthur M. Lea. The specimens bear two sets of numbers, one by Mr. Froggatt, the other by Mr. Lea. I have cited both, placing the Froggatt number first in each case.

(1.)*Callomelitta picta* Smith.   Magnet(140, 6456).

(2.)Parasphecodes excultus, n.sp.   Magnet(134, 6459).

♀.Length about 9 mm.; head, thorax and legs black; abdomen with the second and third segments, and apical part of first very broadly, bright red, the red also extending along the sides of first segment; rest of abdomen black, the fourth segment with a very faint, hardly noticeable, reddish band across the middle, and the broad hind margin slightly brownish; on the ventral side the fourth segment is red at sides except apically; head and thorax with rather long pale hair; some fuscous hair about the ocelli, and fuscous hairs intermixed on face; hair of legs moderately abundant, orange-tinted on inner side of tarsi, purplish-fuscous on outer side of basitarsi; hind femora with a large curled creamy-white floccus; hind tibiæ with shining white hair on inner side, contrasting with the purplish-fuscous behind; flagellum obscurely ferruginous beneath, longitudinally depressed or furrowed; rest of head, and thorax, dullish, minutely rugose; mesothorax rather coarsely rugose-punctate; area of metathorax distinctly defined behind, covered with dense irregular longitudinal rugæ, the wrinkles variously incomplete or anastomosing; tegulæ rufous with a fuscous spot; wings reddish-hyaline, first recurrent nervure meeting second transverso-cubital; outer nervures not weakened;

abdomen shining, with sparse exceedingly minute punctures; apex with dark purplish-fuscous hair, but glittering pale hairs at sides of apical half.

In my Table, in Annals and Magazine of Natural History, September, 1904, this runs to no species, because the first r.n. meets second t.c., and the red of abdomen is bright. The dark legs separate it at once from *P. lacthius* and *P. lithusca*; in the black apex of abdomen it resembles the Tasmanian *P. tuchilas* and *P. tilachus*; but *P. tuchilas* has the hind margins of the first two abdominal segments darkened, and the sculpture is different, while *P. tilachus* has a much darker abdomen. The insect is also quite distinct from the various Australian species, I have described in recent years.

(3.) *Halictus lanarius* Smith. One male. Devenport (138, 10714). *Halictus lanuginosus* Smith, is apparently the same.

(4.) *Paracolletes carinatus* (Smith). One male "Tasmania" (135, 10709). The abdomen is a fine dark blue, instead of green, and the second segment is more closely punctured; but the insect agrees so closely with female *P. carinatus*, that it is safe to regard it as its male.

(5.) *Paracolletes melbournensis* Cockerell. One female. Mt. Wellington (141, 6458).

(6.) PARACOLLETES LEAI, n.sp. Ulverstone (139, 10712).

♀. Length about 12 mm.; slender, black, the abdomen obscurely metallic, the fifth segment entirely greenish, the hind margins of the others suffused with reddish-purple; scanty hair of face, sides of thorax, and metathorax, glittering whitish, but dorsally and especially about tubercles fulvous, on vertex fuscous (perhaps some fuscous on mesothorax, but it is apparently denuded); head, thorax and abdomen shining; clypeus shining, with large punctures, and a median ridge, failing on the lowest fourth; mandibles with a red subapical ring, and slightly reddish at apex; a sharp keel between antennæ; flagellum reddish beneath at apex; front with very distinct rather dense punctures, except at sides, where they are sparse; vertex sparsely punctured; mesothorax shining, with scattered punctures, hardly any in middle; parapsidal grooves very distinct; area of metathorax dullish, with slight oblique striae; mesopleura with sparse punctures, very shiny and practically impunctate posteriorly; tegulae piceous; wings hyaline, a little brownish in the region of the cells; basal nervure meeting transverso-medial, a little to the outer side; first recurrent nervure joining second submarginal cell about the end of its first third; second recurrent joining third submarginal about as far from end as first recurrent from base of second submarginal; stigma piceous, nervures dark fuscous; legs with hairs mostly pale, ferruginous on inner side of anterior tibiae and tarsi, mainly fuscous on middle tibiae and tarsi; long and white on hind femora, creamy-white on inner and posterior side of hind tibiae, but purplish-brown and very strongly plumose behind, pale on inner side of hind basitarsi, but fuscous on anterior edge; abdomen sparsely and feebly punctured, scantily pubescent, without hair-bands; second and third segments with extremely narrow testaceous hind margins; apical hair dark fuscous. Hind spur with long oblique teeth.

A male from King Island(136, 6457) is provisionally referred here, though it may represent a very closely allied but distinct species. It has exactly the same form and appearance as the female, but differs as follows: face much narrower, eyes prominent; face covered with long fulvous hair, but black at sides above; vertex, mesothorax and scutellum with black or dark fuscous hair, but fulvous about tubercles; first recurrent nervure joining second submarginal cell nearer base; first two abdominal segments with much long light hair.

In my Table, in Trans. American Entom. Society, September, 1905, this runs nearest to *P. versicolor*(Sm.), which it resembles in the relatively narrow abdomen of the female, differing, however, by the ridged clypeus, and the very dark smooth (not silky) abdomen. In my Table, in Annals and Magazine of Natural History, January, 1906, it runs to the vicinity of *P. spatulatus*, a considerably smaller, broader species, with various differences. There is a good deal of resemblance to several other species, but it is impossible to identify it with any of them.

I give a check-list of the bees at present known from Tasmania.

PROSOPIS
  alcyonea (Erichs.).
  honesta Smith.
  hobartiana Ckll.
  vicina Sichel (in part).
EURYGLOSSA
  walkeriana Ckll.
PARACOLLETES
  chalybeatus (Erichs.).
  obscurus (Smith).
  viridicinctus Ckll.
  obscuripennis Ckll.
  hobartensis Ckll
  carinatus (Smith).
  melbournensis Ckll.
  leai Ckll.
CALLOMELITTA
  picta Smith.
HALICTUS
  orbatus Smith.
  cognatus Smith.
  limatus Smith.
  globosus Smith.
  repræsentans Smith.

HALICTUS
  familiaris (Erichs.).
  warburtoni Ckll.
  mitchelli Ckll.
  burkei Ckll.
  lanarius Smith.
  tasmaniæ (Ckll.).
"ANDRENA" (? HALICTUS)
  infima Erichs.
PARASPHECODES
  tilachus Smith.
  lithusca Smith.
  talchius Smith.
  stuchila Smith.
  altichus Smith.
  taluchis Smith.
  excultus Ckll.
MEGACHILA
  leucopyga Smith.
  chrypsopyga Smith.
  ordinaria Smith.
EXONEURA
  bicolor Smith.

Although this list is small, Tasmania is evidently much richer in bees than New Zealand. No doubt, many species remain to be discovered, and the local naturalist who will take up the bees in Tasmania will not only have a rich harvest of new forms, but also an opportunity to determine the habits of all the species, nothing having been done in this direction. It will also be very interesting to determine how many of the Australian genera are actually absent from Tasmania, and what proportion of the Tasmanian species is precinctive.

SYNONYMICAL NOTES ON SOME RECENTLY DESCRIBED AUSTRALIAN *CICADIDÆ*.

By W. L. Distant.

(Communicated by W. W. Froggatt, F.L.S.)

Since Goding & Froggatt published their monographic revision of the Australian Cicadidæ, the path has been cleared for other workers in that continent. Mr. Howard Ashton has recently published descriptions of new species; but, as a large proportion of these have been previously described, I am sure Mr. Ashton will be glad to have these errors corrected.

Cyclochila virens.

Cyclochila virens Dist., Entomologist, 1906, p.148.
Cyclochila laticosta Asht., Proc. Roy. Soc. Vict.(N.S.), xxiv., p.221, Pl.xlix., fig.1*a*, *b*, 1912.

Arunta interclusa.

Thopha interclusa Walk., List Hom., Suppl. p.5(1858).
Thopha n.sp. Walk., List Hom., iv., t.1, f.6(1852).
Arunta flava Asht., Rec. Aust. Mus., ix., p.76, Pl.vii., figs. 1, 2 (1912).

My reasons for regarding *A. flava* Asht., as a synonym of *A. interclusa* Walk., are as follows. Ashton's description accords with Walker's type, from which he says it differs "in its lighter colour, smaller size, less produced front to head, powdered white penultimate segment, and unspotted tegmina." The measurements given by Ashton, represent those of Walker's type; the head is not less produced (judging by Ashton's figure); *A. interclusa* has the anal segment powdered white, and also the tegmina unspotted.

Ashton's figures are somewhat difficult to reconcile with his description; he gives the expanse of tegmina as "90 mm.," which agrees with that of Walker's type, but his figures expand, ♂ 110,

♀ 97 mm., which is probably the responsibility of the artist. The tympanal coverings in the ♂ figured, are clearly inexact, and do not agree with the description.

It is probable that Mr. Ashton has confused Walker's species.

LEMBEJA BRUNNEOSA.

Lembeja brunneosa Dist., Ann. Soc. Ent. Belg., 1910, p.418.
Lembeja australis Asht., Rec. Austr. Mus., ix., p.77, Pl.vii., f.3 (1912).
Prasia vitticollis Asht., Proc. Roy. Soc. Vict.(N.S.), xxiv., p.228, Pl. li., f.4a, b, 1912 (the female of *Lembeja brunneosa*).

I had previously described this species from North Queensland, in 1910, which Mr. Ashton had overlooked, as he states that his *L. australis* is the first species of the genus described from Australia.

MELAMPSALTA CONVERGENS.

Cicada convergens Walk., List Hom., i., p.114(1850).
Melampsalta cylindrica Asht., Mem. Nat. Mus. Melb., No.4, p.31, Pl. iv., fig.1(1912).

Genus FROGGATTOIDES.

Froggattoides Dist., Ann. Soc. Ent. Belg., 1910, p.417.
Larrakeeya Asht., Rec. Austr. Mus., ix., p.77(1912).

FROGGATTOIDES TYPICUS.

Froggattoides typicus Dist., Ann. Soc. Ent. Belg., 1910, p.418.
Larrakeeya pallida Asht., Rec. Austr. Mus., ix., p.78, Pl. vii., f.4(1912).

The typical form was sent to me by my friend, Mr. Froggatt, who had received it from North Queensland. Mr. Ashton has localised his specimen as "Lawler, Western Australia."

By a clerical error, the name of this genus was published as *Froggattoids*. I now amend it.

REVISION OF THE AUSTRALIAN CURCULIONIDÆ BELONGING TO THE SUBFAMILY CRYPTORHYNCHIDES. Part XI.

By Arthur M. Lea, F.E.S.

This part* deals with a small group of genera that cluster around *Idotasia*, and nearly all of whose members are small or very small, and usually polished. If large scales are present, the derm beneath them is never opaque; in all, the mesosternal receptacle is highly raised, and the metasternal episterna are very small. They are usually apterous, strongly convex, and without prominent shoulders. Most of the genera and species are ex-Australian. *Idotasia* was referred to the *Zygopides* by Mr. Pascoe; I know comparatively few genera of that subfamily, but its distinct pectoral canal, bounded behind by a raised mesosternal receptacle, and scrobes terminating at the eyes, convince me that it belongs to the *Cryptorhynchides*. Mr. Pascoe described the metasternum as "normale," but it is, in fact, very peculiar, whether the genus is regarded as belonging to the *Cryptorhynchides* or to the *Zygopides*. The nearest genus to it, known to me, is *Ampagia*, referred, without hesitation, to the *Cryptorhynchides* by Mr. Pascoe.

The Australian allied genera may be tabulated as follows:—

Hind femora strongly dilated; abdomen with a semicircular shining ridge.
    Club of antennæ short.. Ampagia.
    Club long.. Amydala.
Femora not specially dilated; abdomen without a shining ridge.
    Scutellum present; winged............................... Alatidotasia.
    Scutellum absent; apterous.
        Metasternum moderately long..................... Idotasia.
        Metasternum short... Ampagiosoma.

---

* For convenience, *Camptorrhinus*, an isolated genus, is dealt with at the end of this part. But, except that it belongs to the same subfamily, it has little in common with *Idotasia*.

Genus AMPAGIA Pascoe, Trans. Ent. Soc. Lond., 1870, p.208.

Head partially concealed by prothorax. Rostrum short, straight, wide and flat. Antennæ short and stout; club briefly ovate, less than half the length of funicle. *Prothorax* more or less conical. *Scutellum* absent.* *Elytra* closely applied to prothorax, sides regularly decreasing in width to apex. *Pectoral canal* deep and wide. *Mesosternal receptacle* strongly raised, narrow, curved, emargination transverse; cavernous. *Metasternum* shorter than following segment, its episterna concealed except posteriorly. Basal segment of *abdomen* large, its disc flattened and masked outwardly by a subcircular rim or ridge. *Legs* long; femora angular, compressed, edentate, widely grooved, posterior suboblong, angularly produced on their outer upper edge. Elliptic, strongly convex, squamose,† apterous.*

Mr. Pascoe founded this genus on a weevil from King George's Sound, having very remarkable femora and abdomen. Subsequently,‡ he described a second species (*A. rudis*) from New Zealand, referring it to a new genus (*Acallopais*) which he compared with *Acalles*, a genus with which, other than in density of clothing, it has scarcely anything in common. Comparing Mr. Pascoe's two species together, (I do not know Major Broun's *A. sculpturatus*) it will be seen that both *A. erinacea* and *A. rudis* agree in the mesosternal receptacle, abdomen, legs, eyes, rostrum, antennæ, and, in fact, in all characters on which genera are founded. In the Memoirs of the Australian Museum, Mr. Olliff, in dealing with the insects from Lord Howe Island, described another species, *A. montigava*, referring it, however, to *Idotasia*, to the species of which genus it bears a very strong superficial resemblance; a second species, referred by him to *Idotasia*, possibly belongs to *Ampagia*; unfortunately, I omitted to examine the type when last in Sydney, but Mr. Olliff describes the femora as "strongly thickened." It is certainly not an *Idotasia*. *Cryptorhynchus femoralis* Erichs., is also an *Ampagia*. Of the two new species described below, I have not ventured to regard *A. alata* as belonging to a new genus, despite its possession of

---

* Except in *A. alata*. † Except in *A. montivaga*.
‡ Ann. Mag. Nat. Hist., 1877.

scutellum and wings. Although the genus is a very distinct one, several of the species are very closely allied, differing but little in anything but size and clothing. In the appended tabulation, I have been compelled, consequently, to make use of some very trivial characters.

Alate...	*alata*, n.sp.
Apterous.	
Glabrous...	*monticaga* Oll.
Squamose.	
Not less than 4 mm. in length...	*femoralis* Erichs.
Less than 4 mm. in length.	
Scales sooty and almost uniform in colour...	*erinacea* Pasc.
Elytra with a distinct patch of whitish scales at basal third...	*cognata*, n.sp.

AMPAGIA FEMORALIS Erichs., Mast. Cat., Sp.No.5544.

Cryptorhynchus femoralis Erichs.

Black, shining; antennæ and tarsi dull red. Rather densely clothed with coarse scales varying in colour from ochreous-white to sooty-brown or black; a moderately large sooty patch about the summit of posterior declivity, head and base of rostrum densely squamose. Under surface and legs densely clothed with large, soft and somewhat ochreous scales, the metasternum and basal segment of abdomen with long setæ.

Head with the ocular fovea and rostrum at the base entirely concealed by clothing. Rostrum dilated towards base and apex, very feebly carinate along middle; rather strongly, but not very densely punctate. Scape the length of four basal joints of funicle; club briefly ovate, scarcely longer than the three preceding joints. *Prothorax* densely and strongly punctate, punctures round, deep, and very close together, but not at all confluent. *Elytra* very feebly rising along suture to slightly beyond middle, and then descending at an angle of about 60°; each with ten deep, narrow, and very distinct striæ, containing moderately distinct but distant punctures, elsewhere impunctate. *Under surface* and *legs* with similar punctures to those on prothorax. Mesosternal receptacle not keeled posteriorly. Abdomen with basal segment less than half total length, apex rounded and slightly produced on to second, its middle feebly concave, and less strongly punctate than elsewhere. Posterior *femora* strongly dilated near their outer apex, where their width is more than half their total length. Length 4¾, rostrum 1¼, width 2 mm.

Hab.—Tasmania and King Island, on several shrubs growing close to sea-beaches.

AMPAGIA ALATA, n.sp.

Black; in places (including the rostrum) piceous-brown; antennæ and tarsi reddish. Densely clothed with pale brown, intermingled with semierect sooty scales; a distinct patch of snowy scales on basal third of elytra scarcely extending halfway to sides, and a few small and indistinct spots on suture beyond middle. Under surface with paler scales than above; apices of all the femora with whitish scales.

Rostrum densely and coarsely punctate; with a feeble median ridge. *Prothorax* with dense, round, clearly cut punctures, which, however, are entirely concealed by clothing. *Scutellum* small. *Elytra* with compressed striæ, marked at regular intervals by small punctures. *Under surface* with dense, almost concealed punctures. Posterior *femora* scarcely twice as long as their greatest width. Length 3⅔, rostrum ¾; width 1½ mm.

Hab.—N.S.W.: Tamworth.

This species possesses a scutellum and wings, characters which would seem to forbid its being placed in *Ampagia* (I can state positively that both *A. erinacea* and *A. femoralis* are apterous), but I have not ventured to propose a genus for its reception, as in all else (including the femora and abdomen) it is conformable to the genus. The scutellum is small, and, were it not for the clothing, would be scarcely traceable; the elytra are apparently soldered together, but having (in the unique specimen, under examination) forced them apart, gauzy wings are plainly discernible.

AMPAGIA MONTIVAGA Oll.

Idotasia montivaga Oll., Mem. Aust. Mus., 1889, p.19.

Black; antennæ and legs red; each elytron diluted with red in middle. Glabrous except for a few indistinct setose scales at apex and on flanks of prothorax, and setæ on the two basal and the apical segment of abdomen.

Head polished and almost impunctate; eyes larger and less distant than usual. Rostrum very finely punctate, a few coarse punctures at base. *Prothorax* with a few very small punctures on disc towards base, front with larger and moderately long punctures, sides with much larger and moderately elongate punctures. *Elytra* without punctures in vicinity of suture, sides with moderately large ones in feeble striæ. *Metasternum* feebly concave. Basal segment of abdomen with a somewhat triangular plate in middle, on each side of which is a distinct groove, so that this segment appears to be divided into three parts; second segment almost vertical in middle. *Femora* widely grooved, the posterior largely dilated externally, and not twice as long as their greatest width. Length 3, rostrum $\frac{2}{3}$; width $1\frac{1}{3}$ mm.

Hab.—Lord Howe Island (Australian Museum).

The specimen, under examination, appears to be more brightly coloured than those seen by Mr. Olliff, which are described as black with piceous antennæ and legs. In all the other species of the genus, the raised, shining, abdominal carina is semicircular, and rises from a flat or gently convex surface; in the present species, the carina is scarcely marked, the plate is triangular, and bounded outwardly, on each side, by a distinct groove, so that it is rendered even more distinct.

AMPAGIA ERINACEA Pasc., Mast. Cat. Sp.No.5576.

Black or piceous-black, under surface and legs piceous-brown, antennæ red. Rather densely clothed with sooty suberect scales, not as dark on under as on upper surface, and partially clothing the mesosternal receptacle; elytra occasionally with a few whitish scales scattered about.

Rostrum densely and coarsely punctate, punctures more or less concealed. *Prothorax* with dense punctures. *Elytra* with compressed striæ, more distinct towards apex than elsewhere, and with almost angular punctures. *Under surface* densely punctate; basal segment of abdomen with a moderately distinct semicircular elevation. Posterior *femora* not twice as long as their greatest width. Length 3, rostrum ⅔(vix); width 1½; variation in length 2¼-3½ mm.

Hab.—W. Australia: King George's Sound.

In this (the typical) species, the abdominal ridge is less distinct than in the others, which may account for its having been overlooked by Mr. Pascoe in describing it, although subsequently (when describing *Amydala*) its presence was noted.

AMPAGIA COGNATA, n.sp.

Piceous-brown, legs and antennæ paler. Densely clothed with dingy brown scales (paler on under surface and legs), with sooty, suberect scales scattered about on prothorax, and more or less distinctly on the alternate interstices of the elytra; elytra with a patch of whitish scales on basal third, and which is feebly traceable on to shoulders. Pectoral canal almost glabrous.

Sculpture apparently as in the preceding, except that the abdominal ridge is more distinct. Length 2⅔ mm.

Hab.—N. S. Wales: Sydney(A. M. Lea).

A specimen from Eyre's Peninsula (the Rev. T. Blackburn's No.691) differs in being smaller(2 mm.), and rather stouter than the one from Sydney. I have not cared to abrade either of the specimens, except to make sure that the scutellum is absent. The species is evidently close to *A. erinacea*, but it appears to be distinct on account of its clothing, and the more distinct abdominal ridge.

AMPAGIA SQUAMIGERA Oll.

Idotasia squamigera Oll., Mem. Aust. Mus. 1899, p.19.

Hab.—Lord Howe Island.

Genus AMYDALA Pascoe, Journ. Linn. Soc., 1871, p.213.

Club of antennæ cylindrical, as long as funicle, two basal joints long and subequal, two apical very short. All else as in *Ampagia*.

The shape of the club is so strongly at variance with all the species of *Ampagia*, that it is as well, perhaps, to recognise *Amydala*. It is remarkable, however, that two genera should have such abnormal hind femora and abdomen in common.

AMYDALA ABDOMINALIS Pasc., Mast. Cat., Sp.No.5569.

Black, shining. Clothed all over with variously coloured scales. Prothorax with a median triangular ochreous-red patch, speckled with white, four patches of mouse-coloured scales at base, and one on each side of apex. Elytra with irregular patches of ochreous, mouse-coloured, and whitish scales. Under surface with whitish scales, becoming ochreous on abdomen.

Head almost impunctate. Rostrum shorter than prothorax, flat, sides strongly incurved to middle. Scape the length of five basal joints of funicle. *Prothorax* not visibly punctured. *Elytra* each with ten feebly punctured striæ; suture near base with numerous, small, rounded granules. Abdomen with first segment almost half its total length, its middle produced on to second; second, third, and fourth each with a row of about eight strong punctures; fifth with large punctures or small foveæ in middle. Posterior *femora* suboblong, about thrice as long as wide. Length $11\frac{1}{2}$, rostrum 3; width $5\frac{1}{4}$ mm.

Hab.— Queensland : Wide Bay.

Genus IDOTASIA Pascoe.

Ann. Mag. Nat. Hist. vii.(4th Ser.), 1871, p.261.

Head not concealed by prothorax; ocular fovea obsolete or nearly so. *Eyes* widely separated, facets of variable size. *Rostrum* rather stout, not very long, curved. *Antennæ* short, stout; scape* inserted much closer to base than apex of rostrum, less than half the length of funicle; two basal joints of funicle moderately long, the others transverse; club briefly ovate, adnate to funicle. *Prothorax* convex, subconical, sides rounded, base truncate; ocular lobes obtuse. *Scutellum* absent. *Elytra* subcordate, slightly wider than prothorax, base truncate, sides considerably narrowed near apex. *Pectoral canal* deep and moderately wide, terminated immediately behind anterior coxæ. *Mesosternal receptacle* strongly raised, walls thin, emargination strongly transverse, rapidly sloping from apex to base and triareolate,

---

* Mr. Pascoe describes the scape as scarcely attaining the eye, but in the two Australian species, it certainly does.

cavernous.* *Metasternum* large, longer than first segment of abdomen, transversely and largely but shallowly excavated; flanks almost vertical, not much longer than wide, base oblique, apex with coxal emargination; episterna almost entirely concealed, the extreme apex appearing as if belonging to the mesosternum. *Abdomen* moderately large, sutures distinct, two basal segments concave in ♂, the first larger than second, intercoxal process very wide; three apical segments of almost equal width and suddenly depressed below second; third and fourth combined shorter than second or fifth. *Legs* long; posterior coxæ almost touching elytra; femora strongly grooved from base to apex, extreme base strongly compressed, dentate or not;† tibiæ somewhat compressed, straight or almost straight; tarsi stout, third joint wide, not very deeply bilobed, claw-joint thin; claws very minute. Elliptic, convex, highly polished; apterous.

This genus is abundantly represented in New Guinea, and sparingly in New Zealand. The two Lord Howe Island species, referred by Mr. Olliff to *Idotasia*, belong, I believe, to *Ampagia*; one of them certainly does, and here they are dealt with under that genus.

The Australian species may be thus tabulated :—

Prothorax with coarse punctures, no larger (but more
    crowded) on sides than on disc............................ *birta*, n.sp.
Prothorax with punctures much larger at sides than on
    disc.
    Elytra not punctate on hind declivity, except at
        extreme apex... *albidosparsa*, n.sp.
    Elytra distinctly punctate on posterior declivity.
        Striæ invisible from most directions.................... *evanida* Pasc.
        Striæ fine but distinct....................................... *æqualis* Pasc.

IDOTASIA EVANIDA Pasc.; Mast. Cat., Sp.No.5578.

Black, shining. Snowy-white scales in rostral grooves, and forming two rows on femora; apex of femora with scales in punctures, a moderately large patch on the posterior; tibiæ with very small scales; each lateral prothoracic puncture with a scale.

---

    * At least in the Australian species.
    † Edentate in the Australian species.

Head feebly punctate; eyes rather finely faceted. Rostrum with four punctate grooves, leaving three distinctly elevated lines (less distinct in ♀ than in ♂), of which the median one is widest. *Prothorax* about as long as wide; flanks at apex with large round punctures, but at base with very small punctures, disc with small punctures evenly distributed. *Elytra* moderately strongly punctured at apex, scarcely visibly elsewhere; very finely striate, striæ invisible from most directions. *Under surface* sparsely and irregularly punctate. *Femora* with a row of punctures in front and behind, at apex moderately densely punctate, posterior passing apex of elytra; tibiæ with rows of punctures. Length 3, rostrum $\frac{2}{3}$: width $1\frac{1}{3}$ mm.

Hab.—Queensland: Wide Bay, Brisbane - N. S. Wales: Tweed, Richmond, and Clarence Rivers.

IDOTASIA ÆQUALIS Pasc., *l.c.* No.5577.

Colour and clothing much as in *I. evanida*.

Head and rostrum much as in *I. evanida*, but the eyes rather more coarsely faceted, and the rostral grooves and elevated lines less pronounced in both sexes. Flanks of *prothorax* with large round punctures both at apex and base, but more numerous at apex, disc with larger punctures than in *I. evanida*. *Elytra* punctate-striate, the striæ fine but distinct, the punctures small and distant, but moderately distinct, and at apex round and regular. Punctures of *under surface* and *legs* much as in *I. evanida*, but rather coarser. Length $3\frac{1}{3}$ mm.

Hab.—Queensland: Cape York, Rockhampton - N. S. Wales: Tamworth.

Close to the preceding species, but distinguished by the decidedly coarser puncturation, especially of the prothorax, and the striation of the elytra.

IDOTASIA LÆTA, n.sp.

Black, shining. Snowy-white scales in rostral grooves, margining eyes, in punctures of legs, and forming a moderately distinct patch on upper surface of hind femora.

Head with sparse punctures, but moderately large and distinct between eyes; these larger than usual. Rostrum and *legs* as in

I. evanida. *Prothorax* with moderately numerous, very distinct, and rather large (very coarse for the genus) punctures of even size, and evenly distributed, except that at sides they are more crowded than on the disc. *Elytra* impunctate (except for a series at base, and a few small ones at extreme apex); highly polished, and entirely without striæ. Length 2¼ mm.

Hab.—N. Queensland : Endeavour River, Sue Island(Macleay Museum).

The character of the prothoracic punctures, and entire absence of elytral striæ will readily distinguish this species from all the Australian, and most of the New Guinea species.

IDOTASIA ALBIDOSPARSA, n.sp.

Black, shining. Upper surface of posterior femora with a moderately distinct patch of snowy scales; legs elsewhere, and the rostrum very indistinctly squamose.

Head with very indistinct punctures; with or without a feeble shining space between eyes; these more decidedly lateral, and more widely separated than usual. Rostrum smooth, without raised lines; sides seriate-punctate, middle finely, apex rather densely punctate. *Prothorax* with evenly distributed and minute punctures except that on the lower flanks (especially anteriorly) they become rather large. *Elytra* without punctures, except a shallow one marking the base of each of the almost invisibly impressed striæ, and a few small ones at extreme apex. *Legs* as in *I. evanida.* Length 3 mm.

Hab.—N. Queensland : Endeavour River(Macleay Museum).

The rostrum, in three specimens (possibly all females) under examination, is entirely without elevated lines. The punctures on the disc of the prothorax are much smaller than in any other species here described. It is possibly close to, but evidently distinct from, *I. salubris* from New Guinea.

AMPAGIOSOMA, n.gen.

Head not concealed by prothorax; ocular fovea moderately distinct. *Eyes* widely separated, moderately coarsely faceted.

Rostrum rather short and stout, slightly curved. *Antennæ* rather long and thin; scape inserted much closer to apex than base of rostrum, the length of funicle; funicle with the first two joints elongate; club elliptic-ovate, moderately long. *Prothorax* strongly convex, apex moderately produced, base truncate, ocular lobes subobtuse. *Scutellum* absent. *Elytra* strongly convex, raised (but not suddenly) above prothorax, widest near shoulders, thence strongly lessened to apex. *Pectoral canal* deep and moderately wide, terminated between four anterior coxæ. *Mesosternal receptacle* strongly raised, sides thin except at base, emargination semicircular; slightly cavernous. *Metasternum* very short (scarcely half the length of the following segment); episterna narrow. *Abdomen* rather narrow, sutures distinct; first segment moderately large, raised above and so obscuring second that, although it is slightly larger than either of the two following, it appears to be smaller, third and fourth combined slightly less than fifth. *Legs* moderately long; femora not very stout, grooved and edentate; tibiæ compressed, angularly joined to femora, four posterior with a laminate extension on upper edge towards base; tarsi slightly shorter than tibiæ, third joint not very wide, deeply bilobed; claws small. Elliptic, strongly convex, polished, apterous.

Allied to *Ampagia* and *Idotasia*; from the former, it is separated by the abdomen and legs; and from the latter, by the antennæ, metasternum, abdomen, and legs; the tibiæ are faintly reminiscent of *Psepholax*.

AMPAGIOSOMA CONVEXUM, n.sp.

Piceous-black, upper surface with a very feeble bluish iridescence; front of prothorax, rostrum, and legs piceous-brown; antennæ red. Upper surface sparsely and irregularly clothed (denser at apex and base of prothorax and base, middle, and suture beyond middle of elytra than elsewhere) with scales varying from white to a dingy orange. Under surface and legs rather densely clothed, intermediate femora with a feeble ring of white scales, posterior femora with either two apical rings or a large apical patch of whitish scales; pectoral canal with large soft scales.

Head densely and coarsely punctate, but punctures concealed; a short distinct carina in middle; depressed between eyes. Rostrum slightly wider near base than at apex, sides rather strongly incurved to middle; with distinct punctures leaving five raised costæ which are very distinct to just before antennæ, apex with moderately dense but small punctures. Two basal joints of funicle equal in length. *Prothorax* with moderately dense, large, irregular punctures at base and apex; but absent across middle, except for a few on each side of a very narrow, shining, elevated median carina; the carina distinct to apex but not to base. *Elytra* at base no wider than prothorax, but rapidly widening to basal third, thence strongly narrowed (with a feebly rounded outline) to apex; with series of rather shallow punctures (except at sides, where they become almost foveate); without distinct striæ (even at sides) but the spaces between the series of punctures gently convex. *Under surface* and *legs* densely punctate, but punctures of the former entirely concealed. Length 4, rostrum $1\frac{1}{3}$; width $2\frac{1}{3}$, depth $2\frac{1}{3}$ mm.

Hab.—New South Wales (Macleay Museum).

In one of the specimens under examination, the scales form two very feeble and narrow transverse fasciæ at the middle, and the suture thence is very distinctly supplied with a narrow line of scales. The elytral punctures are somewhat irregular, both in disposition and size; on two specimens, they are almost twice as large at the sides of one as of the other; on the flattest part (just before the middle), they are smaller, and more distinct than elsewhere.

A specimen in the Macleay Museum (from King George's Sound) possibly belongs to this species; it differs in being larger ($4\frac{1}{2}$ mm.), rather more convex, the clothing more setose in character, the median crest of the prothorax much more noticeable, and the antennæ thinner; the punctures are also different, but as in the two specimens above described the punctures are not exactly alike, this may not be of much importance. Probably, however, the specimen represents a distinct species, but it is not in the best of condition.

Genus ALATIDOTASIA Lea: Deutsch. Ent. Zeitschr. 1910, p.523.

ALATIDOTASIA RUBRIVENTRIS Lea, *l.c.*, p.524.

Hab.—Queensland.

Genus CAMPTORRHINUS Schönherr.

Curc. Disp. Meth. p.283; Gen. et Spec. Curc. Vol. iv., p.170, Gen.306; Lacord., Gen. Col., Tome vii., p.86.

Head small, not concealed by prothorax. *Eyes* large, widely separated above, almost touching beneath, facets moderately large. *Rostrum* long, thin, feebly curved. *Antennae* moderately stout; scape inserted slightly nearer apex than base of rostrum; two basal joints of funicle moderately long, the others strongly transverse; club elongate, continuous with funicle. *Prothorax* narrowed and produced in front, constriction slight, ocular lobes prominent. *Scutellum* suboblong, very distinct. *Elytra* long, base widely and semicircularly emarginate. Pectoral canal narrow, deep, terminated at base of anterior coxae. *Prosternal receptacle* raised, triangular, walls thin, rounded behind, cavernous. Intercoxal process of *mesosternum* subtruncate at apex. *Metasternum* elongate, episterna longer than three basal segments of abdomen. *Abdominal segments* large, sutures distinct; first about once and one-half the length of second; second, third and fifth subequal, slightly longer than fourth. *Legs* long; coxae large, the intermediate separated less widely than the anterior; femora pedunculate, dentate, posterior passing elytra; tibiae short, subfalcate. Elongate, subcylindrical, squamose, punctate, winged.

Perhaps the most remarkable genus in the subfamily. The receptacle for the rostrum forms part of the prothorax, not - as in almost all the other Australian genera—of the mesothorax; it appears as if forming part of an additional segment, the suture of which is distinct at the sides and is even traceable across the base of the pronotum. The eyes are almost as in *Tranes*. The abdomen appears to be composed of six segments, the fifth being widely emarginate and allowing the apical dorsal segment to be seen; this segment is doubled over and squamose, and might almost be regarded as a true pygidium, the third segment slightly (but still noticeably) longer than the fourth, is also very remarkable.

Of the genus (somewhat numerously represented in the Malay Archipelago), only one species is known to occur in Australia.

CAMPTORRHINUS DORSALIS Boisd.; Mast. Cat., Sp.No.5414.

Cryptorhynchus ephippiger Boisd.

Densely clothed (even including the pectoral canal) with large, soft, overlapping scales, apical half of rostrum bare and shining. Scales on head, rostrum and scutellum uniformly ochreous-brown, a large black patch (in which are a few paler scales) on disc of prothorax; elytra with a large suboblong patch of blackish scales which become paler at the sides, scales on posterior declivity (especially just behind the black patch) paler than elsewhere. Abdomen with rather darker scales than on sterna, and, in addition, with elongate paler ones rather sparsely distributed. Tibiæ and femora feebly ringed with black.

Head convex, depressed between eyes. Rostrum the length of prothorax, somewhat flattened, very feebly incurved to middle; in ♂ rather densely punctate, punctures partially concealed on basal half and leaving a feeble median carina, very feebly punctate and without carina in ♀. *Prothorax* convex, longer than wide; densely and strongly punctate; with a feeble but moderately distinct median carina continuous to apex but not to base. *Elytra* about one-fourth wider than prothorax at base, sides straight and very feebly diminishing to near apex; strongly seriate-punctate or foveate, punctures round and deep, diminishing in size towards base and apex, depressed along suture, over the third and fifth feebly raised, more noticeably at summit of posterior declivity. *Under surface* densely punctate, punctures concealed by scales. Teeth of anterior and intermediate *femora* rather small, of the posterior large, triangular and acute. Length $8\frac{2}{3}$, rostrum $1\frac{4}{5}$; width 3; variation in length 5-9 mm.

Hab. — Queensland — New South Wales.

The apical half or two-thirds of the anterior tibiæ are usually furnished beneath with long sparse setæ, but, in one specimen under examination, the setæ are very dense and long. The colour of the derm (invisible, however, till the scales have been removed) is of a dark chestnut-red.

Var. INORNATUS, n.var.

Clothing of an uniform muddy- or slaty-brown, elytral interstices with distinct seriate granules. Length 10 mm.

Hab.— Queensland : Brisbane(A. J. Coates).

I have seen but two female specimens of this variety.

NOTES ON THE NATIVE FLORA OF NEW SOUTH WALES.

By R. H. Cambage, F.L.S.

Supplementary Lists to Part VIII., Camden to Burragorang and Mount Werong.

(Continued from These Proceedings, 1911, p.583.)

(Plate lxv.)

The following lists contain the names of additional species collected during a second visit to the district, in December, 1911, when many plants were found flowering, which had been previously overlooked, or not identified.

Supplementary List.

Camden to Burragorang.

Hypericineæ: *Hypericum gramineum* Forst.

Leguminosæ: *Acacia decurrens* var. *mollis*, (flowering in October).

Halorageæ: *Halorayis teucrioides* A. Gray.

Myrtaceæ: *Bæckea densifolia* Sm., *Callistemon linearis* DC.

Umbelliferæ: *Hydrocotyle geraniifolia* F.v.M., *Actinotus Helianthi* Labill.,(Flannel Flower).

Rubiaceæ: *Cassinia aurea* R.Br.,(yellow flowers), *Gnaphalium japonicum* Thunb.

Goodeniaceæ: *Goodenia decurrens* R.Br.

Epacrideæ: *Lissanthe sapida* R.Br.,(red fruit, ⅜ inch in diameter, with a somewhat apple-like taste. Burragorang Mountain).

Polygonaceæ: *Rumex Brownii* Campd.

Euphorbiaceæ: *Poranthera corymbosa* Brong., *P. microphylla* Brong., *Breynia oblongifolia* J. Muell.

Orchideæ: *Dipodium punctatum* R.Br.

Commelynaceæ: *Commelyna cyanea* R.Br.

GRAMINEÆ: *Themeda Forskalii* Hack.,(*Anthistiria ciliata* L.).
FILICES: *Blechnum cartilagineum* Sw., *Dryopteris decomposita* (R.Br.) O. Kuntze, (*Aspidium decompositum* Spreng.), *Asplenium flabellifolium* Cav.

Burragorang to Yerranderie and Kowmung.

MENISPERMACEÆ: *Stephania hernandiæfolia* Walp.
VIOLARIEÆ: *Hymenanthera dentata* R.Br.
TREMANDREÆ: *Tetratheca ericifolia* Sm.
POLYGALEÆ: *Comesperma ericinum.*
HYPERICINEÆ: *Hypericum gramineum.*
GERANIACEÆ: *Geranium dissectum* L., *Oxalis corniculata* L., (Sour Grass).
OLACINEÆ: *Olax stricta* R.Br.
STACKHOUSIEÆ: *Stackhousia viminea* Sm.
LEGUMINOSÆ: *Bossiæa prostrata* R.Br., *Zornia diphylla* Pers., *Desmodium varians* Endl., *Glycine clandestina* Wendl.
ROSACEÆ: *Acæna ovina* A. Cunn., *A. sanguisorbæ* Vahl,(Burr).
MYRTACEÆ: *Callistemon lanceolatus* DC.
ONAGRARIEÆ: *Epilobium glabellum* Forst.
UMBELLIFERÆ: *Hydrocotyle geraniifolia*, *Trachymene ericoides* Benth.
COMPOSITÆ: *Cassinia aurea* (yellow flowers), *Podolepis canescens* A. Cunn., *Helichrysum collinum* DC., *H. semipapposum* DC.
GOODENIACEÆ: *Goodenia bellidifolia* Sm., *G. barbata* (pale blue flowers), *G. heterophylla* Sm., (Byrnes' Gap to Kowmung, No. 3131), *Scævola hispida*, *S. microcarpa* Cav.
BORAGINEÆ: *Cynoglossum australe* R.Br.
SCROPHULARINEÆ: *Veronica calycina* R.Br.
LAURINEÆ: *Cassytha glabella* R.Br.(Dodder).
EUPHORBIACEÆ: *Poranthera microphylla*, *Adriana tomentosa* Gaud.
SANTALACEÆ: *Choretrum spicatum* F.v.M.
CONIFERÆ: *Callitris calcarata* R.Br. (Black or Mountain Pine; near Wollondilly River, about ten miles above bridge).
AMARYLLIDEÆ: *Hypoxis hygrometrica* Labill.

LILIACEÆ: *Dianella tasmanica* Hk., *D. revoluta* R.Br., *Thysanotus tuberosus* R.Br., (Fringed Violets).

JUNCACEÆ: *Juncus planifolius* R.Br., *J. pauciflorus* R.Br., *J. pallidus* R.Br., *J. prismatocarpus* R.Br., *J. Fockei*.

CYPERACEÆ: *Scirpus inundatus* Spreng.

GRAMINEÆ: *Andropogon australis* Spreng., *Danthonia penicillata* F.v.M., var. *longifolia*(*D. longifolia* R.Br.).

FILICES: *Adiantum hispidulum* Sw.

Colong to Mount Werong.

RANUNCULACEÆ: *Ranunculus lappaceus* Sm., (Buttercup), and var. near *subsericens*, *R. rivularis* Bks. and Sol.

DILLENIACEÆ: *Hibbertia Billardieri*.

PITTOSPOREÆ: *Bursaria spinosa*, *Billardiera scandens*.

TREMANDREÆ: *Tetratheca ericifolia*.

POLYGALEÆ: *Comesperma retusum* Labill., *C. ericinum*.

MALVACEÆ: *Plagianthus pulchellus*.

GERANIACEÆ: *Geranium dissectum*.

RUTACEÆ: *Correa speciosa*.

STACKHOUSIEÆ: *Stackhousia linarifolia*, *S. viminea*.

LEGUMINOSÆ: *Oxylobium ellipticum* R.Br., var. *alpinum*, *Gompholobium Huegelii* Benth., *G. minus* Sm., *Aotus* sp., *Pultenæa pycnocephala* F.v.M., *Bossiæa heterophylla* Vent.

ROSACEÆ: *Rubus parvifolius*, *Acæna sanguisorbæ*.

MYRTACEÆ: *Kunzea* sp. No.3175, allied to *K. pomifera* F.v.M.).

ONAGRARIEÆ: *Epilobium glabellum*.

UMBELLIFERÆ: *Xanthosia pilosa* var. *glabra*, *H. dissecta* Hk.

COMPOSITÆ: *Brachycome scapiformis* DC., *Cassinia aculeata* R.Br., *Podolepis canescens*, *Helichrysum bracteatum* Willd., *H. elatum* A. Cunn., *H. semipapposum*, *Gnaphalium purpureum* L., *Erechthites mixta* DC., *Senecio velleioides* A. Cunn., *S. dryadeus* Sieb., *Microseris Forsteri* Hk.

STYLIDEÆ: *Candollea serrulata* (*Stylidium graminifolium*).

GOODENIACEÆ: *Velleya montana* Hk., *Goodenia bellidifolia*, *Scævola hispida*.

CAMPANULACEÆ: *Lobelia pedunculata* R.Br.,(flowers white to pale blue), *Wahlenbergia gracilis*.

PRIMULACEÆ : *Anagallis arrensis*(Pimpernel).

LOGANIACEÆ : *Mitrasacme serpyllifolia* R.Br., *M. polymorpha* R.Br.

GENTIANEÆ : *Limnanthemum crenatum* F.v.M. (aquatic plant in Bindook Swamp).

SCROPHULARINEÆ : *Gratiola peruviana* L., *Veronica gracilis* R.Br.(margin of Bindook Swamp).

LENTIBULARINEÆ : *Utricularia dichotoma* Labill., (Mount Werong).

LABIATÆ : *Prunella vulgaris* DC., *Scutellaria humilis* R.Br.(in basaltic soil on top of Mount Shivering).

MONIMIACEÆ: *Hedycarya Cunninghami* Tul.,(Native Mulberry. In Barrallier's Pass).

PROTEACEÆ : *Conospermum taxifolium* Sm.

THYMELEÆ : *Pimelea glauca* R.Br.

EUPHORBIACEÆ : *Poranthera corymbosa*, *P. microphylla*.

ORCHIDEÆ : *Dipodium punctatum*, *Gastrodia sesamoides* R.Br. (on Mount Shivering and east of Mount Colong), *Caleana major* R.Br.

IRIDEÆ : *Patersonia sericea* R.Br.(Wild Iris), *P. glabrata*.

AMARYLLIDEÆ : *Hæmadorum planifolium* R.Br.

LILIACEÆ : *Dianella revoluta*, *D. cærulea* Sims, *Burchardia umbellata* R.Br., *Bulbine bulbosa* Haw., *Cæsia parviflora* R.Br., (blue flowers), *S. umbellata* R.Br.(white flowers), *Sowerbæa juncea* Sm., *Xerotes filiformis* R.Br.

XYRIDEÆ : *Xyris gracilis* R.Br.(yellow swamp-flower).

JUNCACEÆ : *Juncus planifolius*, *J. pallidus* (up to altitude of 3,900 feet), *J. Fockei*, *J.* sp.(No.3142).

RESTIACEÆ : *Restio australis* R.Br.

CYPERACEÆ: *Cyperus sanguineo-fuscus* Hook. f., *Scirpus setaceus* L.(?)(Mount Werong), *Schœnus turbinatus* Poir., *S. Brownii* Hk.

GRAMINEÆ : *Andropogon australis*, *Stipa pubescens* R.Br., *Danthonia penicillata* var. *semiannularis* (*D. semiannularis* R.Br.), *Amphipogon strictus* R.Br.

FILICES : *Lindsaya linearis* Sw., *Blechnum discolor*(Forst.) Keys.,(*Lomaria discolor* Willd.), *Cyclophorus serpens*(Forst.) C. Christ(*Polypodium serpens* Forst.).

Flowering specimens were obtained in December, 1911, of the Hibbertia (No.2259) mentioned in these Proceedings for 1911 (p.576), which show that the plant then referred to, is an erect form of *H. serpyllifolia*.

Quintinia Sieberi was found towards the head of Ruby Creek, just east of Mount Werong. Early Australian botanists soon noticed that the seeds of this tree often germinate in the caudices of Tree-ferns; the young plants thus produced gradually extend to the ground, and afterwards grow into large trees beside the Tree-fern (Plate lxv.).

An interesting species of Kunzea (No.3175) from 2-3 feet high and somewhat straggling, was found flowering in December on the Big Plain, at an altitude of about 3,800 feet, and is probably a new species. The specimens collected are in the National Herbarium, Sydney.

EXPLANATION OF PLATE LXV.

Quintinia Sieberi (on the right) growing from a seed which germinated in the caudex of *Alsophila australis* (leaning to the left).

NOTES ON THE NATIVE FLORA OF NEW SOUTH WALES.

By R. H. CAMBAGE, F.L.S.

PART IX. BARRABA TO NANDEWAR MOUNTAINS AND BOGGABRI.

(Plates lxvi.-lxvii.)

The notes for this paper were obtained during a short visit to the locality in November, 1909, and although many small plants were doubtless overlooked, sufficient were noticed to enable a good general impression of the character of the vegetation to be formed. One of the chief features of interest of the locality, from a geographical standpoint, is that, although the Nandewar Mountains are situated about 90 miles west of the Great Dividing Range, and are connected with New England by the Nandewar Range, which is in places a comparatively low spur, yet they reach an altitude of about 5,000 feet above sea-level, an elevation only exceeded in a few instances in New South Wales, outside the Kosciusko and surrounding area. It is this elevation, and partial isolation, which give additional interest to the locality from a botanical point of view, for the increased height enables plants to flourish there, which would otherwise be absent from the district; while the isolation makes it both difficult and interesting to account for some of the species being there at all.

The Nandewar Mountains were discovered by Surveyor-General Oxley on the 8th August, 1818, when on his exploratory journey easterly from the Macquarie River to Port Macquarie. As an evidence of their comparative height, and the generally lower nature of the intervening country, they were first seen and named from a distance of upwards of one hundred miles. Oxley had just previously discovered the Warrumbungle Mountains, which he named Arbuthnot's Range, and he writes, that when standing on Mount Exmouth, the highest point of the Warrum-

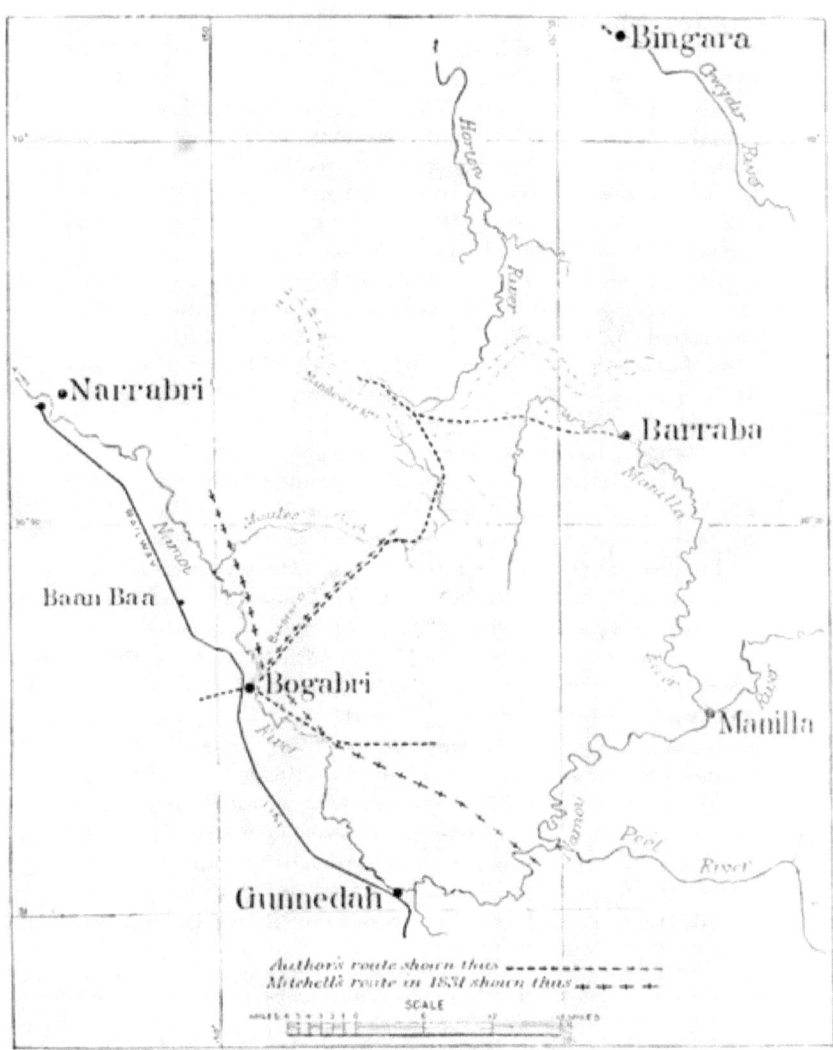

bungles, and which has an elevation of over 4,000 feet :—" To the north-east, commencing at N.33°E., and extending to N.51°E., a lofty and magnificent range of hills was seen lifting their blue heads above the horizon. This range was honoured with the name of the Earl of Hardwicke, and was distant on a medium from one hundred to one hundred and twenty miles: its highest elevations were named respectively Mount Apsley and Mount Shirley."* Accompanying Oxley, on this expedition, was Charles Fraser, Colonial Botanist, who collected many new species of plants. Oxley passed to the south of Hardwicke's Range, now known as the Nandewar Mountains, and on 2nd September, 1818, discovered and " named Peel's River, in honour of the Right Hon. Robert Peel,"(p.248), and which he crossed near Gidley, to the north-west of Tamworth. The native name of the river is Callala.

Allan Cunningham.—The second botanist to visit the vicinity of the Nandewar Mountains, was Allan Cunningham, who passed northwards near Barraba and Bingara in May, 1827, when on his journey from the Upper Hunter to Queensland, which resulted in his discovery of the Darling Downs. On returning in the following July, he crossed the Gwydir River some 10 miles below its junction with Horton's River, discovering and naming both rivers during this expedition, the former in honour of the Right Hon. Lord Gwydir, and the latter in honour of R. J. Wilmot Horton, M.P., Under Secretary of State for the Colonies. In continuing his journey southwards, partly up Horton's River, Cunningham passed over the Nandewar Range and over the eastern spurs of the Nandewar Mountains, which latter he referred to as Hardwicke's Range, and spoke of the elevations as "curiously formed cubical and chimney-shaped summits."†

Surveyor-General Sir Thomas L. Mitchell.—The third explorer to visit the neighbourhood of the Nandewar Mountains, was Sir

---

* Oxley's Expedition, p.261. According to Oxley's map, the northern elevation was named Apsley, and the southern, Shirley, and they were about 17 miles apart.

† Journal of the Royal Geographical Society, London, Vol. ii., p.115, with map.

Thomas L. Mitchell, in December, 1831, but he kept along the western side, and refers to them throughout as the Nundawàr Range, this evidently being the native name, although Mitchell does not say so in his journal. He gives an outline drawing of these mountains as viewed from the westward, and quotes names for the most prominent peaks from north to south in the following order:—Riddell, Couràda, Lindesay, Kaputar, and Forbes. Mitchell writes:—"That great range terminates in three principal heads, of which Mounts Riddell and Forbes are the northern and southern, the central or highest being named Mount Lindesay."* Mount Forbes, which is near the south-western extremity, was named after Captain Forbes, of the 39th Regiment, and it is not unlikely that Mount Lindesay was named after the then Acting Governor, Sir Patrick Lindesay, while Couràda is a native name. Mount Kaputar, or more especially the bluff towards its south-eastern side, is now locally known as Mount Lindsay (spelt without an e).

Barraba occupies an area of Devonian and Carboniferous formations, the former containing fairly abundant fossils of *Lepidodendron australe*, and is about 1,650 feet above sea-level. From Barraba past May Vale to Mount Lindsay Station is a distance westerly of nearly 30 miles, the altitude at the homestead being about 3,000 feet, and the ascent from May Vale, which is situated about half-way, nearly 1,000 feet. Carboniferous shales are met with between Barraba and May Vale, and afterwards areas of basalt and acid volcanic agglomerates are passed.

The Nandewar Mountains consist of a series of peaks composed largely of alkaline rocks, and which have, for the most part, a general N.N.west and S.S.east direction, while the western side presents a steep face towards the plains around Narrabri.†

From the eastern side, a range less than 2,500 feet high in places, and known as the Nandewar Range, passes between Barraba and Bingara and connects with southern New England.

---

* Mitchell's Eastern Australia, Vol. i., p.136.
† For a paper on "The Geology of the Nandewar Mountains" by H. I. Jensen, D.Sc., see These Proceedings for 1907, p.842.

Plants were collected by the roadside from Barraba to Mount Lindsay Station, on the head of the Horton River, and also on the alkaline and acid rocks up to elevations of about 5,000 feet, and including the summit of Kaputar. From the homestead, the route afterwards followed was partly down Maule's Creek from near its source, over rhyolites and Permo-Carboniferous formation, and some black-soil plains to the Namoi River at Boggabri which is about 820 feet above sea-level.

Rainfall.—According to the records at the Sydney Observatory, the following are the average rainfalls, and the number of rainy days at some localities in and around the area described in this paper. The figures are :—

	Inches.	Rainy days.
Manilla	26·5	64·
Barraba	27·4	49
Bingara	30·5	78
May Vale	31·3	79
Mount Lindsay Station	36·5	60
Gunnedah	25	64
Boggabri	23·5	59
Narrabri	26·5	57

Barraba to May Vale.

During a hurried drive from Barraba to May Vale, at elevations varying from about 1,650 to 2,000 feet, the following plants were noticed :—

RANUNCULACEÆ: *Ranunculus lappaceus* Sm.(Buttercup), *R.* sp.
DILLENIACEÆ: *Hibbertia linearis* R.Br.
MALVACEÆ: *Modiola multifida* Moench (introduced), *Pavonia hastata* Cav.
LEGUMINOSÆ: *Swainsona tephrotricha* F.v.M., *Hardenbergia monophylla* Benth.(False Sarsaparilla), *Acacia armata* R.Br.
ROSACEÆ: *Rubus parvifolius* L.
MYRTACEÆ: *Angophora subvelutina* F.v.M.(Apple Tree), *Eucalyptus melliodora* A. Cunn.,(Yellow Box), *E. albens* Miq.,(White Box), *E. tereticornis* Sm.,(Forest Red Gum), *E. melanophloia* F.v.M., (Silver-leaved Ironbark), *E. macrorrhyncha* F.v.M.,

(Stringybark), *E. Bridgesiana* R. T. Baker, (one of the trees recognised by Baron von Mueller as *E. Stuartiana* F.v.M.; the name is still retained by Mr. Maiden).

UMBELLIFERÆ : *Hydrocotyle hirta* R.Br.
RUBIACEÆ : *Asperula oliyantha* F.v.M.
COMPOSITÆ : *Leptorrhynchus squamatus* Less., *Helichrysum apiculatum* DC., *Helipterum anthemoides* DC.
GOODENIACEÆ : *Velleya paradoxa* R.Br.
CAMPANULACEÆ : *Wahlenbergia gracilis* DC.,(Blue Bell).
VERBENACEÆ : *Verbena officinalis* L.
LABIATÆ : *Ajuga australis* R.Br.
THYMELEÆ : *Pimelea glauca* R.Br., *P. curviflora* R.Br.
EUPHORBIACEÆ : *Adriana tomentosa* Gaud.
URTICEÆ : *Urtica incisa* Poir.,(Nettle).
CASUARINEÆ : *Casuarina Cunninghamiana* Miq.,(River Oak).
CONIFERÆ : *Callitris calcarata* R.Br.,(Black Pine).
LILIACEÆ : *Xerotes longifolia* R.Br., *X. multiflora* R.Br., *Arthropodium strictum* R.Br.
CYPERACEÆ : *Cyperus vaginatus* R.Br.

Eucalyptus melanophloia, the Silver-leaved Ironbark, is a fairly common tree on the lower parts of the western slopes of New England, coming up from the Narromine district towards Boggabri and Bingara, and though absent from the table-land, it occurs again on the eastern watershed, being common on the Upper Clarence east of Wilson's Downfall. Although plentiful all around the Nandewars, it was not noticed at or above the 3,000 feet level.

Casuarina Cunninghamiana(River Oak), though common on the large creeks around Barraba and at May Vale, was absent from the head waters of the Horton River at the 3,000 feet level, and apparently does not ascend much above an altitude of 2,800 feet in this latitude.

The Nandewar Mountains.

The following plants were found on the Nandewar Mountains from May Vale to the summit of Mount Kaputar (locally called Lindsay), and chiefly at altitudes between 3,000 feet, around Mount Lindsay Homestead, and 5,000 feet at the summit of the

Nandewars. Authors' names not repeated, were previously used for the same plant.

RANUNCULACEÆ: *Clematis glycinoides* DC., *Ranunculus lappaceus* (Buttercup), *R. plebeius* R.Br.

DILLENIACEÆ: *Hibbertia acicularis* F.v.M., *H. serpyllifolia* R.Br., *H. linearis*.

VIOLARIEÆ: *Viola betonicafolia* Sm., (Wild Violet), *V. hederacea* Labill., (Wild Violet), *Ionidium filiforme* F.v.M.

PITTOSPOREÆ: *Pittosporum undulatum* Vent., (scarce), *Billardiera scandens* Sm., (Roly Poly Vine).

TREMANDREÆ: *Tetratheca ericifolia* Sm.

POLYGALEÆ: *Comesperma sylvestre* Lindl.

CARYOPHYLLEÆ: *Stellaria pungens* Brongn., *S. flaccida* Hook., (with leaves unusually narrow).

HYPERICINEÆ: *Hypericum gramineum* Forst.

MALVACEÆ: *Modiola multifida* (Naturalised).

STERCULIACEÆ: *Sterculia diversifolia* G.Don, (Currajong).

GERANIACEÆ: *Geranium dissectum* L., var. *potentilloides*, *Erodium cicutarium* Willd., *Oxalis corniculata* L., (Sour Grass).

RUTACEÆ: *Asterolasia correifolia* Benth., var. *Muelleri* F.v.M., (*A. Muelleri* Benth.), *Correa speciosa* Andr.

STACKHOUSIEÆ: *Stackhousia linarifolia* A. Cunn., *S. viminea* Sm.

RHAMNEÆ: *Cryptandra amara* Sm., *Discaria australis* Hook.

SAPINDACEÆ: *Dodonæa viscosa* L., and var. *attenuata* (Hopbush).

LEGUMINOSÆ: *Oxylobium ellipticum* R.Br., (?) var. *minor* (at 4,500 feet), *Gompholobium Huegelii* Benth., var. *leptophyllum*, *Daviesia latifolia* R.Br., *D. ulicina* Sm., *Pultenæa scabra* R.Br., *P. setulosa* Benth., *Dillwynia ericifolia* Sm., var. *phylicoides*, *Hovea linearis* R.Br., *Indigofera australis* Willd., (Indigo), and var. *platypoda*, *Glycine clandestina* Wendl., *Hardenbergia monophylla*, *Acacia lanigera* A. Cunn., (at 4,600 feet), *A. armata*, *A. neriifolia* A. Cunn., *A.*

obtusata Sieb., *A. rubida* A. Cunn., *A. lunata* Sieb., *A. viscidula* A. Cunn., (at 4,500 feet), *A. melanoxylon* R.Br., (Tasmanian Backwood), *A. dealbata* Link, (Silver Wattle).

ROSACEÆ: *Rubus parvifolius.*

CRASSULACEÆ: *Tillæa verticillaris* DC.

HALORAGEÆ: *Haloragis* sp.

MYRTACEÆ: *Calythrix tetragona* Labill., *Micromyrtus microphylla* Benth., (at 4,600 feet), *Leptospermum flavescens* Sm., *L. scoparium* Forst., (A Teatree), *L. stellatum* Cav., (?), *Kunzea opposita* F.v.M., *Angophora subvelutina* (Apple Tree), *A. intermedia* DC., (Apple Tree), *Eucalyptus coriacea* A. Cunn., (Scribbly Gum, Snow Gum of Kosciusko and Kiandra), *E. dives* Schauer, (Peppermint), *E. Andrewsi* Maiden, (a Peppermint), *E. nova-anglica* Deane and Maiden, (Red Peppermint), *E. Bridgesiana*, *E. macrorrhyncha* (Stringybark), *E. melliodora* (Yellow Box), *E. albens* (White Box), *E. Cambayei* Deane and Maiden, (Bundy of Burraga and Bathurst districts), *E. viminalis* Labill., (Manna Gum), *E. rubida* Deane and Maiden, (White Gum, chiefly a multi-flowered form; *E. Gunnii* var. *rubida* Maiden), *E. tereticornis* (Forest Red Gum), *E. Bancrofti* Maiden, (*E. tereticornis* var. *brevifolia* Benth., Brittle, or Tumbledown Gum).

UMBELLIFERÆ: *Hydrocotyle hirta.*

ARALIACEÆ: *Panax sambucifolius* Sieb.

RUBIACEÆ: *Coprosma hirtella* Labill., *Asperula oligantha.*

COMPOSITÆ: *Olearia rosmarinifolia* A. Cunn., *O. viscidula* Benth., *O. elliptica* A. Cunn., (Shiny Leaf), *Brachycome multifida* DC., *Craspedia Richea* Cass., (Batchelor's Buttons), *Cassinia aculeata* R.Br., *C.* sp. (No. 2414), *Podolepis acuminata* R.Br., *P. canescens* A. Cunn., *Leptorrhynchos squamatus*, *Helichrysum bracteatum* Willd., (Everlasting Flower), *H. apiculatum*, *H. semipapposum* DC., *H. obcordatum* F.v.M., *Helipterum anthemoides*, *H. incanum* DC., *H. dimorpholepis* Benth., *Gnaphalium japonicum* Thunb., *Senecio lautus* Forst., var. *capillifolius* (*S. capillifolius* Hook.).

CANDOLLEACEÆ: *Candollea serrulata* Labill., (*Stylidium graminifolium* Sw., Trigger Flower).

GOODENIACEÆ: *Goodenia geniculata* R.Br., *Dampiera* sp.

CAMPANULACEÆ: *Lobelia* sp., *Wahlenbergia gracilis* (Blue Bell).

EPACRIDEÆ: *Melichrus urceolatus* R.Br., *Brachyloma daphnoides* Benth., *Lissanthe strigosa* R Br., *Leucopogon attenuatus* A.Cunn.,(at 4,500 feet), *Monotoca scoparia* R.Br.

JASMINEÆ: *Notelæa microcarpa* R.Br.

SCROPHULARINEÆ: *Veronica Derwentia* Andr., (above 2,100 feet), *V. calycina* R.Br., *V.* sp., (a small plant like *V. gracilis*), *Euphrasia Brownii* F.v.M.

BIGNONIACEÆ: *Tecoma australis* R.Br., (Bignonia or Wonga Vine).

MYOPORINEÆ: *Myoporum acuminatum* R.Br., (towards May Vale).

LABIATÆ: *Scutellaria humilis* R.Br., *Prostanthera lasianthos* Labill., (Wild Lilac), *P. nivea* A. Cunn., (at 4,500 feet), *Ajuga australis, Oncinocalyx Betchei* F.v.M.

PLANTAGINEÆ: *Plantago varia* R.Br.

POLYGONACEÆ: *Muhlenbeckia rhyticarya* F.v.M.

PROTEACEÆ: *Persoonia* sp. (at 4,300 feet), *Hakea eriantha* R Br., (at 4,300 feet), *H. microcarpa* R.Br., *Lomatia ilicifolia* R.Br.

THYMELEÆ: *Pimelea glauca, P. linifolia* Sm., *P. pauciflora* R.Br., *P. curviflora, P.* sp. (No. 2383).

EUPHORBIACEÆ: *Poranthera microphylla* Brongn.

URTICEÆ: *Urtica incisa* (Nettle).

SANTALACEÆ: *Exocarpus cupressiformis* Labill., (Native Cherry), *E. stricta* R.Br.

CONIFERÆ: *Callitris calcarata* (Black or Mountain Pine).

CYCADEÆ: *Macrozamia heteromera* C. Moore, (with pinnæ divided at the ends. Not a common species).

ORCHIDEÆ: *Thelymitra ixioides* Sw., (?) (flowers smaller than in the type, and sepals not spotted), *Diuris maculata* Sm., *Prasophyllum patens* R.Br.

IRIDEÆ: *Patersonia sericea* R.Br., (Wild Iris), *Libertia paniculata* Spreng., (at 4,500 feet).

AMARYLLIDEÆ: *Hypoxis hygrometrica* Labill.

LILIACEÆ: *Dianella revoluta* R.Br., *Eustrephus latifolius* R.Br., *Anguillaria (Wurmbea) dioica* R. Br., *Bulbine bulbosa* Haw., (at 4,500 feet), *B. semibarbata* Haw., *Stypandra glauca* R.Br., *Xerotes longifolia*, *Xanthorrhœa arborea* R. Br., (Grass Tree), *X.* sp. (No. 2369).

JUNCACEÆ: *Luzula campestris* DC., *Juncus homalocaulus* F.v.M., *J. pauciflorus* R.Br.

CYPERACEÆ: *Scirpus* sp., *Lepidosperma laterale* R.Br., *Carex inversa* R.Br., *C. appressa* R.Br.

GRAMINEÆ: *Andropogon affinis* R.Br., *Themeda Forskalii* Hack., (*Anthistiria ciliata* L., Kangaroo Grass), *Arundo Phragmites* Dod., *Poa caespitosa* Forst.

FILICES: *Alsophila australis* R.Br., (Tree-Fern), *Adiantum Aethiopicum* L., (Maiden-Hair Fern), *Hypolepis tenuifolia* Bernh., *Cheilanthes tenuifolia* Sw., *Pellaea (Pteris) falcata* (R.Br.) Fée, (Fish-bone Fern, near The Waterfall), *Pteridium aquilinum* (L.) Kuhn, (*Pteris aquilina*, Bracken), *Blechnum discolor* (Forst.) Keys., (*Lomaria discolor*), *B. capense* (L.) Schlecht., (*Lomaria capense*), *Doodia aspera* Mett., *Asplenium flabellifolium* Cav., *Polystichum aculeatum* Sw., (*Aspidium aculeatum*).

One of the most attractive flowering plants found on the Nandewar Mountains, during the first week in November, was *Asterolasia correifolia* var *Muelleri*, which belongs to a genus closely allied to Eriostemon. This particular plant, which Bentham regarded as a distinct species, while Mueller considered it a variety of *A. correifolia*, is growing on Mount Kaputar, locally called Lindsay, above the 4,500 level and up to the summit of The Bluff at about 4,800 feet, occurring in masses about three feet high, and crowned with a profusion of beautiful bright yellow flowers. Var. *Muelleri* has much smaller leaves than *A. correifolia*, and these, as well as the branchlets, are more tomentose. The flowers of the former are yellow, while those of the latter are white, and, as pointed out by Maiden and Betche, the stigma of the former is entire or nearly so, while that of the latter is more or less lobed, or nearly entire.*

The discovery of this variety of Asterolasia, on the Nandewar Mountains, is of special interest, as although it is not uncommon in Victoria, it has only once previously been recorded for New South Wales, having been collected by Mr. Forsyth at Lobb's Hole near Kiandra, in November, 1900. Its occurrence at Mount Lindsay extends its range northerly a distance of about 400 miles, and it still remains unknown to botanists in the intervening area.

In order to try and account for the present distribution of this plant, particularly its isolation on the Nandewar Mountains, several possible causes have to be considered, and the problem is difficult of final solution. Examples of isolated occurrences of plants, such as this, all furnish some slender evidence of what former land-surfaces or climatic conditions may have been, and an aggregation of similar facts, obtained by constant observation and collecting, largely assists in the solution of such problems.

Three of these possible causes, which suggest themselves, are: first, dispersal by birds; second, gradual spreading from parent-plants; and third, stranding through change of climate in intervening areas.

Possible distribution by birds is an important factor, which should never be overlooked, as seeds may be dispersed over a very wide area, and young plants may only grow where the conditions are suitable for the particular plant. This variety of Asterolasia, however, is so rare in New South Wales, that if its occurrence on Mount Lindsay is the result of dispersal by birds, it is difficult to understand why it does not occur in many more localities much less than 400 miles northerly from Kiandra. It is possible that it may have been overlooked in some spots, but various collectors have been over a great portion of this area, so that it is unlikely that its occurrence is other than rare within the limits mentioned.

---

* J. H. Maiden, F.L.S., and E. Betche, These Proceedings, 1901, p.80; and 1902, p.56.

Little, therefore, can be said in favour of dispersal by birds being responsible for the distribution in this case.

The second suggestion, that it may have gradually spread from parent-plants, assisted by birds, presents certain points which are exceedingly difficult of proof, but nevertheless provide material for some interesting lines of thought. Adopting Mueller's opinion that this plant is only a variety of *A. correifolia*, which species occurs in the coastal area from about Sydney and the Nepean northwards, it might perhaps be considered a mountain-form which has climbed to its present height, and gradually developed differences owing to environment. Its present north and south extremes of range would then have to be regarded as having been connected through the coastal species. There are such large breaks in the continuity of this range of distribution, between coastal and mountain localities, so far as at present known, that this explanation cannot be considered as very satisfactory.

A further possibility and theory of its having gradually spread from parent-plants would involve its antiquity. Physiographers have reason to believe that, in early Tertiary time, New South Wales was an almost level tract of land, a peneplain, not raised much above sea-level; and that the mountains which form the present Main Divide, north and south, were not elevated until late Tertiary.[*] If *A. correifolia* had spread from the east coast, inland for two or three hundred miles prior to this uplift, and while the climatic conditions over that area were fairly uniform, then the occurrence, to-day, of resultant forms or varieties of that species in the elevated or western areas, with altered climatic conditions, would seem by no means an impossibility. In regard to the antiquity of the species, all that can be said at present, is that representatives of the genus are spread over, at least, parts of New South Wales, Victoria, and Western Australia, while the closely allied genus, *Eriostemon*, has representatives in all the

---

[*] "Geographical Unity of Eastern Australia," by E. C. Andrews, B.A. Journ. Proc. Roy. Soc. N. S. Wales, 1910, p.420. Presidential Address by C. Hedley, F.L.S., these Proceedings, 1911, p.13.

States of Australia, and one species in New Caledonia.† In this connection it is interesting to note that a third plant, *A. mollis* Benth., which is also regarded as a variety of *A. correifolia* by Maiden and Betche (These Proceedings, 1902, p.56), and which bears white flowers, occurs on the somewhat isolated Warrumbungle Ranges, a group of mountains lying just over 100 miles to the south-west of the Nandewars, and which, as pointed out by Dr. Jensen, bear close resemblance to them in their physiographic features, as well as being made up largely of alkaline rocks.

This hypothesis, therefore, that *A. correifolia* may have had an extensive range as far back as late Tertiary time, and that the varieties *Mulleri* and *mollis* are adaptations to environment as a result of the latest uplift, appears to have some reasonable grounds for consideration, which, however, must only be regarded as being put forth tentatively for the present.

The third suggestion, that the plants of var. *Mulleri* now found on the Nandewars may have become stranded owing to change of climate, seems also to be worthy of investigation. It must not be overlooked that the home of this variety to-day is in Victoria, largely in the Buffalo Ranges, and that, so far, it has only been recorded from two localities in New South Wales, one being fairly near Victoria, at Lobb's Hole, in the Kiandra district, and the other 400 miles northerly, but at an elevation of over 4,500 feet. Viewing the distribution of this plant or variety alone, there seems ground for assuming that, in prehistoric time, its range was more continuous between Kiandra and the Nandewars and that its disappearance from the intervening area may have resulted from some climatic change along this line. If it originated as a cold-loving plant, it may not be necessary to claim such great antiquity to account for its distribution, as it may have developed since the uplift in late Tertiary time.

A change of climate from cold to warm might have been produced in two ways: one being by a lowering of the mountain-levels by either tectonic movement or denudation, and the other by a general raising of temperature through the closing of a

---

† B.Fl., Vol. i., p.331.

glacial period. A structural study of the mountains between Kiandra and the Nandewars, points to the conclusion that, since the latest uplift, there has been no tectonic movement which has resulted in any general lowering of the surface throughout this area, consequently no modification of temperature has been effected in this manner.

Turning next to consider the possible effects of denudation, and seeing that the dissection of the mountains is still in a relatively youthful stage, as evidenced by the presence of gorges, the time-factor since the uplift does not seem to have been sufficiently great to admit of any considerable general lowering of summits by denudation such as would result in producing climatic changes. There is one local exception to this, as pointed out by E. C. Andrews[*] and by T. Griffith Taylor,[†] in the geologically recent formation of the Goulburn River valley, or Cassilis Geocol, which has resulted from the softness of the strata through which the river has had to cut. Considerable denudation in this locality is undeniable, though judging by the northerly and north-easterly dip of the strata towards this area from the southern side, it seems probable that the original site of this valley presented a slightly warped surface, or syncline, and was not uplifted quite as much as the New England and Blue Mountain plateaus. It would seem, therefore, that there may not have been much general lowering of mountain summits since the last uplift, and that the cause for climatic change must be looked for elsewhere.

It is suggested that sufficient change of climate to have allowed var. *Muelleri* to have occurred intermittently or perhaps continuously throughout the area extending from Kiandra to the Nandewar Mountains, may have been provided by the latest glacial period in Pleistocene time. Professor David has pointed out that the evidence of Pleistocene glaciation on Mount Kosciusko shows that there was a lowering of temperature of about 10° Fah., and that the snow-line came down about 3,000 feet

---

[*] "Tertiary History of New England." By E. C. Andrews, B.A. Records Geological Society of N. S. Wales, Vol. 7 (1903), pp. 183-187.
[†] These Proceedings, 1906, p. 522.

(printed 300 erroneously) below its present limit.* Should the snow-line have come down only about 2,000 feet, with a consequent lowering of temperature of 6-7° Fah., such a change would have provided all the climatic conditions necessary for the spread of this particular variety of Asterolasia over practically all the present land-surface between Kiandra and Nandewar Mountains, and the closing of the glacial period, with the consequent warming of the climate, might have had the effect of gradually exterminating all the plants of this variety, excepting those at altitudes which still ensure cool conditions. This hypothesis, if correct, would show that var. *Muelleri* is a relic, or stranded plant, as a result of the termination of the last glacial period, but in our present state of knowledge nothing definite can possibly be said on the matter, though continued investigation of similar occurrences should assist in some solution of the problem.†

Another plant of considerable interest, in regard to its distribution, found towards the top of Mount Lindsay, is *Pultenea setulosa*, which had never previously been collected in New South Wales. It grows in masses about 5-6 feet high, and is covered with yellow flowers during the first week in November. Its previously known habitat is Broad Sound, Queensland, about 750 miles northerly from the Nandewar Mountains, though it probably occurs in portions of the unexamined intervening area.

Eight species of Acacia were noticed between the 3,000 and 5,000 feet levels, *A. dealbata* occurring on the actual summit of Mount Kaputar at about 5,000 feet, while *A. rubida* and *A. melanoxylon* were found up to 4,900 feet. *A. armata* was seen up to an altitude of about 2,500 feet, and *A. neriifolia* ascends to about 3,000 feet This latter species, like *A. rubida*, retains its juvenile foliage (pinnate leaves) until the shrubs are 6-8 feet high, and this dimorphic foliage often assists in the identification of the plant. *A. neriifolia* is well worthy of cultivation as a Golden-Wattle, as it

* "Geological Notes on Kosciusko, with Special Reference to Evidences of Glacial Action." By T. W. Edgeworth David, B.A., F.R.S., etc. These Proceedings, 1908, p. 668.

† See remarks by Mr. A. G. Hamilton, in regard to the occurrence of *Eucalyptus globulus* near Mudgee. These Proceedings, 1887, p. 260.

bears a profusion of blossoms which are of a darker yellow colour than those of many Acacias. Its flowering time is about the first of September.

Eucalyptus coriacea, the Snow-Gum of Kosciusko, was found on alkaline rocks from the 4,600 feet level up to the actual summit of Mount Lindsay or Kaputar, the later being about 5,000 feet above sea-level. This is the Eucalypt which climbs above all others in New South Wales, and reaches the greatest altitude of any Eucalypt in Australia. In various isolated situations, as on some of the narrowest parts of the Liverpool Range, and on the Nandewar Mountains, its occurrence is suggestive of its being a relic or stranded plant. Although it reaches an elevation of 6,500 feet on Mount Kosciusko,* it by no means takes the highest land in Tasmania, being absent from the summit of Mount Wellington (4,166 feet), and also from the summit of Mount Roland at nearly 4,000 feet, where it was specially searched for by Mr. E. C. Andrews and myself in February, 1911. On Mount Roland, rather stunted forms of *E. Gunnii* Hk., and *E. coccifera* Hk., are common, while *E. coccifera* and *E. vernicosa* Hk., occur on the summit of Mount Wellington.

Taking those plants which are common to the coldest parts only of this State, and to Tasmania, my observations go to show that such plants require an increased minimum altitude of about 1,000 feet for every 300-330 miles in their distribution northerly from Tasmania to northern New South Wales. *E. coriacea* is one of these cold-loving plants, and as the direct distance from Hobart to Mount Kosciusko is about 450 miles, the presence of this Snow-Gum at 6,500 feet on Kosciusko should imply its occurrence in Tasmania at levels up to about 5,000 feet, provided the geological formation and aspect were suitable. So far as the former is concerned, the rocks of Mount Wellington appear such as would support the growth of this species in New South Wales, while those of Mount Roland may be too acid. This Snow-Gum is also a lover of open country, usually avoiding scrubby land, and will, in some situations, occupy large areas almost exclusively. It may, therefore, be

---

* J. H. Maiden, F.L.S., Agricultural Gazette of N. S. Wales, 1899.

absent from some localities because other plants have obtained possession, and, following the law of the "survival of the fittest," retain such possession to the exclusion of the Snow-Gum.

E. albens was found flowering on the Nandewar in November, at an altitude of about 2,800 feet, its usual flowering period in the western districts being in the autumn. As an evidence of the effect of climate on plant distribution, it may be mentioned that south of the Murrumbidgee, this species is usually below an elevation of 1,500 feet, while at a point on the Nandewars, about 350 miles northerly, it is able to reach an altitude about 1,300 feet higher.

The discovery of *E. dives*, the Peppermint of our western mountains, on Mount Lindsay, is of very great interest, as hitherto it had been considered by botanists to be restricted to the southern side of the Hunter Valley. It was shortly afterwards (December, 1909) collected by Mr. J. L. Boorman at Guy Fawkes, east of Armidale, the specimens being now in the National Herbarium, Botanic Gardens, Sydney. This species, although a mountain plant, rather prefers the western to the eastern aspect in New South Wales, and extends from the Nandewars southerly at least as far as Ballarat in Victoria. It is usually found at elevations from about 2,000 feet upwards in this State, some of its lowest points of occurrence being in the Goulburn to Yass district. On Mount Lindsay it was found intermittently from about 3,500 to 4,500 feet, but does not occur on the summit.

It had always seemed remarkable that *E. dives* had not been recorded from New England, and its absence from that locality had been previously attributed to its inability to cross the comparatively warm valley of the Goulburn River, a tributary of the Hunter. The Liverpool Range, in which the Goulburn River rises, is in one place only about 1,700 feet above sea-level, which appears to be too low for the growth of *E. dives* in latitudes north of Sydney; and the Main Divide for many miles, where it winds past Murrurundi towards New England, is very narrow, in places amounting to only a few hundred yards, thus reducing the possibilities of this tree spreading on to New England. Another point is that the higher parts of the Liverpool Range are largely capped with basalt, a basic rock which *E. dives* always avoids, preferring a sedimentary formation considerably acid, but not necessarily containing a high proportion of free silica.

In order to flourish in the latitude of Mount Lindsay, this Peppermint would probably require an altitude of nearly 3,000 feet, and as most of the country between the Liverpool Range and the Nandewar Mountains including part of the Liverpool Plains, is much below that elevation, its occurrence on the latter mountain is difficult to explain. There is, however, a much denuded range running north-westerly past Currabubula, known as the Peel Range, and connecting the Nandewar Mountains with the Liverpool Range to the north of Murrurundi, through a gap in which the Namoi River passes near Carroll, and *E. dives* may possibly have spread from the south along this range, although it is now, for the most part, not sufficiently elevated for the growth of this species. Considering the amount of basic rock, however, on the high land between Coolah or Cassilis and Murrurundi, its passage along this stretch of the Liverpool Range for such a great distance, 60-70 miles, on to the Peel Range would be very difficult of explanation. At present, there is no record of this species between the Mudgee district and the Nandewars, a distance of about 150 miles, and it is difficult to understand how it ever could have occurred continuously under present climatic conditions, without the intervening hills had been formerly much higher than now.

There is the possibility, which seems not unreasonable, that the species may have spread to the Nandewar Mountains towards the close of the glacial period in Pleistocene time, but the evidence in support of this theory is very meagre. At the same time this hypothesis is supported by the fact that there is another southern plant, viz., *Asterolasia correifolia*, var. *Muelleri*, in company with this tree, which was hitherto unknown as far north, and the probability of their isolation being due to accidental dispersal by birds becomes, therefore, somewhat discounted. However, *E. dives* has, by some means, reached the Nandewars, and is sparsely represented on southern New England, but its rarity in the latter locality is possibly largely owing to the fact that much of the geological formation along the Main Divide, extending from Cassilis to southern New England, is of too basic a character to support the growth of this particular Peppermint. The curious distribution of this tree in the north, furnishes an interesting subject for investigation, which might be considered in conjunction with the study of local physiographic problems, and climatic changes.

E. Cambagei was found unexpectedly on Mount Lindsay, extending from about the 3,500 feet level to nearly 4,900 feet, or practically on the summit. In its distribution, this species is not unlike *E. dives*, favouring the western side of the Main Divide and extending into Victoria, but descending to lower levels, and sometimes growing on more basic formations. Its most northern limit previously known to me was near Murrurundi, and close to the Liverpool Range, where it is growing on basaltic formation at an elevation of about 1,500 feet; but I have recently found it at Currabubula, on Carboniferous formation, at an altitude of 2,500-2,900 feet. It is remarkable that, so far, this tree has not been recorded from New England, while, however, it has found its way to the Nandewars, and should be looked for in the Nundle Swamp Oak district, on the southern portion of New England. (For previous remarks concerning this species, see these Proceedings for 1902, p. 199.)

E. Andrewsi and *E. nova-anglica* were found at about the 3,000 feet level, the former on the acid, volcanic agglomerate formation, and the latter on the alluvial flats near the Horton River. The occurrence of these two species in this locality is of interest, as neither has been recorded south of the Hunter Valley, and both are regarded as typical New England trees. They have, however, found their way westward to the Nandewars, although some of the intervening country is lower than the elevations at which they usually flourish. Curiously they have here met with two southern Eucalypts which do not occur on northern New England, viz., *E. dives* and *E. Cambagei*, although owing to considerations of soil and moisture requirements they do not actually associate with them, though only separated by a mile or so. (For previous remarks concerning *E. Andrewsi* and *E. nova-anglica*, see these Proceedings for 1904, pp. 791, 795.)

The finding of *E. Bancrofti* (*E. tereticornis* var. *brevifolia*) on mountains chiefly composed of alkaline rocks, was a matter for some surprise, as the species is one which appears to thrive only where there is an abundance of free silica. It was first noticed between May Vale and Mount Lindsay Station, and was growing on basalt, a basic rock with a minimum of free silica. As this was such an unusual occurrence, some investigation was made, which resulted in disclosing the fact that the basalt was thin, and was overlying extensive beds of acid, volcanic agglomerate, into which the roots had, no doubt, penetrated. In cases of this kind it is not unlikely that many seeds would germinate in the basalt, but only those plants would eventually survive which happened to be provided with suitable drainage until their roots reached the siliceous rocks below. The species, which throughout, had very glaucous buds, was afterwards found on other areas of acid agglomerate formation. The presence of this tree may be taken as an indication that the rock upon which it is growing contains upwards of 70 per cent. silica. (For previous remarks, see these Proceedings, 1908, p. 55.)

Coprosma hirtella was noticed on the summit of Kaputar at an altitude of about 5,000 feet. This is a typical Tasmanian plant, and has been recorded as far north as the Blue Mountains, but according to specimens kindly shown me by Mr. Maiden, it occurs on Bald Hills Station, about 65 miles easterly of Armidale; and on the 17th April, 1843, was collected by Dr. Leichhardt at the head of the Gwydir River. Members of this genus are most numerous in New Zealand, and the Australasian species are found chiefly in the colder parts.

Oncinocalyx Betchei, a somewhat rare plant of a few feet high, was found just above the 3,000 feet level, northerly from the homestead, and about half a mile southerly from The Waterfall.

On the summits of Mount Lindsay and the hill across the gorge to the north-east, at 4,500 feet, an almost aborescent form of *Lomatia ilicifolia* was noticed, growing to a height of about 8-10 feet, with stems 2 inches in diameter.

An interesting little Pimelea shrub (No. 2383), with glabrous flowers, is growing on Mount Lindsay at about 4,500 feet, but, in the absence of fruiting specimens, has not been identified.

A species of Xanthorrhœa (No. 2369, Grass-Tree) with a caudex of a few inches, and a flowering spike of 1 foot 9 inches, was found near the homestead at an altitude of about 3,000 feet. It differs from described New South Wales species in having quadrangular leaves, which are about 1 foot 8 inches long, and in this respect, though differing in others, somewhat resembles X. *quadrangulata* F.v.M., of the Mount Lofty Ranges in South Australia.

Among the hills across the gorge to the north-east of Mount Lindsay, and quite concealed from west winds, is a picturesque glen, which is beautified by a number of graceful Tree-Ferns (*Alsophila australis*). The altitude of the spot is about 3,700-4,000 feet, and I know of no place in this State, where this Tree-Fern occurs so far westerly of the Main Divide, and which, in this instance, is about 90 miles.*

Head of Maule's Creek to Boggabri.

The following notes refer to the country extending from the valley in which the head-waters of Maule's Creek collect, at about 2,000 feet above sea-level, and past the old Willuri woolshed to Boggabri at 820 feet. Maule's Creek takes its rise in the south-eastern portion of the Nandewar Mountains, and flows, first southerly and then westerly, to the Namoi River, joining it about a dozen miles below Boggabri. In the earlier part of its westerly course, it passes between sandstone escarpments (Plate lxvii.) of probably Permo-Carboniferous age, extending for several miles, and this portion of the creek was followed by me, after which a direct course was taken across the flat country south-westerly to Boggabri.

The first explorer to visit this locality was Sir Thomas L. Mitchell, and according to his journal he discovered Maule's Creek on the

---

* His Honor Judge Docker informs me that there are some Tree-Ferns in a sheltered nook on the Warrumbungles, but though south-westerly from the Nandewars, this spot is closer to that portion of the Main Divide which sweeps round from Murrurundi to Cassilis.

18th December, 1831, and named it on the following day; though after whom he named it is not stated. On this journey, he followed the right bank of the Namoi River, and also of the lagoon or billabong, just east of Boggabri. Mitchell clearly shows that Namoi, which he spelt "Nammoy," is the native name of the river below the junction of the Conadilly. Special mention is made of a remarkable peak, which he had first seen from a distance of about 25 miles, the native name of which is Tangulda, and which is now identified as Barber's Pinnacle, north of Wilberoi House (Plate lxvi.).* A list of the flora on this peak is given in this paper.

After proceeding north-east by north from Barber's Lagoon, for over 20 miles towards the Nandewars, Mitchell found the country beyond Maule's Creek almost inaccessible for horses, and returned. He then continued his journey down the Namoi, passing eastward of Narrabri, and thence northerly, until reaching the Gwydir some 6-8 miles above Moree.

On the 2nd January, 1832, somewhere to the eastward of Narrabri, Mitchell discovered the species which was afterwards named *Capparis Mitchelli*, and specially remarks that he only saw one tree of it during the whole of the expedition. He next found it on the Lower Bogan in 1835 (Vol. i., p. 284). The species is not uncommon in the Boggabri district.

The following plants were found chiefly between the head of Maule's Creek and Boggabri, by far the greater number occurring below an altitude of 1,200 feet:—

RANUNCULACEÆ: *Clematis aristata* R.Br., *C. microphylla* DC., *Ranunculus lappaceus* (Buttercup).

DILLENIACEÆ: *Hibbertia linearis*, var. *obtusifolia*.

PAPAVERACEÆ: *Argemone mexicana* L., (Mexican Poppy. Naturalised), *Papaver horridum* DC.

CRUCIFERÆ: *Capsella bursa-pastoris* Mœnch (Shepherd's Purse), *Lepidium pseudo-ruderale* Thell., *Senebiera didyma* Pers., (Pepper-wort, naturalised).

CAPPARIDEÆ: *Capparis Mitchelli* Lindl., (Wild Orange), *Apophyllum anomalum* F.v.M., (Warrior or Currant-bush).

* Mitchell's Eastern Australia, Vol. i., pp.47, 51.

VIOLARIEÆ : *Viola hederacea.*

PITTOSPOREÆ : *Pittosporum phillyræoides* DC., *Bursaria spinosa* Cav.,(Blackthorn).

CARYOPHYLLEÆ: *Stellaria glauca* With., *S. flaccida* Hk.

HYPERICINEÆ : *Hypericum gramineum.*

MALVACEÆ: *Sida corrugata* Lindl., and vars. *orbicularis, pedunculata* and *angustifolia, Hibiscus Sturtii* Hk.

STERCULIACEÆ : *Sterculia diversifolia* (Currajong), *Melhania incana* Heyn.,(evidently rare in New South Wales and belongs to the interior).

LINEÆ : *Linum marginale* A. Cunn.,(Australian Flax Plant).

GERANIACEÆ : *Erodium cygnorum* Nees, *Oxalis corniculata* (Sour Grass).

RUTACEÆ : *Eriostemon difformis* A. Cunn.,(on sandstone hills west of Boggabri), *Correa speciosa* (Maule's Creek), *Geijera parviflora* Lindl.,(Wilga).

CELASTRINEÆ : *Celastrus Cunninghamii* F.v.M.

STACKHOUSIEÆ : *Stackhousia muricata* Lindl., *S. viminea, S. spathulata* Sieb.

RHAMNEÆ : *Alphitonia excelsa* Reiss.,(Red Ash).

SAPINDACEÆ: *Nephelium subdentatum* F.v.M., *Heterodendron olefolium* Desf.,(Rosewood), *Dodonæa viscosa* and var. *spathulata* (Hopbush), *D. tenuifolia* Lindl., *D. boroniæfolia* G. Don.

LEGUMINOSÆ : Suborder i., PAPILIONACEÆ ; *Hovea linearis, H. longifolia* R.Br.,(a charming little shrub when covered with purple flowers in spring), *Psoralea adscendens* F.v.M., var. *parva* Benth., (*P. parva* F.v.M.), *Indigofera australis* and var. *signata*(Indigo), *Swainsona coronillifolia* Salish.,(commonly called Darling Pea), *S. luteola* F.v.M., *Hardenbergia monophylla, Melilotus parviflorus* Desf.,(naturalised).

Suborder ii., CÆSALPINIEÆ : *Cassia australis* Sims, *C. eremophila* A. Cunn.

Suborder iii., MIMOSEÆ : *Neptunia gracilis* Benth., (a small sensitive plant on the plains), *Acacia triptera* Benth., (Wait-a-While), *A. armata, A. neriifolia* (up Maule's Creek), *A. hakeoides* A. Cunn.(about 15 miles N.E. of Boggabri), *A. salicina* Lindl.,(the Cooba of the Lachlan River, up Maule's Creek), *A. decora* Reichb.,

A. homalophylla A. Cunn.,(Yarran), *A. pendula* A.Cunn., (Myall), *A. Oswaldi* F.v.M., *A. implexa* Benth., *A. Cunninghamii* Hk.,(Curracabark, on Barber's Pinnacle and other hills), *A. dealbata* (not the glaucous form found on the mountains).

ROSACEÆ: *Rubus parvifolius.*
CRASSULACEÆ: *Tillæa verticillaris.*
HALORAGEÆ: *Halorayis elata* A. Cunn.
MYRTACEÆ: *Calythrix tetragona* (on hills east of Boggabri), *Melaleuca bracteata* F.v.M.,(along the banks of Maule's and Goonbri Creeks. Identified by Mr. R. T. Baker*), *Angophora intermedia* (Apple Tree), *Eucalyptus melliodora*(Yellow Box), *E. populifolia* Hook.,)Bimble or Shiny-leaved Box), *E. albens* (White Box), *E. Woollsiana* R. T. Baker (Narrow-leaved Box), *E. melanophloia* (Silver-leaved Ironbark), *E. crebra* (Narrow-leaved Ironbark), *E. dealbata* F.v.M., *E. rostrata* Schl.,(River Red-gum), *E. tereticornis* (Forest Red-gum), *E. Bridgesiana* (only seen on upper part of Maule's Creek), *E. viridis* R. T. Baker,(Mallee, on sandstone hills three or four miles west of Boggabri).

ONAGRARIEÆ: *Jussiæa repens* L.,(an aquatic plant with beautiful, yellow, buttercup-like flowers, on the Lagoon near Wilberoi).
CUCURBITACEÆ: *Cucumis myriocarpus* Naud.,(Native Melons).
UMBELLIFERÆ: *Eryngium rostratum* Cav., var. *paludosum, Daucus brachiatus* Sieb.
LORANTHACEÆ: *Loranthus linophyllus* Fenzl,(on *Casuarina Cunninghamiana*), *L. pendulus* Sieb.,(on *Eucalyptus crebra*), *L.* sp.(on *Santalum lanceolatum*).
RUBIACEÆ: *Canthium oleifolium* Hk.,(often called Wild Lemon, and covered in early November with a profusion of strongly sweet-scented, white flowers). *Asperula oligantha.*
COMPOSITÆ: *Centaurea melitensis* L.,(Saucy Jack. Naturalised), *Olearia elliptica, Calotis microphylla* Benth., *C. lappulacea* Benth., *Brachycome graminea* F.v.M.,(a very tall form, 20 inches high), *Siegesbeckia orientalis* Linn., *Cotula australis* Hk., *Craspedia*

---

* See a paper "On the Australian Melaleucas and their Essential Oils," by R. T. Baker, F.L.S., and H. G. Smith, F.C.S., Journ. Proc. Roy. Soc. N. S. Wales, 1910, p.601.

Richea (Batchelor's Buttons), *Cassinia* sp., *Leptorrhynchos squamatus*, *Helichrysum apiculatum*. *H. semipapposum*, *H. obcordatum* F.v.M., *H.* sp., *Helipterum anthemoides*, *H. dimorpholepis*, *Gnaphalium japonicum*, *Senecio capillifolius* Hk., *Carduus pycnocephalus* L.,(naturalised).

GOODENIACEÆ: *Velleya paradoxa*, *Goodenia glauca* F.v.M., *G. ovata* Sm.

CAMPANULACEÆ: *Lobelia pedunculata* R.Br., *Isotoma axillaris* Lindl., *Wahlenbergia gracilis*(Blue Bell).

EPACRIDEÆ: *Melichrus urceolatus*.

PRIMULACEÆ: *Anagallis arvensis* L.,(Pimpernel. Naturalised).

JASMINEÆ: *Jasminum suavissimum* Lindl., *Notelæa microcarpa*, *N. linearis* Benth.

APOCYNEÆ: *Alstonia constricta* F.v.M., (Quinine or Bitter Bark), *Lyonsia eucalyptifolia* F.v.M. (a tall woody climber).

GENTIANEÆ: *Erythræa australis* R.Br., *Limnanthemum crenatum* F.v.M.,(an aquatic plant with orbicular leaves, and beautiful yellow, fringed flowers, upwards of one inch in diameter. In Barber's Lagoon).

BORAGINEÆ: *Cynoglossum australe* R.Br.

CONVOLVULACEÆ: *Convolvulus marginatus* Poir.

SOLANEÆ: *Solanum esuriale* Lindl., *S. cinereum* R.Br., *S. esculum* F.v.M., *S. parvifolium*, R.Br., *Nicotiana glauca* (a tobacco-plant introduced from South America).

SCROPHULARINEÆ: *Mimulus gracilis* R.Br.,(little blue flowers growing in clusters on the plains), *Morgania glabra* R.Br., *Verbascum blattaria* L.,(naturalised).

BIGNONIACEÆ: *Tecoma australis*(Wonga Vine).

ACANTHACEÆ: *Justicia procumbens* Linn.

MYOPORINEÆ: *Myoporum platycarpum* R.Br., *Eremophila Mitchelli* Benth.,(Budtha or Budda, sometimes called Sandalwood), *E. longifolia* F.v.M.

VERBENACEÆ: *Verbena officinalis* L.

LABIATÆ: *Scutellaria humilis*, *Prostanthera rotundifolia* R.Br., *Ajuga australis*, *Oncinocalyx Betchei* (on Robertson's Mountain), *Stachys arvensis* L.,(Stagger-weed, naturalised).

PLANTAGINEÆ: *Plantago varia*.

PHYTOLACCACEÆ: *Codonocarpus australis* A. Cunn., ("Bell Fruit." On hills east of Boggabri).

CHENOPODIACEÆ: *Rhagodia hastata* R.Br.,(Saltbush), *R. nutans* R.Br., *R. linifolia* R.Br., *Kochia microphylla* Moq., (Cotton-bush).

AMARANTACEÆ: *Ptilotus exaltatus* Nees, *Alternanthera triandra* Lam.

POLYGONACEÆ: *Rumex Brownii* Campd., *Polygonum minus* Huds.

NYCTAGINEÆ: *Boerhaavia diffusa* L.,(Tarvine, an excellent fodder plant).

PROTEACEÆ: *Hakea leucoptera* R.Br.,(Needlewood).

THYMELEÆ: *Pimelea glauca*, *P. pauciflora*, *P. curviflora*.

EUPHORBIACEÆ: *Euphorbia Drummondii* Boiss., *Beyeria viscosa* Muq., *Phyllanthus subcrenulatus* F.v.M., *P. thesioides* Benth.,(on Ironbark hills, 10-12 miles N.E. of Boggabri. Rare in New South Wales.) *Breynia oblongifolia* J. Muell., *Adriana tomentosa*.

URTICEÆ: *Trema cannabina* Lour., *Ficus rubiginosa* Desf., (Figtree), *Urtica incisa*(Nettle).

CASUARINEÆ: *Casuarina Cunninghamiana*(River Oak, along the banks of Maule's Creek and the Namoi River), *C. Cambagei* R. T. Baker,(Belah, regarded by Mr. Maiden as *C. lepidophloia* F.v.M.,*), *C. Luehmanni* R. T. Baker(Bull Oak).

SANTALACEÆ: *Santalum lanceolatum* R.Br., *Exocarpus cupressiformis*(Native Cherry), *E. aphylla* R.Br.

CONIFERÆ: *Callitris robusta* R.Br.,(White or Cypress Pine. Regarded as *C. glauca* R.Br., by Mr. R. T. Baker),† *C. calcarata* (Black or Mountain Pine).

ORCHIDEÆ: *Cymbidium canaliculatum* R.Br.

LILIACEÆ: *Dianella revoluta*, *Eustrephus latifolius*, *Anguillaria* (*Wurmbea*) *dioica*, *Bulbine bulbosa*, *B. semibarbata*, *Stypandra glauca* R.Br., *Arthropodium strictum* R.Br., *Xerotes longifolia*, *Xanthorrhoea* sp. (No. 3603, with almost quadrangular leaves, on Robertson's Mountain).

---

* Forest Flora of N. S. Wales, by J. H. Maiden, F.L.S., Part xiii., p.74.

† See "A Research on the Pines of Australia," by R. T. Baker, F.L.S., and H. G. Smith, F.C.S.

JUNCACEÆ: *Juncus pauciflorus, J. pallidus* R.Br.,(Rushes).
NAIADEÆ: *Potamogeton crispus* Linn.
CYPERACEÆ: *Cyperus gracilis* R.Br., *C. concinnus* R.Br., *C. vaginatus, C. fulvus* R.Br., (a viscid form with long spikelets), *Lepidosperma laterale, Carex inversa, C. Gaudichaudiana* Kunth, *C. appressa*.
GRAMINEÆ: *Andropogon sericeus* R.Br., *A. affinis* R.Br., *Themeda Forskalii* (*Anthistiria ciliata*, Kangaroo-Grass), *Stipa verticillata* Nees, *S. aristiglumis* F.v.M., *S. scabra* Lindl., (Silver Grass), *Deyeuxia Forsteri* Kunth, *Danthonia penicillata* F.v.M., *Chloris truncata* R.Br., (Umbrella-Grass), *Arundo Phragmites, Poa caespitosa*, (White tussocks), *Bromus arenarius* Labill., *Festuca bromoides* Linn.,(naturalised), *Hordeum murinum* L.,(Barley Grass, naturalised).
MARSILEACEÆ: *Marsilea Drummondii* A.Br.,(in damp places on the plains, and often known as Nardoo).
FILICES: *Adiantum Aethiopicum*(Maiden-hair Fern), *A. hispidulum* Sw.,(under sandstone cliffs near Maule's Creek), *Cheilanthes tenuifolia, Pellaea(Pteris) falcata, Pleurosorus(Grammitis) rutafolius*(R.Br.), Fée.

Tangulda or Barber's Pinnacle.

(Plate lxvi.)

The hill now known as Barber's Pinnacle, is a conspicuous peak of decomposing rhyolite, rising about 360 feet above the level of the surrounding plain. Upon it the following plants were noticed:—

Clematis microphylla, Bursaria spinosa, Melhania incana, Geijera parviflora, Alphitonia excelsa, Heterodendron olaefolium, Hardenbergia monophylla, Acacia decora, A. Cunninghamii, Haloragis elata, Angophora intermedia, Eucalyptus albens, E. melanophloia, E. dealbata, Loranthus sp.,(on *Geijera parviflora* and *Santalum lanceolatum*), *Canthium oleifolium, Helichrysum obcordatum, Isotoma axillaris, Wahlenbergia gracilis, Notelaea microcarpa, Cynoglossum australe, Verbascum blattaria, Tecoma australis, Prostanthera rotundifolia, Rhagodia hastata, Kochia microphylla, Beyeria viscosa, Ficus rubiginosa, Urtica incisa, Santalum lanceolatum, Exocarpus cupressiformis, Callitris robusta, Xerotes longifolia, Cyperus fulvus, Lepidosperma laterale, Stipa verticillata, S. scabra, Cheilanthes tenuifolia.*

A species of some interest in regard to distribution, which is growing on Barber's Pinnacle and other hills, and also near the upper portion of Maule's Creek, is *Alphitonia excelsa*, the Red Ash of the coastal district; and the little trees are easily identified by the clusters of berry-like fruits, and leaves with an almost white underside. The fact that this species will flourish in the brush-lands of the moist coast, in places where there is an annual rainfall of 50 inches, and also in the much drier west, where the rainfall is reduced to about 24 inches annually, is evidence of its adaptability to environment.

It seems undoubted that this species has worked its way into New South Wales from the north. It is recorded from several islands off the north and north-east coast of Australia, amongst others being Borneo, Celebes, New Guinea, New Caledonia, Hawaii and Fiji,[*] and is known to occur in various portions of Eastern Queensland; but on coming into New South Wales, the cold heights of the Main Divide have caused it to spread westwards towards Boggabri on the one hand, and along the coastal eastern slopes on the other, where it appears to reach its greatest southerly extension. At the same time it is known to occur in various localities in the Goulburn and Hunter River Valleys near the Liverpool Range, and this range is sufficiently low in places to allow this plant access to both sides. Its most southern point known to me is Milton, where it is growing on a doleritic basalt formation, containing under 55% silica, while at Boggabri it is found on acid rocks, some of which contain an abundance of free silica.

Whether this species had the same range east and west, in this State, prior to the final uplift in late Tertiary time, or has spread along both sides of the Main Range since that period, there does not appear to be at present definite evidence to show; but considering the great similarity between the eastern and western forms, its

---

[*] "The Montane Flora of Fiji," by Lilian S. Gibbs, F.L.S., Journ. Linn. Soc. London, 1909, p.143.

somewhat limited extent east and west, and present possibilities of migration to the places where it now occurs in this State, it seems probable that much of this distribution has occurred under conditions of present-day topography.

Melaleuca bracteata is the common Tea-tree along the creeks north-east of Boggabri, growing in groups or clusters up to 20 feet high, and flowering late in November. The clustering habit of these trees causes a bending over and bunching of the heads, which render them useful for shade purposes. (Plate lxvii.)

The presence of such trees as *Acacia pendula* (Myall), and *Eucalyptus populifolia* (Bimble or Shiny-leaved Box), east of Boggabri, shows that typical western conditions come eastward to this locality, which marks a point on the eastern margin of the habitat of both these species.

Ficus rubiginosa, usually a moist-climate or coastal tree, is well established on the dry summit of Barber's Pinnacle, and on other hills.

The selective qualities of plants, when seeking suitable conditions for subsistence, are exemplified in the Eucalypts and other genera around Boggabri, and accord with what may be seen in a similar climate elsewhere in this State. Certain trees find it necessary that their roots should reach abundant moisture, while others have adapted themselves to subsist where the soil-moisture is slight indeed. Taking the three conditions of moisture at Boggabri, viz., that of the river-banks, the alluvial flats, and the hills, it is found that the river-banks are occupied by *Eucalyptus rostrata*, while the flats are covered with *E. populifolia, E. Woollsiana, E. melliodora* and *E. tereticornis*, the hills and even slight ridges being the home of *E. albens, E. crebra, E. melanophloia, E. dealbata* and *E. viridis*.

The local Casuarinas have distributed themselves in the following manner:—*C. Cunninghamiana* along the river-banks, *C. Cambagei* on the flats, and *C. Luehmanni* on the elevations. Other genera descriminate in a similar manner.

From a study of this distribution, and adaptation to environment, it is easy to conceive how a process of evolution may be originated by earth-movements or climatic changes, as well as by the proximity of different geological formations.

Percentage of Tasmanian Plants.

Of about 210 species noticed around Boggabri, at elevations from about 800-1,200 feet above sea-level, 36% chiefly of the smaller plants, are recorded from Tasmania, which, considering the disparity of climates, seems a fairly high percentage; while, on the Nandewar Mountains, at altitudes varying from 3,000-5,000 feet, and with much greater similarity of climates, 60% of about 160 species seen, occur in Tasmania. This affords an instructive example of the regulating influence of climate on plant-distribution.

It is also worthy of note that not a single Eucalypt, and only one Acacia noticed around Boggabri, in a warm, fairly dry climate, are known to occur in Tasmania; while only two species were found of each of these genera, which are common to both Tasmania and the Nandewars.

I wish to express my thanks to Mr. J. H. Maiden, F.L.S., and Mr. E. Betche, for assistance and corroboration in the identification of a number of plants, and also to Mr. W. J. Markwell, of Mount Lindsay Station, for affording facilities to visit the Nandewar Mountains.

EXPLANATION OF PLATES.

Plate lxvi.

Tangülda or Barber's Pinnacle, Boggabri.

Plate lxvii.

Groups of *Melaleuca bracteata* F.v.M., and Permo-Carboniferous(?) sandstone cliffs, Maule's Creek.

ORDINARY MONTHLY MEETING.

November 27th, 1912.

Mr. W. W. Froggatt, F.L.S., President, in the Chair.

Mr. Francis Edward Burbury, Launceston, Tas.; Miss Myall Cadell, Beecroft, Sydney; and Mr. A. A. Girault, Nelson (Cairns), N.Q., were elected Ordinary Members of the Society.

The President reminded Candidates for Fellowships, that Saturday, 30th inst., was the last day for sending in applications.

A communication from the Secretaries of Section D (Biology), Melbourne Meeting of the Australasian Association for the Advancement of Science, January, 1913, asking intending contributors of papers to communicate the titles as soon as convenient, and also to forward the papers, with abstracts, not later than one week before the meeting, was read from the Chair.

The Donations and Exchanges received since the previous Monthly Meeting (30th October, 1912), amounting to 16 Vols., 74 Parts or Nos., 15 Bulletins, and 11 Pamphlets, received from 54 Societies and two Individuals, were laid upon the table.

NOTES AND EXHIBITS.

Mr. A. A. Hamilton showed specimens of four species of plants from the National Herbarium, Sydney, of which two, it is believed, are new for Australia, and two new for New South Wales, namely: *Atriplex hastata* Linn., Cook's River (A. A. Hamilton; October, 1912); new for Australia.—*Senecio crassiflorus* DC., Waratah railway embankment (J. Gregson; March, 1910); The Dyke, Newcastle (Mrs. Hamilton; October, 1912); new for Australia.—*Galenia secunda* Sond., Geelong Coast, Victoria (Chas. Walters; January, 1902); recorded from Victoria in Ewart's Census of Weeds, etc., p.144; West Maitland (J. C. Burges; January, 1911); Stockton Beach (Mrs. Hamilton; October, 1912); new for New South Wales.—*Malva nicæensis* All., Government Domain, Sydney(J. H. Camfield; October, 1902); Cook's River(A. A. Hamilton; October, 1912); recorded from South Australia in J. M. Black's "Naturalised Flora of South Australia"; new for New South Wales.—The specimens from Newcastle, *Senecio crassiflorus*, a native of South America, and *Galenia secunda*, a South African species, have doubtless been introduced in ballast unloaded from vessels.

Mr. E. Cheel exhibited, a series of interesting grasses infested with "Smut"—*Ustilago bullata* Berk., on the inflorescence of *Agropyrum scabrum* Beauv.; Nattai River, viâ Hill Top (E. Cheel; February, 1912). It is recorded for New South Wales in Cooke's "Handbook of Australian Fungi"(p.326) on the inflorescence of *Triticum*, but it is not mentioned for this State by McAlpine("The Smuts of Australia," p.151), although he records it for Victoria, Tasmania, and South Australia. It was originally recorded from New Zealand, and afterwards from Murray River, by Rev. M. J. Berkeley (*vide* Journ. Linn. Soc., Bot., xiii., p.174, 1872).—*Urocystis stipæ* McAlp., on leaves and stems of *Stipa aristiglumis* F.v.M.; Hill Top (E. Cheel; January, 1912). The only other record is on *S. Luehmanni* Reader, from Victoria (*vide* McAlpine, *op. cit.*, p.198).—*Urocystis tritici* Koern., the Flag-Smut of wheat, on leaves, leaf-sheaths, and stems of wheat (*Triticum vulgare* Vill.), from Long Sally, Eugowra(D. O. Douglas; November, 1912). Mr. Douglas says, "There are ninety acres in one paddock, and one-tenth of it blighted like this sample I am sending you." It is probably the *U. occulta* of Cobb, recorded from New England in Agric. Gaz. N. S. Wales, iii., p.731, 1892). McAlpine (*op. cit.*, p. 199) says it is common in New South Wales, but does not give any specific locality.—*Sorosporium eriachnes* Thuem., on inflorescence of *Eriachne* sp. [? *E. pallida*] from South Australia (Department of Agriculture, May, 1900.—*Tolyposporium bursum* (Berk.) McAlp., on inflorescence of *Anthistiria imberbis* Retz., [*Themeda Forskalii* Hack., var, *imberbis* Hack.]; Hawkesbury Agricultural College, Richmond (C. T. Musson; November, 1912). Previously recorded for this State in these Proceedings (1910, 137) as *T. anthistiriæ* Cobb.—Also two exotic grasses: *Avena barbata* Brot., Hunter's Hill, and

University grounds, Sydney, (W. M. Carne; October, 1912); specimens of the common Wild Oats (*A. fatua* Linn.), which is closely allied, were exhibited for comparison.— And *Poa bulbosa* Linn., Bulbous Meadow Grass: Cowra (E. Breakwell; October, 1912). This, like *P. nodosa* Nees, has peculiar bulbous-based stems, and should be a very useful grass for the dry districts. The latter is fairly common in South and West Australia, but *P. bulbosa* has not been previously recorded for Australia, as far as is ascertainable.

Mr. E. I. Bickford sent for exhibition, a specimen of the West Australian pitcher-plant, *Cephalotus follicularis* Labill., portion of a growing plant in his possession.

Mr. W. W. Froggatt showed specimens of a small black and red Cicada (*Melampsalta incepta* Walk.) which appeared in great numbers in parts of New South Wales, in the early part of the month. From Dapto, they were reported as swarming like house-flies. At Kingwood, near Penrith, numbers appeared in the peach-orchards, puncturing the bark of the trees in search of sap, and causing the trees to gum badly. Near Lismore the same species swarmed through the forest in millions, almost like a grasshopper-plague, and, in consequence, many trees were looking sickly and unhealthy.

CONTRIBUTIONS TO OUR KNOWLEDGE OF SOIL FERTILITY.

vi. *The Inactivity of the Soil-Protozoa.*

By R. Greig-Smith, D.Sc., Macleay Bacteriologist to the Society.

In papers i., iv., and v. of this series, I have shown that soils contain bacteriotoxins, and fatty substances collectively named agricere. These are affected differently by heat and by the volatile antiseptics. Heat destroys the bacteriotoxins more or less, the extent of the destruction depending naturally upon the temperature and the exposure, but there is an interference through the production of certain toxins developed in some unknown manner during the heating. While, therefore, a moderate heat destroys the natural bacteriotoxins that are in the soil, a higher temperature, or possibly a longer exposure, produces toxins that were not originally present. The volatile disinfectants, on the other hand, have no direct action upon the bacteriotoxins. They act upon the agricere, carrying it to the surface, where it is irregularly deposited upon the angular fragments of soil. Indirectly, the nutrients are rendered more accessible to the solvent action of soil-water, and especially to the attacks of the bacteria, while the bacteriotoxins are more easily dissolved, and, therefore, more easily decay.

By their protozoal hypothesis, Russell and others claim that the soil-bacteria are prevented from multiplying freely by such soil-protozoa as the ciliates (among which *Colpoda cucullus* is very active), and as the soil-amœbæ. The action of heat and of the volatile disinfectants, according to these authors, is chiefly to destroy the protozoal phagocytes, other agencies having only a slight effect.

In the present paper, I have endeavoured to test the action of the soil-phagocytes by adding them purposely to soil, and by using the extracts of raw soil, as was done by Russell and Hutchinson.

But I have taken care to use soil that had not been overheated, and to have controls of unfiltered soil-extracts to compare with the filtered, presumably protozoa-free, extracts. Taken as a whole, my experiments show that Russell's contention cannot be sustained; the protozoa have little or no action in limiting the number of soil-bacteria. This is in agreement with Fred,* who, in one experiment upon the nitrification of compost-soil, found a slight gain in the test which had been treated with ether; he ascribed this to the stimulating effect of the disinfectant, rather than to the destruction of phagocytes.

The action of the soil-bacteriotoxins has been little investigated, although their effect has been known for a considerable time. Martin, for example, found that typhoid bacteria disappeared from raw soil in two days, but persisted for over a year in sterilised soil. Although ascribed to the competition of other bacteria, there can be little doubt that the typhoid bacteria were destroyed by the bacteriotoxins in the raw soil. When some kinds of actively-growing bacteria are added to soil, they rapidly increase, and then die down. For example, *Bac. prodigiosus*, is at the height of its growth between the second and third day at 28°; after that, the numbers rapidly fall away. In experiments with soil bacteria, the height of the rise is generally greatest at a later period, on account of the smaller number of bacteria at the start, and also on account of the slower growth of the natural microbes. In plate-cultures, the toxic influence of bacteria, such as *Bact. putidum*, is readily seen, for when many are present upon a plate, few colonies of other bacteria develop. Thus it comes about that the weaker dilutions show a greater number of bacteria than the stronger, for, in the presence of relatively fewer colonies of *Bact. putidum*, the other bacteria are not inhibited. The actual diminution of bacteria, by the products of *Bac. prodigiosus*, was numerically shown in a previous paper.†

The spore-producing soil-bacteria, such as *Bac. vulgatus*, *Bac. subtilis*, and *Bac. mycoides*, which resist the action of the volatile

* Centralb. f. Bakt., 26 Abt., xxxi., 233.
† These Proceedings, 1911, p.686.

disinfectants, appear to be little influenced by their own bacteriotoxins, but are affected by the toxins of other bacteria. This indifference was noted by Russell and Hutchinson, and although they claim that no bacteriotoxins are present in soil, they speak of the inhibiting action of bacteria added in the course of their experimental work.

These authors had tested the effect of the protozoa indirectly by comparing the growth of bacteria in raw soils, or in treated soils to which raw soil had been added, with the growth of bacteria contained in suspensions of raw soil freed from protozoa by filtration through cotton wool. The effect of filtered and unfiltered suspensions was not tested, although this appears to be the more reasonable method of testing the matter. Their experiments with heated soils are of little value, for two reasons. First, the temperature and period of exposure were excessive for the object in view, namely, the destruction of the protozoa; and, secondly, they ignored the effect of the bacteriotoxins and heat-toxins. As it appeared that a confirmation of their work was necessary, certain experiments were begun with this object.

In the first, a good arable soil was treated, for two days, with 2 per cent. of chloroform, and 20 grm. portions were weighed into small, wide-necked, ounce-bottles. These were divided into two sets. Each portion of one set received four c.c. of a suspension of a ciliate, *Colpoda cucullus*, while the portions of the other set were treated with the same quantity of the same suspension after it had been heated at 65° for ten minutes. Thus, one set received a suspension of living, the other of dead protozoa. The ciliates had been grown in 4 per cent. bean-infusion, and had been derived from a garden-soil. It was not a pure culture, and had been partly washed in 0·2 per cent. saline, but as this caused an encysting of the ciliates, the washing could not be continued until the great bulk of the bacteria had been eliminated. As it was, each portion received 400 motile forms of *Colpoda cucullus*, besides many bacteria and encysted ciliates. The bottles were covered with a small bell-jar, and incubated at 28°. In this, and the succeeding two experiments, the soils, containing at the start 20·9 per cent. of moisture, slowly dried; the figures obtained after the forty-fourth day are, therefore, not recorded. In the later experiments, the bottles were weighed, and the loss of water made up from time to time. In the last experiments, the loss of moisture was avoided by using corks fitted with a short piece of glass-tubing, terminated with an open point of about 1 mm. bore.

EXPERIMENT i.—THE ADDITION OF PROTOZOA.

Chloroformed soil.	Bacteria grown at 28° in millions per grm.					
	Start.	6 days.	14 days.	20 days.	27 days.	43 days.
Living protozoa ...	1·3	14·3	8	7·5	6·2	6·5
Dead protozoa ...	1·0	6	7·3	4·7	4·3	4·3

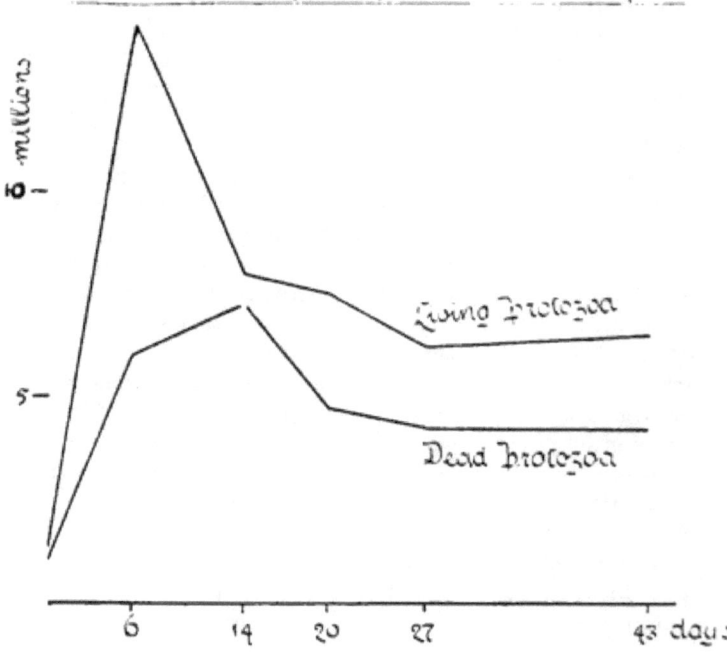

Although living protozoa were added to the soils of the first set, the bacteria increased enormously in six days. A phagocytic activity is not apparent. The subsequent decline may, however, be due to the ciliates, but it is more likely caused by the secretion of toxins by the bacteria. The continued excess of bacteria, in the test containing the living protozoa, in no way confirms the phagocytic hypothesis. Indeed, it is evident that the reason for the rapid increase of the numbers, in the first test, was caused by the introduction of a number of rapidly growing, feebly-resistant bacteria, which soon succumbed to the effect of their own toxin. The resistant bacteria, being also more numerous, probably account for the continuation of the greater number, as time went on. The nature of the colonies upon the plates was instructive. Those derived from the "living" soils were chiefly of the translucent-white or yellowish glistening kind, characteristic of the *coli-fluorescens* group of bacteria, while those from the "dead" soils were mostly opaque, white and granular, indicative of the *subtilis-vulgatus* bacilli. The odour of the plates was also marked. Those of the "living" set had a disagreeable, putrefactive smell, in sharp contrast with the faint odour of the other. By the twenty-seventh day, the distinctive odours had disappeared, and the colonies were very much the same in both tests.

The suspensions had been tested for living protozoa by infecting sterile 4% bean-infusions. The heated suspension contained none, while the raw suspension gave rise to many. On the fourteenth day, the soils were tested in a similar manner. Both contained Colpoda, and the "living" soil contained amœbæ in addition. Upon testing the original chloroformed soil, it was discovered that the protozoa were still alive; a luxuriant growth of *Colpoda cucullus* being obtained. Thus the treatment with 2% chloroform had not been sufficient to destroy the encysted ciliates.

For destroying protozoa, Russell and Golding used 2% of carbon bisulphide or toluol, allowing it to act for two days; while, for field-work, they suggest the employment of from two or three cwt. per acre, as a suitable quantity. This is, roughly, the equivalent of from 0·01% to 0·02%. Russell and Hutchinson used 4% of toluene to kill off all protozoa, but, in the later part of their paper, the statement occurs that toluene does not kill off all the larger organisms, one, at least, a small ciliated protozoon being left; and this is probably concerned with the diminution of the activity of the treated soil, after a long period, as, for example, in the second crop. The impression is left, however, that the disinfectant kills off living and encysted forms of *Colpoda cucullus*, the chief food of which is said to be bacteria.

In my experiments, I found that *Colpoda cucullus* was, of all the soil-protozoa, least affected by disinfectants. It occurred in infusions seeded with soils which had been treated for three days with 20% of toluene (Kahlbaum), or with 10% of chloroform (Schering).

With regard to its food, the partiality for bacteria is open to question. From observation, they appear to feed upon organic débris of any kind, and any bacteria that they consume are drawn in accidentally. They are specially fond of the slimy matter exuded by the encysting cell. It should not be forgotten that the digestion of the organic débris will give rise to waste products containing nutrients available for bacteria, thus augmenting the food at the disposal of the remaining microbes, which will respond by growing more quickly. The bacterial increase should not, for this reason, be lessened by the presence of Colpoda. It appears that, if any real phagocytic effect in reducing the bacterial numbers is to be ascribed to any protozon, it should be to the amœbæ rather than to the ciliates. The amœbæ are destroyed by comparatively small amounts of disinfectants; they were detected in infusions seeded with soils which had been treated with 1% of chloroform, but not with 2%.

It is unfortunate that Russell and Hutchinson did not use enough disinfectant to ensure the complete destruction of all the protozoa in their experimental work, as there is the doubt raised that, so far as the protozoa are concerned, their disinfection had been abortive. And yet the point claimed by these authors is, that the protozoa, and especially Colpoda, had been destroyed, and, in consequence, the bacteria had increased. Might not the proportion of protozoa that had been destroyed, have been proportional to the bacteria that were killed; and that, so far as numbers are concerned, the *status quo* remained after the treatment with disinfectants?

From the appearance of the protoplasm and the absence of food-granules, Goodey* concludes that the Colpoda first to appear in soil-cultures, have emerged from the encysted condition, and that they, therefore, do not functionate as a factor in limiting the bacterial activity in soils.

As the ciliates, such as *Colpoda cucullus*, cannot be credited with the limitation of the soil-bacteria, we must examine the claims of the amoebae; and be it remembered, that we are not so much concerned with phagocytosis as with the limitation of the bacteria.

Even if the amoebae do actively ingest bacteria, in the soil, there is no evidence that the net result may not be an increase of the residual microbes from the stimulating influence of the excreted products of the digested bacillary protoplasm.† On the other hand, it is possible that substances of the nature of immune bodies may be secreted or excreted by the amoebae. The matter clearly cannot be decided *ex cathedra*, and, accordingly, an experiment was begun, in which a number of amoebae were added to a soil that had been freed from protozoa by heating at 65° and treatment with chloroform. Subsequent tests showed that the soil was free from protozoa. A suspension of amoebae, *Amoeba limax*, from a

---

* Proc. Roy. Soc. B.84, 18/8/11, p.179.

† The amoebae undoubtedly are phagocytes, but they certainly do not englobe every microbe they chance to meet, for I have watched soil-amoebae moving in plant-infusions, and in no case have I seen the undoubted ingesting of a bacterium. I have seen the protruding pseudopodia push aside the living bacteria, and pass over the dead microbes [a trace of methylene blue added to the drop under examination colours the dead cells but not the living] which can be traced under the amoeba as it glides along, and which are left upon the spots they originally occupied. A motile bacterium may touch the protozoon, and dart off again, or it may be caught, presumably by the flagella, and after wriggling about for some seconds, swim away. Again, a protruding pseudopodium may touch a bacterium and immediately retract, or a distinct angular bay may be formed as the pseudopodium meets and passes the microbe. Rotating

garden soil, had been seeded into a bean-infusion, and, after a time, a rich growth of amoebae was found. The suspension was centrifugalised, and the sediment rapidly washed with 0·2% saline. The amoebae were suspended in saline, a part of which was heated for 10 minutes at 62° to 64°. To each 20 grm. portion of soil, 4 c.c. of suspension were added. This contained, in the case of the unheated suspension, 6,089 living motile amoebae, no motile ciliates, many cysts, presumably of the latter, and many bacteria.

EXPERIMENT ii.—THE ADDITION OF AMOEBAE.

Heated soil.	Bacteria grown at 28° in millions per grm.					
	Start	1 day	5 days	7 days	15 days	36 days
Living amoebae ...	0·3	42·5	39	35	26	25
Dead amoebae ...	0·2	0·9	11	20	24	24

The experiment was repeated and confirmed at a later date, with a poor sandy soil. The tests were contained in small bottles closed with wooden corks, through which passed glass tubes furnished with open capillary ends of approximately 1 mm. bore. The evaporation from the soil was very small, the loss being equal to only 0·37% in 73 days at 22°. Each test received four c.c. of a suspension of *Amoeba limax* in 0·2% saline. This quantity contained 2,720 moving and 800 encysted amoebae, together with a mixed

---

pairs of bacteria cease their motion as the protozoal arm touches them, but in a few seconds they are as active as ever. I have seen an amoeba, in moving forwards, touch a rod-shaped microbe which adhered to the surface, sliding over but still maintaining its position in the field, until the terminal was reached. There it remained attached. Meanwhile, another microbe was similarly treated, but somehow became detached from the terminal. In its circumambient wandering, the amoeba touched the same bacterium, and both became fixed to the terminal tuft of barely visible slime, until a fragment of débris, encountered by the protozoon, proved too weighty, and fragment and bacteria were left behind. Mouton [Ann. de l'Inst. Past., xvi., p.476] seems to have seen, in this entanglement, an agglutination of the microbes by an agglutinin secreted by the pulsating vacuole.

bacterial flora, but with no other protozoa. Half of the suspension was heated at 65° for 30 minutes. The soil had been treated with 10% of chloroform to destroy any native amœbæ.

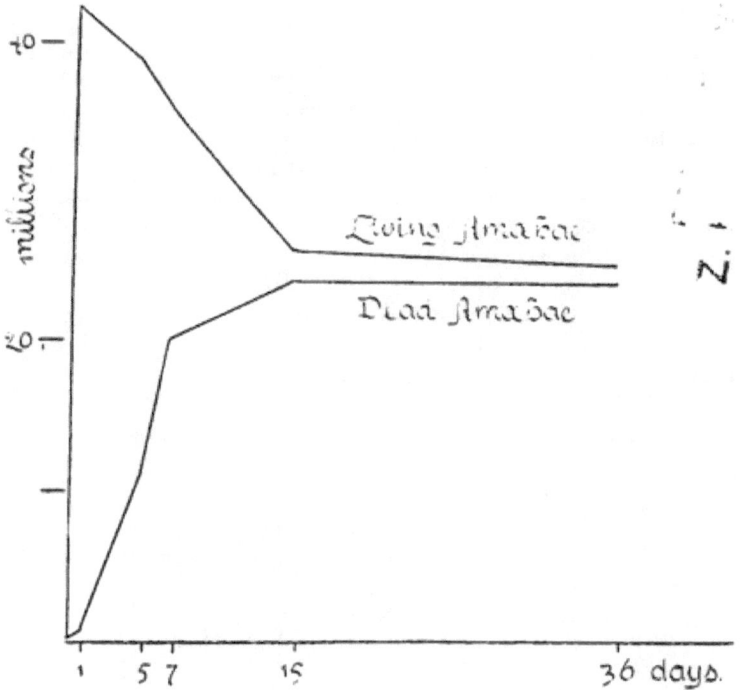

Experiment iia.—The Addition of Amœbæ.

	Bacteria grown at 22° in millions per grm.						
	Start	5 days	14 days	21 days	33 days	45 days	73 days
Living amœbæ ...	3·0	44·0	8·4	3·8	3·1	1·0	5·2
Dead amœbæ ...	0·8	5·9	2·1	3·9	1·4	0·4	1·2

The bacteria in the soils, seeded with living amœbæ and bacteria, multiplied very rapidly during the first day. This was due to the quickly growing nature of the added microbes, which, from the examination of the colonies upon the plates, were seen to be of the *coli-fluorescens* type, and, among them, *Bact. putidum* was prominent. The decline in the numbers may have been caused by the phagocytic propensities of the amœbæ, but it was more probably the result of the action of the bacteriotoxins secreted by the bacteria themselves. In this, as in the first experiment, there is no evidence of any rapid increase in the amœba-free soil.

A general observation of the behaviour of the bacteria in soils, leads one to believe that the kinds resistant to heat and disinfectants, are little influenced either by their own toxins or by those of other groups. Such, however, does not appear to strictly hold, for their growth is certainly restricted by the presence of toxins of other groups, as the following approximate count of the rough, opaque colonies upon the plates, shows.

EXPERIMENT ii.—BACTERIA OF THE *Subtilis-vulgatus* TYPE.

In millions per grm.

	At start	1 day	5 days	7 days	15 days	36 days
Unheated suspension	0.13	0.50	10	7	12	10
Heated suspension	0.13	0.53	11	15	18	17

On comparing the numbers with those of the total bacteria, it is seen that the non-resistant have a decided inhibiting action upon the resistant bacteria, and, although the latter increase as time goes on, their multiplication is not so rapid in the presence as in the absence of the toxins of the less resistant and more rapidly growing forms.

Upon noting that *Bact. putidum* was one of the chief bacteria in the unheated suspension, a series of portions of soil were seeded with a pure culture of this organism, and, for the purpose of control, a second series received water. The soil had been treated with toluene, and had been heated to 65°.

EXPERIMENT iii.—THE ADDITION OF *Bact. putidum*.

Heated and toluened soil.	Bacteria grown at 28° in millions per grm.						
	Start	1 day	2 days	3 days	10 days	24 days	44 days
Bacteria	0·098	24	35	37	29	14	9·5
Control	0·095	0·3	9·4	16	21	12	10

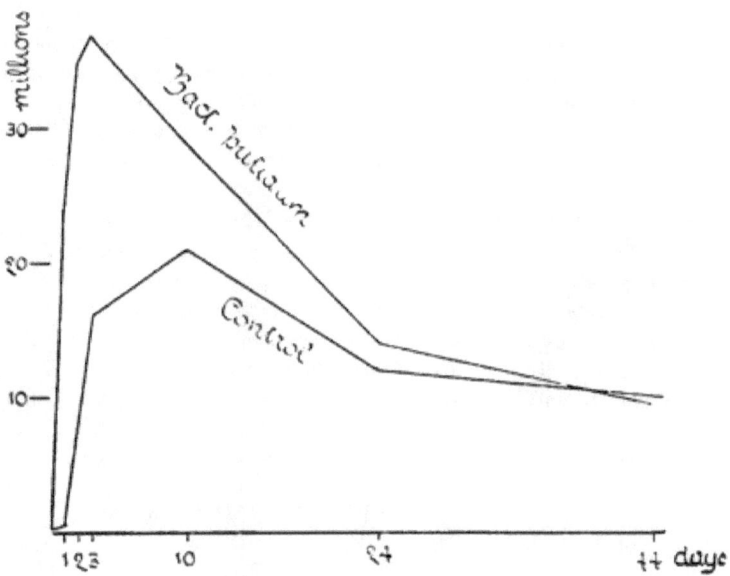

The experiment shows the same rapid rise following the addition of one of the components of the suspension used in Expt. ii., and the control is similar in its behaviour to the heated suspension series. As a whole, the experiment tells us that the same general multiplication of bacteria occurs in the presence, as in the absence of amœbæ.

In the apparent absence of protozoal activity in these experiments, it seemed necessary to confirm some of Russell and Hutchinson's results. The most telling of their experiments was one in which, as the result of adding a filtered suspension to a toluened soil, the bacteria rose from 66 millions on the 20th, to 166 millions on the sixtieth day. No test was, however, made with the unfiltered as against the filtered suspension. The experiment was not confirmed, and, as it is possible that the results might have been abnormal, a repetition of a certain portion of it was decided upon.

An alluvial soil was air-dried, and treated for two days with 5% chloroform. After the evaporation of the solvent, a number of 20 grm. portions were weighed out into small bottles, and moistened with 4 c.c. of water or extract, a proportional quantity of water being added to the tests which received the gram of air-dried, untreated soil. The amount of water lost by evaporation was calculated weekly or biweekly from the loss of weight of eight bottles, two from each set, and the loss was made good. The moisture in the soils varied up and down from 19·6 to 15·4. The extract was made by shaking 100 grm. of soil with 500 c.c. of water for 20 minutes, and filtering half of it through five inches of tightly packed, cotton wool. This removed the larger protozoa, such as *Colpoda cucullus*, but the cysts of smaller ciliates were not retained, as was shown by their growth in bean-infusion. The experiment was made in duplicate, one set being incubated at 28°, the other at 15°.

EXPERIMENT iv., *a*—THE ADDITION OF SOIL AND ITS EXTRACTS.

Chloroformed soil (alluvial).	Bacteria grown at 28° in millions per grm.							
	Start	2 d.	6 d.	13 d.	35 d.	42 d.	57 d.	69 d.	83 d.
1, Water control ...	1·33	4·8	4·9	9·0	14	16	19	28	29
2, Unfiltered extract.	1·36	6·0	6·3	9·2	15·3	19	22	25	29
3, Filtered extract ...	1·34	5·7	6·4	10·2	15·8	18	21	31	29
4, 5% untreated soil..	1·40	5·7	5·3	9·2	15	18	20	24	28

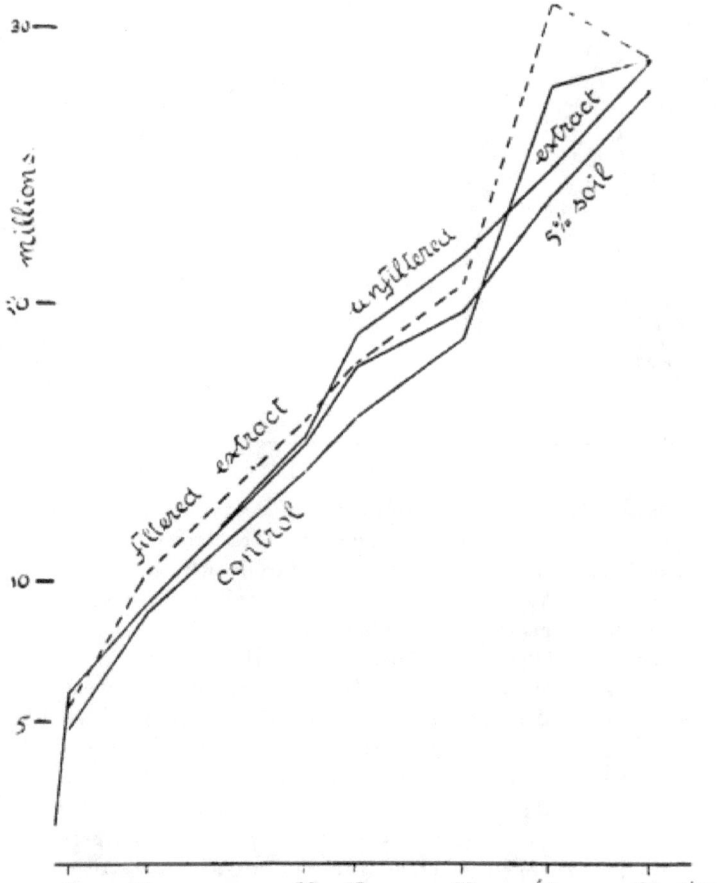

EXPERIMENT iv., b—THE ADDITION OF SOIL AND ITS EXTRACTS.

Chloroformed soil (alluvial)	Bacteria grown at 15° in millions per grm.								
	Start	6 d.	9 d.	13 d.	35 d.	42 d.	57 d.	69 d.	83 d.
1, Water control	1·33	2·7	6·5	7	11	12	13	12	12
2, Unfiltered extract	1·36	6·9	12	14	12	12	13	12	12
3, Filtered extract	1·34	6·7	13	12	13	14	14	12	12
4, 5% untreated soil	1·40	3·5	7	7·5	10	10	11	12	10

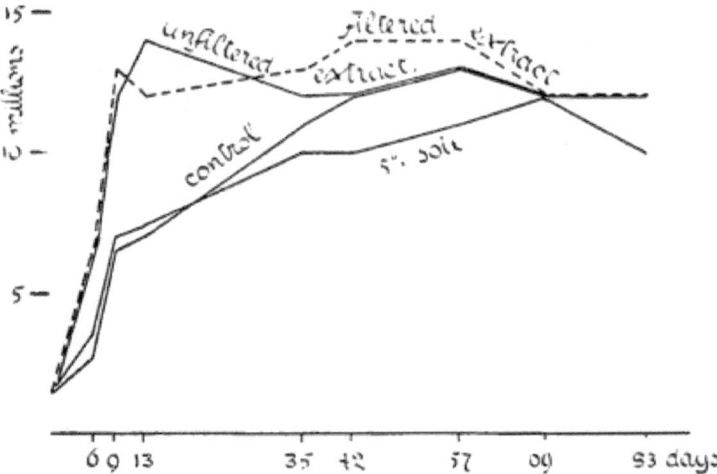

These soils had not been heated, and do not show the rapid rise that occurred in the earlier experiments. The curves of iv. a, for the most part, rise fairly steadily, and there is little difference between them. We see no indication of any influence having been exerted by phagocytic protozoa derived either from the unfiltered extract or from the untreated soil. Beyond the fact that Nos. 2, 3, and 4 received originally more bacteria than the control, and consequently obtained a lead, these tests practically give the same result. The protozoa cannot be said to have any action upon the soil-bacteria at 28°, at which temperature they are very active.*

The curves of the tests at 15° differ from those at 28°. Those which received the extracts, gave a more rapid bacterial growth within the first ten days, but, as at the higher temperature, there is no pronounced evidence of protozoal activity.

One of the points brought out, is the influence of temperature upon bacterial growth. At 15° the numbers never rose above 15 millions, and remained constant between 10 and 15 millions per

---

* The period of multiplication for *Amœba limax* was found to be 1¾ hours at 37°, 8 hours at 28°, and 28 hours at 15°.

grm. At 28°, the rise was steady, and by the eightieth day, the numbers lay between 25 and 30 millions.

A variation of the preceding experiment was made by using a poor sandy soil, and incubating the tests at 22°. The soil, which contained *Amœba limax*, was treated with 4% of chloroform for two days, and the moisture was brought up to 17%. As, however, a strong growth of moulds developed upon the surfaces of the soils in the tests, the moisture was, by the thirty-seventh day, allowed to fall to 13%, at which it was maintained.

EXPERIMENT V.—THE ADDITION OF SOIL AND ITS EXTRACTS.

Chloroformed soil (poor sandy).	Bacteria grown at 22° in millions per grm.							
	Start	7 d.	20 d.	37 d.	66 d.	85 d.	106 d.	121 d.
1, Water control ...	0·14	0·3	2·8	3·7	(0·2)	6·2	6·4	4·4
2, Unfiltered extract	0·17	0·5	11·0	8·3	5·2	4·9	7·0	5·8
3, Filtered extract	0·15	0·5	3·4	8·9	3·5	5·5	4·3	4·7
4,5% untreated soil	0·17	0·5	2·1	3·2	6·0	5·3	(1·6)	4·5

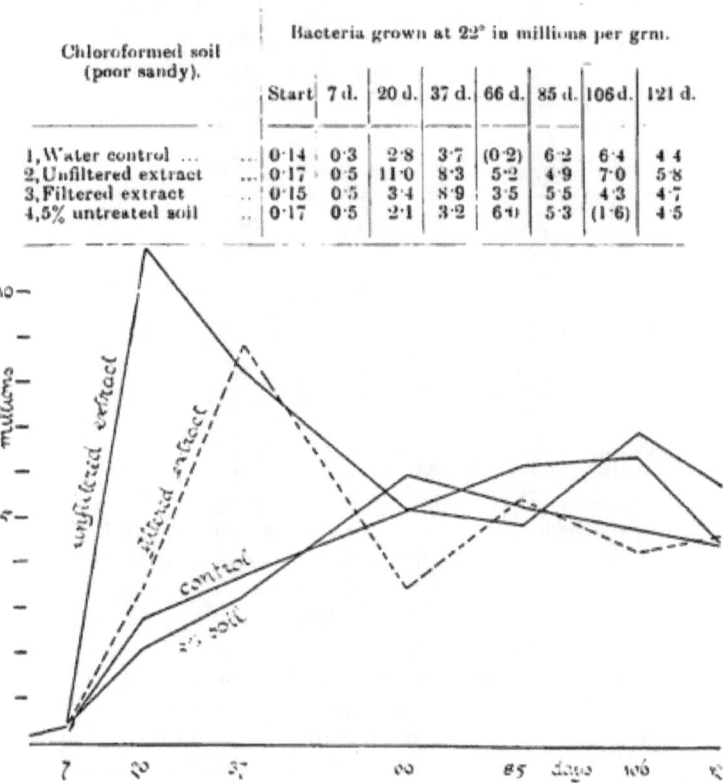

The experiment generally confirms the previous ones, and shows that the removal of some of the protozoa, by filtering the soil-extract through cotton wool, has little influence upon the multiplication of the bacteria in the soil, beyond what is to be expected from the behaviour of the microbes in the extracts.

The curves of the last two experiments do not show the sharp rise noted in the experiments with protozoa, etc., in the earlier part of this paper. There is little doubt that the rapid rise was occasioned by the destruction of the soil-toxins by heat, and, in a confirmatory experiment, the soil was heated to show that such was actually the case. The same alluvial soil was used as in experiment iv. a, and the incubation temperature was the same, viz. 28°. It was heated at 60° to 70° for half-an-hour, but otherwise the conditions were the same. A fifth test was included to show the effect of chloroform.

EXPERIMENT vi.—THE USE OF HEATED SOIL.

Heated soil (alluvial).	Bacteria grown at 28° in millions per grm.						
	Start.	5 dys	14 dys	22 dys	41 dys	55 dys	70 dys
Chloroformed							
1, Water control	1·24	60	48	19	7	16	19
2, Unfiltered extract	1·27	56	47	12	9	15	19
3, Filtered extract	1·25	55	47	15	8	16	17
4, 5% untreated soil	1·54	65	43	17	14	10	17
Not chloroformed							
5, Water control	1·22	51	54	14	7	13	15

The numbers are so near to one another, especially with Nos. 2 and 3, which received the unfiltered and filtered soil-extracts, that the inactivity of the soil-protozoa is well demonstrated. The results with heated soils have confirmed those obtained in the previous experiments with unheated soils.

The effect of heat alone, and of chloroform alone, is very marked, as can be seen by comparing the curves of the control tests in Experiments iv., a, and vi. These tests were made upon the same soil, containing the same amount of moisture, and were incubated at the same temperature. I believe the moisture and temperature are of more importance in modifying the bacterial content of soils than one would imagine, and experiments concerning these influences are in progress. In heated soils, the bacteria grow very rapidly at first, then, as the toxin accumulates, the numbers fall almost as sharply, after which they slowly rise. With chloroform alone, the numbers increase slowly and steadily, as if nutrients were being slowly utilised.

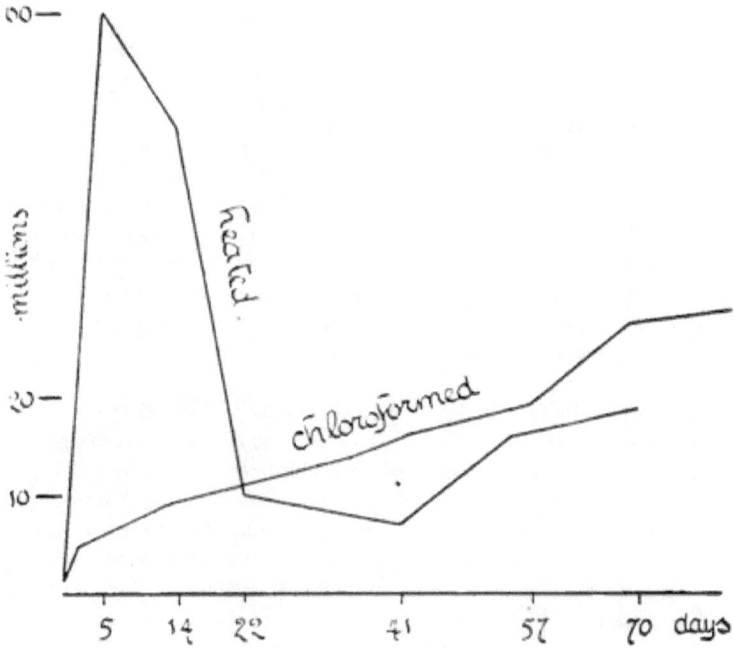

The extracts with which the soils had been treated, in these experiments, contained not only protozoa and bacteria, but also nutrients and toxins, as I have already shown in the first paper of this series. As it is just possible that these two latter substances might have a certain, though small, influence in increasing or decreasing the numbers of bacteria, an experiment was made to test the matter. The same alluvial soil, after chloroforming, received four c.c. of water, and of porcelain-filtered extracts of the strength used, viz., 100 grm. to 500 c.c. After filtering, a portion was boiled for an hour under an aërial condenser, and cooled. The moisture-content of the tests was 19·1%.

EXPERIMENT vii.—THE EFFECT OF PORCELAIN-FILTERED EXTRACTS.

Alluvial soil (chloroformed).	Bacteria grown at 15%, in millions per grm.				
	At start.	2 days.	7 days.	14 days.	36 days.
Water control	0·5	2·5	6·7	9·8	10·2
Filtered extract	0·5	2·3	5·7	8·5	11·6
Filtered extract, heated	0·5	2·6	8·7	12·0	12·4

The unheated filtered extract had, at first, a toxic action when the numbers were lower than the control. But, as the added toxin decayed, the numbers rose. The heated extract had a pronounced nutritive effect. The differences are not great, but they indicate that the soluble substances in the extracts have a certain, though small, influence upon the growth of bacteria.

From the foregoing, it will have been seen that the larger ciliates, as *Colpoda cucullus*, are not destroyed when comparatively large amounts of volatile disinfectant are added to soil. Upon adding suspensions of protozoa, there was no evidence of any limitation in the numbers of the soil-bacteria. Any enhanced effect was due to the addition of the bacteria contained in the suspensions. The filtration of a soil-extract had no influence, beyond that of removing some of the bacteria in the suspension. Any phagocytic tendencies that the soil-protozoa possess, have no influence in limiting the numbers of bacteria in the soil. So far as the growth of bacteria is concerned, the effect of heat is of a different character from that of a volatile disinfectant. Inferentially, the toxins and nutrients of the soil are alone concerned with the changes that occur when soils are heated, or treated with volatile disinfectants.

A NEW ENDOPARASITIC COPEPOD: MORPHOLOGY AND DEVELOPMENT.

By H. Leighton Kesteven, D.Sc., Lecturer in Physiology, Technical College, Sydney.

(Plates lxviii. lxx.)

Introduction.—The parasitic copepod herein described occurs, as far as is yet known, only in *Ptychodera australis* Hill, and in the genital ridges thereof. The Enteropneust has only been recorded from the type-locality, that is, the coast of New South Wales, a few miles north of Port Jackson.

For my material, I have to thank Professor J. P. Hill. It comprises entire specimens and serial sections, some of the latter *in situ* in the host. The fixation is exceedingly good in most of the specimens, and the staining all that could be desired, so that, for any imperfections in the description, I alone am responsible.

This material was given me in 1905; the long delay which has occurred has been due to want of detail of the structure of certain of the appendages. After many fruitless trips in search of further material, on the part of myself and friends, in desperation I dismounted some of the whole specimens, and after treating them with one per cent. aqueous solution of sodium hydroxide, obtained from the clarified exoskeleton floating in glycerine the required details; the pictures so obtained were checked by subsequently cutting the exoskeleton along the length dorsally, so that it could be flattened out, and examined with an oil immersion, so small and flexible are the appendages that nothing short of such high magnification gave one faith in one's observations. The appendages as seen under the oil (Reichert, $\frac{1}{12}$) were traced with the camera lucida.

U b i u s, gen. nov.

A genus of Copepod crustaceans typified by *U. hilli* (*postea*), closely allied to the montoypical genus *Ire* Mayer(5), but differing from that in the possession of a paired ovary, the absence of a chitin-lined "end-gut," and great reduction of the nervous system. Type, *U. hilli* Kesteven.

UBIUS HILLI, sp. nov.

External Features.— Form cylindrical, more or less abruptly truncated anteriorly, and tapering to a point; bifid in the male, posteriorly (Fig. 4). The size is variable; following are the averages of six measurements: female 6.4 x 0.8; male 2.6 x 0.4 mm. If the diameter be taken as the unit of measurement, then, with fair constancy, the length of the female is eight, and that of the male six. In living specimens, the length was probably greater and the diameter less, since longitudinal body-muscles are alone well developed, and must have contracted when the animals were killed.

Colour opaque white.

Cuticle thin, very flexible, and showing very fine, closely set, annular hair-like thickenings.

External apertures: the mouth (Fig. 2) is situated ventrally, almost at the extreme anterior end. Anus absent. The vulvæ are situated ventrally on either side of the mid-line, well towards the posterior end; each is surrounded by three laterally compressed jointless appendages, two on either side of, and one directly behind the orifice (Fig. 3).

The appendages (Fig. 2) number five pairs; two are situated immediately in front of the mouth, the remainder equidistant behind it; the fifth pair being situated almost at the junction of the anterior and middle thirds of the length of the body.

The antennules (Fig. 5) are short and flattened, composed of a single segment, and provided with a toothed cutting inner edge. The musculature is composed of two bands of striated muscle, which arise from an endoskeletal cuticular rod above, and are inserted well towards the distal extremity of the appendage.

The antennæ (Fig. 6) are three-jointed chelæ, the first segment short and broad. The arrangement of the musculature is shown in Fig. 2. The third pair, mandibles (Fig. 7), are two-jointed, the first joint short and stout, the second flattened, of triangular outline, but with the apex notched; the musculature of these is also shown in the same figure. The fourth and fifth pairs (Fig. 8) are exactly alike; they are biramous, the protopodite of one segment is broad and short. The endopodite, also unisegmented, is flattened, and has all the appearance of being chelate, but no joint is present. The expodite is chelate, of two segments: superficially it bears a close resemblance to the endopodite. These appendages are doubtless legs.

With the exception of a slight constriction, not always present, between the third and fourth pairs of appendages, there are no indications of segmentation whatsoever.

The appendages present striking peculiarities, which has called for special care in their description. Difficulty has been caused, too, by their flexibility, so that though, between thirty and forty specimens have been examined, only in three are the second pair clearly discernible; whilst, in four of the specimens only, does one see the third pair clearly. The first, fourth, and fifth pairs are clearly visible in some eight or nine specimens.

In the absence of any evidence to aid me, I have adopted Mayer's names for the appendages (*l.c.*).

Body-Wall.—Beneath the cuticle is a syncytial (?) flattened epithelium, difficult to make out on account of its delicacy. Deep to the epithelium are the longitudinal muscle-bands; each of these is composed of three or four plain muscle-fibres, as seen in transverse section. There is apparently no anastomosis of these muscle-strands.

Perforating the body-wall are the ducts of numerous excretory (?) glands. Each gland is composed of several large, flask or spindle-shaped cells, whose cytoplasm is very granular, and whose nucleus is relatively small, and poor in chromatic material, with one well defined nucleolus. The "duct" is formed by the fusion of the necks of the component cells, and in its wall are several intensely staining granules resembling *cocci* in size and shape (Fig. 17). There is no true duct formed, the condition being rather, a group of unicellular glands perforating the body-wall by a common aperture. Similar glands are described in *Ire balanoglossi* by Mayer. These glands are most abundant anteriorly.

The body-cavity (hæmocœl) is more or less filled by branched, connective tissue cells, in some places more so than others. Corpuscles of two kinds are present in the cœlomic fluid; small, spherical, hyaline corpuscles about 3μ in diameter, with intensely staining nucleus, and larger forms with more opaque cytoplasm and vesicular nucleus, and varying in size from 8 to 15μ. These latter are irregular in outline, and are probably amœboid.

From place to place along its length, the alimentary canal is slung to the dorsal and ventral body-wall by bundles of clear fibres of some thickness (about 1μ), which closely resemble plain muscle-fibres, but are devoid of nuclei.

Alimentary Canal.—Within the mouth is a small chitin-lined, buccal cavity (Fig. 15), from which the œsophagus passes directly dorsad (Fig. 2), to the centre of the body, and there opens into the digestive tract, which, divided by three constrictions into four compartments, extends backward in a straight line through the trunk, and ends blindly a short distance posterior to the genital apertures (Fig. 1).

Immediately within the oral aperture is a sphincter muscle, and radiating to the body-wall and endoskeletal rods previously mentioned are six strands of muscle, constituting together a dilator oris. These muscles are striated (Fig. 2).

The œsophagus is lined by a columnar epithelium, whose component cells are, for the most part, completely hyaline, some, however, having granular cytoplasm (Fig. 16).

The general arrangement and relative size of the various compartments is sufficiently evident from the diagram (Fig. 1) and transverse sections (Figs. 20 to 25); it remains to describe the epithelium lining it, and a peculiar digestive(?) gland secreting into the second compartment.

The anterior portion of the first compartment is lined by an exceedingly irregular epithelium, depicted in Fig. 19. The cells, of extremely variable size, have a very granular cytoplasm, the granularity being variable. The largest granules (zymogen) are found in the enlarged bulbous ends of the larger cells, and are apparently shed by actual abstriction, since structures precisely similar to the enlarged ends just mentioned, are found free in the lumen of the gut. This calls to mind the secretion from the digestive glands of Molluscs and Crustaceans as described by MacMunn(4); and the histological resemblance between the epithelium here, and that of Limax(*l.c.*), is doubtless correlated with similarity of function. This epithelium recalls that of *Lernaea branchialis* Linn., as described by A. Scott(7).

The remainder of the digestive tract is lined by a minutely granular, squamous epithelium, which, however, becomes cubical and even columnar at the constrictions. The continuity of the epithelium on the dorsal wall of the second compartment is broken by the orifices of a cluster of elongated, cylindrical, unicellular glands; in fact, so numerous are these, that it would be as correct to say that they constitute the dorsal epithelium in this situation. The form of these cells is depicted in Fig. 26; their cytoplasm is finely granular, and their nuclei, as in the cells of the subdermal glands, appear disproportionately small.

The blind termination of the digestive tract is succeeded by a fibrous strand, the remnant of an aborted rectum.

In the absence of a fully developed digestive gland, the glandular first compartment may perhaps be regarded as its homologue as well as analogue.

Nervous System.—As in the adult *Lernaea*, there are no elements present which can be recognised as nervous.

Reproductive Organs.—The disposition of these organs is essentially similar in the two sexes. Paired reproductive glands are situated on either side of the anterior portion of the first compartment of the digestive tract; the glands are hollow, when not filled by reproductive cells, and communicate, without any intervening constriction, with oviduct or vas deferens. The situation of the external orifices has already been described.

The situation of the oviduct, which is the same as that of the vas, can be gathered by a reference to the diagram (Fig. 1), and the various figures of the transverse sections(Figs. 20 to 25). The oviduct presents two well-differentiated segments. The anterior, which is apparently uterus rather than oviduct, is of large lumen, is lined by a flattened epithelium, and is usually distended with more or less matured ova. The posterior segment or oviduct proper is lined by a columnar epithelium (Fig. 29), is of small lumen or its walls are in contact, and does not contain ova. Extending anteriorly from the junction of the two segments is a short blind diverticulum, which *may* be a receptaculum seminis, but does not contain spermatozoa in any of my specimens (Fig. 1). For a portion of its course, the oviduct proper is freely open to a gland situated dorsal to it (Figs. 1 and 31), and which probably supplies the material which serves to agglutinate the ova into strings.

Just within the vulva are two bundles of plain muscle-fibres, which are capable of depressing the floor of the last portion of the duct. Their contraction possibly creates a vacuum which helps in the passage of the ova along the duct (Fig. 32).

The vas deferens is lined by a columnar epithelium (Fig. 28). Ventral to the digestive canal, there is a tubular connection between the two external male orifices. This tube may be a vesicula seminalis; it is lined by a syncytial epithelium, and in its walls are a few plain muscle-fibres (Figs. 27 and 30).

Development.—The mature ovum is of the typical egg-shape, even to having a thicker and a thinner end; its subsequent history shows the thicker end to correspond to the posterior pole of the embryo. The nucleus is large; a chromatin network and nucleolus are plainly visible in a perfectly hyaline nucleoplasm. Yolk-spherules are plentiful, and are quite evenly distributed throughout the cytoplasm.

Cleavage.—The first and second cleavages are parallel to the long axis of the ovum, and at right angles to each other.

Figure 33 is drawn from a section made at right angles to the long axis, through an embryo in the two-cell stage. The nuclei in this and other early cleavage-stages (four- and eight-cell stages) are surrounded by areas of cytoplasm comparatively devoid of yolk-spherules; this area is probably traversed by achromatic astral rays that are too fine to be seen in my preparations. Fig. 10 is a drawing of the reconstructed two-celled embryo.

A section of the four celled-embryo is shown in Fig.34, and the reconstructed embryo in Fig. 11.

Fig. 34 gives one the idea that there has been unequal segmentation; this, however, is due to the fact that the section is not absolutely at right angles to the long axis.

Cleavage next takes place twice successively at right angles to the long axis, resulting in the eight- and sixteen-cell stages.

In the sixteen-cell stage, the embryo still retains its egg-shape, though it has increased slightly in size, owing to the separation of the blastomeres to give rise to a blastocœl (Figs. 35 and 36). Fig. 37 is a longitudinal section through a compacted embryo, in which the blastocœl has not yet appeared.

The appearance of the embryo in the sixteen-cell stage is shown in Fig. 12.

The rotational movement of the polar blastomeres, which leads to the even capping of the poles, is well shown in Fig. 35.

The fifth cleavage is again parallel to the long axis, and results in the thirty-two celled embryo. The blastocœl has increased a good deal in size (Fig. 38).

There now follow two more total and equal cleavages, the first in the longitudinal plane, the second in the transverse plane. These cleavages result in the formation of the hollow blastula.

There next follows a cleavage which does not affect a few cells situated at the posterior pole, about eight in number. The blastula is further enlarged at this division by increase of the blastocœl.

The larger cells, at the posterior end, now divide actively, their daughter-cells being shed into the blastocœl, where they, in turn, divide, to give rise to a solid mass of small cells, more or less completely filling the blastocœl (Figs. 39, 40, and Fig. 14).

Meanwhile, the parietal cells have undergone further division, and the embryo has decreased in size.

In this stage, the embryo is a solid gastrula, gastrulation having been by a much modified involution. The blastopore is represented by a saucer-like depression at the posterior pole (Fig. 13).

Histogenesis and Organogeny.—In the hollow blastula, those eight cells, the budding of which is to give rise to the solid core of the gastrula, stain a lighter colour with borax carmine, than do the remaining cells. Even in the sixteen-celled embryo, in some cases, the posterior quad has a lighter tinge than the other twelve, and almost invariably a certain number of the posterior cells of the sixty-four celled embryo take this lighter tinge. From these cells are derived the whole of the internal organs; they constitute an *endo-mesoderm* rudiment.

The embryo as we left it in the last section, therefore, consisted of a wall of ectodermal cells, at the blastopore, exposing cells of the endo-mesoderm rudiment, the main body of which form a solid core to the embryo.

Whether the ectoderm grows over, and closes the blastopore, or whether the endo-mesoderm remains exposed here even in the nauplius, I was unable to decide. Some sections appear to evidence one condition and others the other, so that I leave the matter unsettled, but with a decided inclination to assert that the former condition exists, *i.e.*, the blastopore is closed.

The cells of the solid endo-mesoderm core soon increase in size, more especially those around the central axis.

Meanwhile, the ectoderm cells of the anterior pole become so differentiated, that a cap of them take a darker stain from hæmatoxylin than the rest.

There next follows a fatty degeneration of certain of the more centrally-placed endo-mesoderm cells, resulting in a mass of fat globules. Fig. 41 represents the embryo just before the fatty degeneration has properly set in. Along with the fatty degeneration of some of the cells of the endo-mesoderm core, there is growth posterior-wards of the anterior cap of differentiated ectoderm, together with a bilaterally symmetrical disposition of the margin of the same; of this symmetrical disposition, the most obvious feature is a division on the ventral side in the midline, and a pair of capes, to use a geographical term, which project beyond the general outline on either side of the median bay.

A rearrangement, and differentiation of the endo-mesoderm cells next takes place, accompanied by an intensification of the bilaterality of the ectoderm, and the first appearance of the appendages, on either side of the "bay." (See Fig. 42.)

The rearrangement of the endo-mesoderm is complex, and effected so quickly that I can do little more than describe the result; but, first, let me say that the undifferentiated ectoderm-cells have become very thin and transparent, and they certainly overlie the large mesoderm-cells presently to be described; but, as already stated, I am unable to say whether the blastopore closes, though strongly inclined to say it does.

The first result of the differentiation of the endo-mesoderm appears at the posterior end; here, five cells on each side and three at the end, which form, as it were, a belt on a level with the midline, and lying immediately beneath the ectoderm, increase in size and take a deep stain from hæmatoxylin. Of the lateral cells, the fourth, on each side, counting from the front, is larger than the others, and these decrease in size on each side of it (Fig. 42).

Lying deeper in the embryo, dorsal to the belt just mentioned, and directly dorsal to the large cell, but nearer the sagittal plane, there is, on each side, another large cell, which differs from those composing the belt, in staining a very little more lightly (Fig. 42,g).

Meanwhile, certain of the cells of the core placed towards the posterior end, have grown in size, apparently at the expense of their neighbours; they have collected up the fat globules, and apparently aggregated to themselves the whole of them.

These cells take practically no stain; their ultimate position is shown in Figs. 45 and 46. As a reference to those figures will show, these cells are of large size and not numerous. They are so arranged that, did they not touch at their inner ends, they would bound a cavity. A few similar but smaller cells extend back from the larger ones, between the deeply staining cells of the mesoderm band.

Whilst these cells have been assuming the above proportions and situation, the endo-mesoderm, or, as their change now shows, more correctly, the mesoderm-cells of the anterior end have become modified into muscle-strands (Figs. 45 and 46). The brain has appeared as a darkly staining hyaline area, composed, it would seem, of four or five large cells.

Two eye-spots are present over the brain. Each of these is a granular elongated cell, one end coming to the dorsal surface and pigmented, the other, in contact with the brain. On either side of the brain dorsal thereto, there is a medium-sized cell, with coarsely granular contents, and taking borax-carmine stain deeply. These are evidently glandular, perhaps larval kidneys.

The darkly staining belt is doubtless a paired mesoderm-band. The two cells dorsal to them are also mesodermal, and in the nauplius occupy practically the same position, and have altered only in that they take the stain more deeply. They are probably the primordial germ-cells. Their stability through a period of complex changes in all other regions, was what first suggested this to me, and it has since occurred to me that they are situated one on each side of the archenteron, at what must ultimately become the anterior end, and silghtly dorsal to the midline.

The large cells which have aggregated to themselves the fat of the degenerated mass, are doubtless the endoderm cells, and constitute a potential archenteron.

The origin of the brain and of the larval kidneys, is quite unknown to me from actual observation; though one might discuss their probable origin from analogy. It is, however, worthy of note that the cells of the larval kidneys are essentially similar to the adult subdermal glands described on page 675.

Though I have the stages of development fairly complete, (see Figs. 41-44), and although I have examined those specimens carefully, I am quite unable to describe a single phase in the formation of the muscles. The suddenness of their appearance is truly surprising; in one stage, no trace of muscle is visible; in what would otherwise appear to be a stage closely following, the whole of the muscles are present.

I have now described, as far as my material permits, the internal organisation of the Nauplius; it remains to describe, as far as is possible, the history of the external form and the appendages.

The embryo, until the appearance of the ectodermal cap, presents only an anterior pole (thinner), and a posterior pole (thicker), dorsal and ventral sides being indistinguishable. Very soon after the appearance of the cap, there appears, on one side, a bay in its margin; this, as further changes show, is on the ventral side; it, therefore, gives us the second axis, and is the first appearance of the bilateral symmetry of the adult.

There now follows a slow dorsi-ventral compression, which probably reaches its maximum with the nauplius. Concurrent with this, there has been a broadening of the anterior end and a narrowing of the posterior end, so that, in some cases, the head-end becomes decidedly broader than the posterior end; this, however, is variable.

Meanwhile, the appendages have been assuming the forms depicted in Fig. 46.

At first (Fig. 42) the appendages appear as thickenings of the ectoderm, situated far forward on either side of the ventral bay in the ectodermal cap. Later they pass back, and the two posterior pairs exhibit already their future biramous character (Fig. 43). The eye-spots are also now apparent.

Fig. 9 is derived from a mutilated embryo of the stage of development of Fig. 43; but which of the two pairs of biramous appendages it represents, I have been unable to decide.

The external features of the nauplius are depicted in Fig. 46. As mounted in balsam and in glycerine-jelly, the little animal is of a yellow colour, transparent, showing the situation of the archenteron with its large intracellular fat globules, also the muscles, the mesoderm-cells and primordial germ-cells of the posterior end. At the anterior end, the eye-spots appear as small pigment-spots surrounded by a very clear hyaline area. The granule-laden larval kidneys are visible, but the brain not so.

No external openings are discernible, mouth and anus not having formed, but between the first two pairs of appendages is a curved prominence, which might be interpreted as a labrum. The whole nauplius is enclosed in a very delicate cuticle, the first exoskeleton, which extends beyond the body proper, or, rather, encloses the body loosely, as the perisarc to the coenosarc in a zoophyte.

The appendages are three pairs, anteriorly situated. The exoskeleton is smooth, and devoid of spines, so that the appendages are, with the exception of the labrum, the only structures which break its even surface.

The antennules are uniramous, blunt-ended, two-jointed limbs. The blunt distal end of the second joint bears two long, stiff bristles.

The antennæ are biramous, composed of a single-jointed protopodite, and of two rami, each two-jointed. Both rami are blunt-ended, and bear each two bristles very similar to those of the antennules.

The mandibles differ from the antennæ only in being smaller, and in that the inner side of the last joint of the anterior ramus bears two or three of the long bristles, as well as the usual two on the blunt end.

This completes the account of the development, as far as I am able to take it; the stages between the nauplius and the adult, are probably passed through as a free-living period of the life-history. It, therefore, only remains to review this development, and to classify *Ubius*. Before passing to review the development, I would like once more to draw attention to the absence of the digestive gland, or rather to its occupying a very primitive embryonic situation, and to suggest that this may be found to be correlated with a very abbreviated ontogeny.

Review of the Development.—The cleavage is of Korschelt and Heider's first type(3, p. 108), characterised by them as being very rare among the Crustacea. This type of cleavage, however, occurs in two other copepods of which the development has been studied. I refer to *Cyclops*(2), and *Chondracanthus*(6). In both of these, not only is the cleavage total, but it follows very much the same lines as in *Ubius*. There may be a difference in the arrangement of the cells in the eight-cell stage in *Chondracanthus*.

In all these three copepods, invagination takes an almost identically similar form, which form reappears in *Lucifer* (1), though here toned down, as it were, and connecting the extreme modification of the above copepod type with typical embolic gastrulation, I am unable to find tissue-differentiation appearing at so early a stage in *Ubius* as Häcker was able to demonstrate in *Cyclops*. The endo-mesoderm "*anlage*" is early recognisable, but only in the early nauplius-stage, does it become possible to separate endoderm and mesoderm.

It is worthy of note that histogenesis has not progressed so far in *Ubius* at the nauplius stage as in *Chondracanthus*. This difference is most striking at the posterior end. In *Ubius* the ectoderm is so extremely thin as to be actually doubtfully present at the extreme posterior end, whilst the mesoderm-belt is composed of not more than twenty-five large cells. In *Chondracanthus*, the ectoderm is so well developed that the rudiment of the ventral ganglion (Bauchganglienanlage) may be identified. Mesoderm and endoderm, however, are not so far advanced in differentiation.

Comparative.— A brief comparison with *Ive balanoglossi* Mayer, has already been made in the generic description; in view of their close relationship and similarity, it may be well to tabulate the outstanding differences.

Ive balanoglossi.	*Ubius killi.*
Body presenting annular thickenings, suggesting segmentation.	Body cylindrical, without trace of segmentation.
Oesophagus chitin-lined.	Oesophagus lined by columnar epithelium.
Mid-gut strongly muscular.	Mid-gut devoid of obvious muscles.
End-gut lined by chitin.	End-gut absent.
Double ventral nerve-cord.	No nerve-cord visible.
Ovary single.	Ovary paired.
Testes large, reniform.	Testes small, cylindrical.

Systematic.- The systematic position of *Ubius* must remain more or less in doubt, until the stages between the nauplius and the adult are known; meanwhile, an attempt must be made to assign it a position on the characters of the adult. Notwithstanding the important differences between *Ive* and *Ubius*, it seems evident that they both belong to the same family. I agree with Mayer that it is not necessary to found a new family for the reception of *Ive*, but unlike him, I am unable to see that its adult features point to a relationship with *Lernæa*.

I fail to see much significance in the resemblance between the mouth-organs of *Ire* and those of the young *Lernæa*, nor am I able to see that the remaining appendages may be brought into line with those of *Lernæa*.

It appears to me preferable to class *Ire* and *Ubius* as members of the *Chondracanthidæ*.

In *Chondracanthus*, the body is unsegmented but lobed, and the appendages are antennules, antennæ, mandibles, maxillæ, and two pairs of legs. In *Ire*, the body is unsegmented but lobed, and the appendages are antennules, antennæ, mandibles, and two pairs of legs. In *Ubius*, also, five pairs of appendages are present; and, in view of the general similarity between *Ire* and *Ubius*, one is justified in applying Mayer's identification to the appendages in this species also. So that the absence of maxillæ is the only feature which contra-indicates the classification suggested, when weighing external features for and against.

Mayer describes having found male *Ire* attached to the female, a phenomenon constantly presented by *Chondracanthus*.

The segmentation of *Ubius* presents a type rare among the crustacea, and is similar to that of *Chondracanthus*, differing completely from that in *Lernæa* (Korschelt and Heider, Pt.ii., p.117).

The unpaired genital gland in *Ire* is opposed to the classification here suggested, but holds equally strong as an objection to classifying the genus with *Lernæa*.

BIBLIOGRAPHY.

(1) BROOKS, W. K.—"*Lucifer*, a Study in Morphology." Phil. Trans. Roy. Soc., clxxii., 1882.
(2) HAECKER, V.—" Die Keimbaum von Cyclops." Arch. für mikr. Anat., xlix., 1897.
(3) KORSCHELT & HEIDER.—Textbook of the Embryology of Invertebrates (M. F. Woodward Edit.), Pt. ii., 1899.
(4) MACMUNN, C.A.—Phil. Trans. Roy. Soc., cxciii., 1900.
(5) MAYER, P.—Mith. Zool. Stat. Neapel, i., 1879.
(6) SCHIMKEWITSCH, W.—" Studien über parasitische Copepoden." Zeits. für wiss. Zool., lxi., 1896.
(7) SCOTT, A.—Memoir vii., Liverpool Marine B. Com., 1901.

EXPLANATION OF PLATES LXVIII.-LXX.

Plate lxviii.

Fig. 1.—Diagrammatic representation of the arrangement of the internal organs: *a*, mouth—*b*, ovary—*c*, uterus—*d*, receptaculum seminis(?)—*e*, oviduct—*f*, vulva—*g*, slime-gland—*h*, solid posterior end of gut.

Fig. 2.—Anterior third of a female specimen: *a*, mouth—*b*, oesophagus—*c*, endoskeletal rod of chitin—*d*, antennule—*e*, antenna—*f*, mandible—*g*, *h*—legs.

Fig. 3.—Posterior third of a female specimen: *a*, vulva—*b*, genital appendages—*c*, slime-glands—*d*, posterior end of gut.

Fig. 4.—Outline of a male specimen.

Fig. 5.—Antennule.

Fig. 6.—Antenna.

Fig. 7.—Mandible.

Fig. 8.—First leg.

Fig. 9.—Antenna or mandible, from an embryo about the same stage of development as that represented in Fig. 43.

Fig. 10.—The two-celled embryo.

Fig. 11.—The four-celled embryo.

Fig. 12.—The sixteen-celled embryo.

Fig. 13.—The gastrula.

Fig. 14.—Showing evidence of rapid division of the endomesoderm anlagen during gastrulation(*cf.* Fig. 39).

Plate lxix.

Fig. 15.—Transverse section at the level of the oral cavity: *o*, oesophagus—*cav.*, oral cavity.

Fig. 16.—Longitudinal section in the region of junction of oesophagus and first compartment.

Fig. 17.—A subdermal gland.

Fig. 18.—Transverse section just in front of the ovaries.

Fig. 19.—Epithelium of the anterior portion of the first compartment.

Fig. 20.—Transverse section at the level of the ovaries: *Ov.*, ovary—*ut.*, uterus.

Fig. 21.—Transverse section at the level of the posterior end of the first compartment.

Fig. 22.—Transverse section at the level of the second compartment: *gl.*, digestive(?) gland.

Fig. 23.—Transverse section at the level of the junction of uterus and oviduct(*ovd.*).

Fig. 24.—Transverse section at the level of the posterior end of uterus and commencement of the oviduct(*ovd.*).

Fig. 25.—Transverse section at the level of the posterior end of the alimentary canal(*al.*).
Fig. 26.—Two cells from the digestive(?) gland related to the second compartment.
Fig. 27.—Transverse section at the level of the external orifice of the vas deferens(*ap.*) and the vesicula seminalis(*v.s.*).
Fig. 28.—Vas deferens in transverse section.
Fig. 29.—Epithelium of the oviduct.
Fig. 30.—Portion of the section drawn in Fig. 27, under higher magnification: *vas.*, vas deferens.
Fig. 31.—Transverse section at the level of the vulva (*v.*) on one side: *s.gl.*, slime-gland.
Fig. 32.—The region of vulva(*v.*) *Mus.*, plain muscle-bundles.

Plate lxx.

Fig. 33.—The two-celled embryo, transverse section.
Fig. 34.—The four-celled embryo, transverse section.
Fig. 35.—The sixteen-celled embryo, transverse section.
Fig. 36.—The sixteen-celled embryo, longitudinal section.
Fig. 37.—The sixteen-celled embryo, longitudinal section.
Fig. 38.—The thirty-two-celled embryo, transverse section.
Fig. 39.—The gastrulation period of development, longitudinal section.
Fig. 40.—The gastrulation period of development, transverse section.
Fig. 41.—Longitudinal coronal section of the late gastrula.
Fig. 42.—The very early nauplius(A′, antennule; A″, antenna; *mn.*, mandible; *mes.*, mesoderm; *g.*, primordial germ-cell).
Fig. 43.—A more advanced nauplius(*e.*, eye).
Fig. 44.—The nauplius(*lbr.*, labrum).
Fig. 45.—The nauplius, nearly median coronal section (*oc.*, retinal cell; *br.*, brain; *nph.*, larval kidney).
Fig. 46.—The nauplius, median sagittal section (*end.*, endoderm; *mus.*, skeletal muscles).

THE FIBRO-VASCULAR SYSTEM OF THE QUINCE FRUIT COMPARED WITH THAT OF THE APPLE AND PEAR.

By D. McAlpine, Corresponding Member.

(Plates lxxi.-lxxiii.).

The quince agrees with the apple and pear in having five carpels, but, in the cavity of each, there are two rows of ovules, instead of merely two ovules in each chamber (Fig. 4). After fertilisation, the ovules become the well-known pips or seeds, while the walls of the ovaries assume a leathery texture, and the whole represents the "core." In the seed-coat of the quince, the cellulose becomes converted into mucilage, which is said to serve the purpose of attaching the seeds to the soil. The flask-like thickened floral axis becomes the succulent portion of the ripening quince.

The vascular system of the quince will now be considered, and it will be found to agree, in the main, with that already described in connection with the apple and pear.

According to De Candolle, in his *Origin of Cultivated Plants,* "the quince is a fruit which has been little modified by cultivation; it is harsh and acid when fresh, as in the time of the ancient Greeks." The reduction of the number of seeds in the fruit of the apple and pear, as compared with that of the quince, may be due to this very fact of cultivation and selection applied to them, having induced a more succulent and more palatable fleshy portion. The more attractive the fruit becomes to animals and birds feeding upon it, the more certainly will the seeds be widely distributed and deposited under conditions favourable to their germination. A fewer number of seeds will thus suffice for the propagation of the species, and even in the apple and pear, not only is there frequently but one mature seed in each carpel, but there are "seedless" apples in which they have become aborted altogether.

In some of the Natural Orders of plants, this reduction in the number of seeds concurrently with the enhanced attractiveness of the fruit, is clearly shown. In the *Ranunculaceæ* or Buttercup Family, there is every gradation from the numerous one-seeded achenes of the Buttercup itself, which are hard and unattractive, through the Columbine with its follicles reduced to five, and finally, the Baneberry, where the carpels are reduced to one, and the attractive fruit contains only a few seeds. Even in the *Rosaceæ*, or Rose Family, to which the apple, pear, and quince belong, there is a similar gradation, from the numerous carpels becoming the fruits or achenes of the wild rose itself, through the apple, pear, and quince, with only five carpels, down to the peach, plum, apricot, and cherry, with only one carpel containing one seed. The lusciousness and attractiveness of these fruits are well-known.

Transverse and Longitudinal Sections of Quince—young and mature.

In the transverse section of a young quince, the core is seen to occupy the greater part of it, and each of the five cavities contains a double row of seeds. The very centre of the core is hollow, *i.e.*, where the five carpels meet, and even with the naked eye, the ten primary fibro-vascular bundles are seen as dark green spots, five being opposite, and five intermediate to each seed-cavity (Fig. 5).

In the mature quince, the core is surrounded by a dense layer of stone-cells, so that the primary vascular bundles are obscured (Fig. 2). In the longitudinal median section of a young quince (Fig. 4), the seeds are seen to be arranged in two rows. There is a small cavity between the two carpels, which tapers towards the apex, where the styles are given off, and the top of the floral axis forms its base. The core is surrounded by a comparatively narrow fleshy portion, which, however, increases considerably towards maturity. In the full-grown quince, the "core" is seen to be towards the "eye" end, and occupies but a relatively small proportion of the whole (Fig. 3).

Transverse and Longitudinal Sections of Young Apples and Pears for comparison.

In each case, the core forms the conspicuous portion, which becomes relatively small towards maturity. In the transverse section of the apple(Fig. 7), the ten fibro-vascular bundles are distinctly seen, surrounding the core. They almost adjoin the skin, as the flesh is so little developed at this stage. In the pear(Fig. 9), they are somewhat obscured by the stone-cells; still an inner whorl of five may be seen at the tips of the seed-vessels, and an outer whorl of five between. While the "core" is more or less central in the apple (Fig.6), it is more towards the apex of the fruit in the pear (Fig. 8).

Section of Fruit-stalk.

When a transverse section of the stalk is made just at the base of the fruit, the ten fibro-vascular bundles are distinctly seen, just as in the apple and pear(Fig. 1). They are continued into the fruit, and form a vascular system there, which is practically the same as in other pomes. The continuity between the fruit and the parent stem is thus maintained, and the materials necessary for growth, including water, are supplied, until the fruit drops when fully mature.

Fibro-vascular System as a whole.

The softening of the quince, for purposes of dissection, was not an easy matter, as it was necessary that the reagents used should not injuriously affect the structure of the tissue. The pear was readily softened by macerating in water, the apple by using a dilute solution of potassium hydrate, but neither of these methods was suitable for the quince. After steeping in water for some time and simmering for a few hours over a slow fire, it was rendered soft and spongy, but there was still a toughness about the "flesh," which prevented its separation from the vascular bundles.

If we endeavour to find a reason for this toughness, particularly in the outer layers of the flesh, the minute structure requires to be investigated. The numerous groups of stone-cells, even larger than those in the pear, will not account for it.

If a section is made through the skin of the fruit and the underlying tissue, the following structures occur(Fig. 14). There is the thickened cuticular layer, with the columnar epidermal cells. Beneath that, there are several layers of subepidermal cells, oval or elongated, and expanded transversely. Then at the junction of this layer with the pulp-cells, the vascular bundles constituting the plume-like branches spread out in a dense mass horizontally. If this is taken in conjunction with the naked-eye appearance of the plume-like filaments, as they appear when the skin is removed from a rotting quince (Fig. 12), there are good grounds for believing that the cells there are matted together by the permeating vessels, and that the tissue is tough in consequence.

If we turn to the chemical composition of the ash of the respective fruits, some of the constituents are seen to be in very different proportions, which may throw some light on the difference of texture.

The following analyses are taken from Dr. Griffiths' "Manures for Fruit and other Trees" (1908):—

Percentage chemical composition of the ash.

	Apple.	Pear.	Quince.
Potash(K_2O)	56·21	55·00	43·20
Soda(Na_2O)	14·02	8·69	1·68
Lime(CaO)	4·87	7·99	6·32
Magnesia(MgO)	6·53	5·42	10·56
Oxide of Iron(Fe_2O_3)	1·93	1·20	1·54
Chlorine(Cl)	0·68	0·52	0·41
Silica(SiO_2)	2·82	1·52	9·64
Sulphuric acid(SO_3)	3·05	5·73	0·82
Phosphoric acid(P_2O_5)	10·89	13·93	26·33
	101·00	100·00	100·50

This is the composition of the ash of the ripe fruit, for it varies considerably at different stages of growth. Thus, unripe apples contain 0·32% of oxide of iron, and 52% of potash; whereas ripe apples contain 1·93% of oxide of iron, and 56% of potash. In the above analyses, there is considerable excess of silica and phosphoric acid in the quince, and a deficiency of sulphuric acid; but how far these compounds affect the texture of the fruit, it is impossible to say.

The vascular net does not readily separate from the flesh, as in the apple and pear, but is intimately bound up with it. A small portion of the net has been detached (Fig. 11), and the meshes are shown with the delicate veinlets arising from their boundaries. It is situated about one-eighth of an inch beneath the skin, and forms a continuous layer.

There is the same elaborate system of vessels, as in the apple and pear; but the plume-like branchlets towards the circumference are apparently much more numerous, and much more delicate. In a relatively large fruit, such as the quince, and one which has been little modified by cultivation, the green hypodermal cells of the fruit itself (Fig. 14) would contribute a considerable proportion of the starch for storing up, and consequently the means for conveying it, when converted into sugar, would require to be increased.

The vascular net-work is likewise present, and having examined this wonderful structure in the three principal pip-fruits or pomes, we are now in a position to show what part it plays in the economy of the fruit.

This network exists from the earliest stages of the fruit (Fig. 10), and it is similarly developed in connection with the "core" and the "flesh," thus ensuring the harmonious growth of both structures.

As regards the carpels, the primary vascular bundles give off internal branches passing to the dorsal and ventral surface of each. These dorsal and ventral branches spread out over the surface, and unite to form the beautiful network completely enveloping each carpel.

As regards the flesh, which is the bulkiest part of the pome, the primary bundles give off external branches, which form a vascular net at the zone of greatest growth, just beneath the skin. This net must be continually enlarging its meshes, so as to accommodate itself to the ever-increasing area, until the fruit is finally mature. The boundaries of each mesh give rise to plume-like branches, which permeate and bind together the peripheral layers, like a compact turf knit together by the fibrous roots of grasses.

The vascular net, both on the carpels and in the flesh, must be undergoing expansion while growth continues, and the question is, How is this done? It has to be continually readjusted to the increasing size and enlargement of the carpels and the flesh. If we start with the net-work in the fruit just formed, as in Fig. 10, the pressure exerted by the continuous growth of the flesh and conducting tissue combined, will not merely cause the net to stretch, but the conducting tissue will be added to. Just as the cells of the flesh enlarge, so will the conducting tissue which conveys the nutritive material necessary for their expansion, increase, and there will be a mutual accommodation between the growing flesh and the conducting tissue, which conveys the nourishment.

One cannot fail to be struck with the analogy, in a broad sense, between the blood-capillaries in the human body and the vascular or capillary net in the flesh of a pome, both serving to regulate the flow of nutriment, and equalise its distribution.

Professor J. S. Macdonald, in his presidential address before the Section of Physiology at the meeting of the British Association for the Advancement of Science (1911), referred to the blood-capillaries as follows: "They are no more and no less than blood-tissue. In its early days, this blood-tissue, or if you will, this capillary network, is pushed into each portion of the body by pressure due to its growth. In its later stage, the tissues surrounding it, which form the muscular coat of the heart, and the walls of the blood-vessels, are arranged into an external mechanical system providing a new pressure, which still further tends to push the blood-tissue into every available space." Without straining analogy too far, we may say that the capillary net-work in the pome is acted on by pressure, due not only to its own growth, but by the surrounding enlarging tissue; and in this way, it meets the increasing demands made upon it under ordinary conditions, as the fruit grows larger and larger.

Comparison of the Vascular System in Apple, Pear, and Quince.

There is a general resemblance in that of each of the three fruits, but there are differences in detail, largely dependent upon differences in the shape and texture of the respective fruits. There are the same number of primary bundles in each, and the general distribution is the same, but owing to the shape of the fruit in the pear, the vascular bundles run together for a greater distance before spreading out, than in the apple. The nests of strongly-thickened cells or "stone-cells," which occur so plentifully in the pear and form the so-called "grit," also occur in the quince, but not in the apple. The want of this additional skeleton in the apple may be correlated with the fibro-vascular system being generally coarser and tougher in texture.

The vascular system invariably forms a network beneath the skin, with the plume-like branches arising from it; and in the quince, these are particularly noticeable as forming a dense interwoven mass of delicate down-like material.

We can now picture to ourselves, in some measure, the marvellous adjustments necessary to produce the symmetrical, shapely, and healthy pome. The core, at first, is the main portion, in connection with which the vascular system is developed. Then the flesh surrounding it enlarges, and the pressure of growth in both flesh and vessels will cause branches from the main vascular system to permeate it. These branches, at the periphery, must form a regular capillary network, so as to ensure a regular and equable supply of nourishment where the greatest and most rapid growth is taking place. If growth is regular and steady, a shapely fruit is produced; but if it is intermittent, by fits and starts, then the regular formation of the capillary network is interfered with, and at those spots where this occurs, the cells are deprived of their nourishment and die.

There are thus two centres, as it were, to which food-material must be steadily directed, the developing seeds of the core, and the rapidly growing cells of the flesh. There must be an equable distribution of nourishment between them, so that there is proportionate growth in each, otherwise, the balance would be disturbed. The core reaches maturity first, and then the pulp-cells monopolise and store up material for the ripening process to take place.

The fruit becomes soft and succulent, while the sweet taste, the aroma, and the delicate flavour are developed. If there has been harmonious working of the different parts, if the different capillary networks have been completely formed, and if the food has been supplied in due proportion, the result is the symmetrically formed, well flavoured, often highly coloured, nourishing, and usually delicious fruit.

EXPLANATION OF PLATES LXXI.-LXXIII.

Plate lxxi.

Fig. 1.—Transverse section of stalk at base of fruit, showing the ten distinct fibro-vascular bundles ($\times 30$).

Fig. 2.—Transverse median section, showing the five carpels and the "stone cells." In the mature quince, the position of the primary vascular bundles is obscured by the "stone-cells."

Fig. 3.—Longitudinal median section, showing the "core" towards the blossom-end. The primary vascular bundles are seen traversing the flesh from the stalk-end towards the carpels, which are surrounded by a dense layer of stone-cells. The stone-cells are also scattered through the flesh, and there are thin streaks here and there, indicating the vascular bundles.

Plate lxxii.

Fig. 4.—Longitudinal median section of young pear-shaped quince, showing the "core" occupying the greater portion of it, and tiers of seeds in the carpels. There is a cavity between the carpels, tapering towards the styles ($\times 3$).

Fig. 5.—Transverse median section of young quince, showing the ten vascular bundles surrounding the core, which occupies the greater portion of the section, and the cavity is shown in the centre ($\times 3$).

Fig. 6.—Longitudinal median section of young apple, showing "core" and flesh distinct ($\times 3$).

Fig. 7a,b.—Transverse median sections of very young apples, showing distinct "core," and ten fibro-vascular bundles surrounding it ($\times 3$).

Fig. 8.—Longitudinal section of young pear, showing the elongated fleshy portion below the seed-vessels.

Fig. 9.—Transverse section of young pear, showing the fibro-vascular bundles surrounding the core, five being at the outer tips of the seed-vessels, and five intermediate. The stone-cells are scattered all through the flesh.

Plate lxxiii.

Fig. 10.—Young apple-fruit (Cleopatra), just after the petals have fallen, showing the very delicate vascular network beneath the skin, even at this early stage ($\times 3$).

Fig. 11.—Portion of vascular net of quince, enveloping the flesh beneath the skin, and showing the meshes (× 4).

Fig. 12.—Portion of plume-like branches, taken from a decaying quince in water, and appearing like fine fluffy material when the stem is removed. The innumerable branchlets extending to the skin are shown, and the deeper-lying branches from which they originate (× 3).

Fig. 13.—Surface-view of skin of quince, showing the "window-cells," about the same size as those of the pear. There are actual openings in the skin, round or polygonal (lenticels), and here and there, the stomata still persist (× 100).

Fig. 14.—Cross-section through skin and flesh, showing the thickened outer walls(20μ) of the oblong epidermal cells, and several layers of subepidermal cells. The vascular bundles extend to the subepidermal layer, and groups of "stone-cells" are shown, with the elongated parenchyma-cells radiating from them (× 100).

NOTES ON AUSTRALIAN LYCÆNIDÆ.
PART v.
By G. A. Waterhouse, B.Sc., B.E., F.E.S.

Danis syrius Miskin.

Proc. Linn. Soc. N.S. Wales, 1890, p. 34 (N. Queensland): *D. apollonius* Waterhouse, (nec Felder), l.c. 1903, p. 147 (C. York).

I have again examined the types of this species in the Queensland Museum. They are in very poor condition, and I find they are both males, and not a male and a female, as Miskin supposed. In these Proceedings for 1903 (p. 149), I suggested that these examples might be identical with the species I then recorded as *D. apollonius*; I am now quite convinced that this is so, and as the larger Cape York *Danis* is distinct from typical *D. apollonius* from New Guinea, Miskin's name must stand. One of the specimens in the Miskin Collection is labelled C. York.

Danis salamandri Macleay.

Proc. Ent. Soc. N. S. Wales, 1866, i., p. liv.(C. York): *D. Macleayi* Semper, Journ. Mus. Godf., Lep., p. 154, 1878 (C. York).

Further examples of this species have reached me from Cape York, and they show that Semper was right in separating it from *D. taygetus* Felder. The name *salamandri* is the older one, and though the specimen in the Macleay Museum is in too poor condition to clearly show its distinctions from *D. taygetus*, its locality is sufficient to prove its identity.

Miletus euclides Miskin.

Hypochrysops euclides Miskin, Proc. Linn. Soc. N. S. Wales, 1888, p. 1517 (Gippsland, *loc. err.*): *Miletus meleagris* Waterhouse, l.c. 1903, p. 270 (Cardwell).

I have shown[*] that, misled by an erroneous locality, I redescribed this rare species. It is known only from Cardwell, Kuranda, and Port Douglas, all Northern Queensland localities.

[*] Vict. Nat. 1910, p. 158.

CANDALIDES SIMPLEXA Tepper.

Cupido simplexa, Trans. Roy. Soc. S. Aust., 1882, p. 30, t.2, Fig. 10 (Monarto, S. Aust.): *Polyommatus cyanites* Meyrick, Proc. Linn. Soc. N.S. Wales, 1887, p. 828(Geraldton, W.A.).

This is the race of *C. hyacinthina* which occurs in north-western Victoria and in South Australia, as well as in West Australia. I have not been able to compare Geraldton examples with those from South Australia, but there is nothing in Meyrick's description to point to any distinctions. *C. hyacinthina* is confined to Eastern Australia.

PHILIRIS Röber.

Tijd. voor Ent., 1891, p. 317(type *ilias* Felder).

The genus is considered, by Mr. Bethune Baker,[*] to be insufficiently differentiated from *Candalides* Hubner(type *xanthospilos*). In addition to a well-marked facies of the imagines, the pupæ supply good characters by which the two genera can be readily distinguished. The pupa of *P. innotatus* Miskin, is covered with short fine hairs, the head is smooth, and the cross-section of the abdomen (as usual with Lycænid pupæ) is ovoid. The pupa of *C. absimilis*, of *C. gilberti*, of *C. heathi*, and of *C. hyacinthina*(that of *C. xanthospilos* is not yet known) is much flattened, the abdomen being produced to lateral ridges, and the head has two flattened processes. These marked pupal differences, with the shape of the imagines, are quite sufficient to substantiate the genus.

PSEUDODIPSAS CEPHENES Hewitson.

Trans. Ent. Soc. London, 1874, p. 344(India, *loc. err.*): *id.*, Ill. Diurn. Lep. Lyc., p. 219, Pl. 89, fig. 3, 4, 1878 (India, *loc. err.*); *Ps. fumidus* Miskin, Proc. Roy. Soc. Qsld., 1889, p. 264(Brisbane).

Hewitson received his specimen from W. E. Atkinson, to whom Miskin sent many Queensland butterflies. This type is the only specimen recorded from India, and, in the British Museum collection, an example of *Ps. fumidus* from Queensland is placed with it. No points of difference can be detected, and Hewitson's figure so

---

[*] Novitates Zoologicæ, 1904, p.369.

accurately represents Miskin's species, that the only conclusion possible is, that the recorded locality is erroneous, and *Ps. cephenes* is an Australian and not an Indian species.

ZIZERA Moore.

Lep. Ceylon, i., p. 78, 1881.

Dr. Chapman has shown that Moore's diagnosis of this genus is faulty, and does not even agree with the type assigned to it. Three of the species usually placed in *Zizera* belong to three different genera, and these Dr. Chapman defines.*

The Australian species thus become *Zizina labradus* Godart, *Zizina delospila* Waterhouse, *Zizula gaika* Trimen, *Zizeeria karsandra* Moore, and *Zizeeria alsulus* Herrich-Schaeffer.

NACADUBA TASMANICA Miskin.

Lycaenesthes tasmanicus Miskin, Proc. Linn. Soc. N. S. Wales, 1890, p. 40 (Tasmania, *loc. err.*): *N. palmyra* Waterhouse (nec Felder), l.c., 1903, p. 228 (Brisbane, Cairns): *Lycaena elaborata* Lucas, Proc. Roy. Soc. Qsld., 1899, p. 137 (1900) (Brisbane).

The sexes of *N. palmyra* have reached me from the Aru Islands, and I find that our representative is distinct. Miskin's name, therefore, stands, though unfortunately based upon an erroneous locality.

THECLINESTHES ONYCHA Hewitson.

Utica onycha Hew., Ill. Diurn. Lep., Lyc., p. 56, t.24, Figs. 11, 12, 1865 (Australia).

Hewitson's type is a female, and agrees best with specimens from North Queensland, which are taken in company with a blue male. A very similar lilac male, as well as the blue one, occurs at Kuranda, and Mr. Dodd tells me that their food-plants are different. South of Townsville, only the lilac males have been taken, and these have been described by Lucas as *Theclinesthes miskini*. This species is, I am convinced, distinct, and not a geographical race of *T. onycha;* so the name *T. miskini* must be revived for the species with a lilac male and a female with brown underside; this

---

* Trans. Ent. Soc. London, 1910, pp. 479-497.

occurs in New South Wales, and in Queensland as far north as Kuranda.

I propose, therefore, to restrict Hewitson's name to the species with a blue male and a female with whitish underside; this occurs at Kuranda, Cooktown, and Cape York, and its place in New South Wales is probably taken by *T. onycha* var. *atrosuffusa* Waterhouse.

PSEUDALMENUS CHLORINDA Blanchard.

Thecla chlorinda, Voyage Pôle Sud, pl. 3, figs. 15-18, ante 1853 (Tasmania): text, p. 401, 1853: *Thecla myrsilus* Doubleday, Gen. Diurn. Lep., ii., pl. 75, fig. 3, 1852 (Van Diemen's Land).

The figures and localities show clearly that these two names represent the same species, but there has been some little doubt which name held the better claim to priority. The name *chlorinda* first appears on the plates of the Voyage au Pôle Sud, which were published several years before the text.* It is again mentioned on page 401, in the text of Vol. iv., where *Thecla myrsilus* is given as a synonym. The name *myrsilus* first appears without description in Doubleday's List of the Butterflies of the British Museum. It is adopted in the Genera, and figured but not described, and the following species listed is *Thecla chlorinda* Blanchard. This shows that the Pôle Sud figure was earlier than that in the Genera, and, at that time, no description of either species had been published. The first description of *chlorinda* is given in Vol. iv., p. 401, of the Pôle Sud, 1853.

It was under the name *chlorinda*, the species was first figured, and several years later first described; therefore, this name has precedence. Doubleday's List may be of earlier date, but this gave nothing, except the locality, to indicate what species his *myrsilus* represented.

IALMENUS ICILIUS Hewitson.

Ill. Diurn. Lep., Lyc., p. 54, pl. 24, fig. 3, 1865 (Swan River): *I. inous* Waterhouse (nec Hew.), Proc. Linn. Soc. N. S. Wales, 1903, p. 259 (Victoria, South Australia).

---

* Voyage Pôle Sud, Vol. 4, p. 2, 1853.

When my revisional paper was written in 1903, I knew but one *Ialmenus* from West Australia, and as Hewitson's descriptions of *I. icilius* and *I. inous* differed only in very minor points, I wrongly concluded they both represented the same species. I now have two distinct species from the West, and I find that the one to which I applied the name *I. inous*, is correctly *I. icilius*. It may be recognised as follows:—

♂. Above. Forewing smoky-brown; small centrobasal area, metallic green. Hindwing smoky-brown; small centrobasal area, metallic green; tornal spots irregular, small, black crowned with dull orange.

Beneath. Forewing dull pale brown; markings pale brown, sometimes almost obsolete. Hindwing dull pale-brown; markings pale-brown, sometimes almost obsolete; tornal spots as above.

♀. Above as in ♂; centrobasal areas metallic blue. Beneath as in ♂.

Loc.—Perth, Adelaide, Victoria.

This species is distinctly smaller than *I. inous*.

IALMENUS INOUS Hewitson.

Ill. Diurn. Lep., Lyc., p. 54, pl. 24, figs. 1, 2, 1854 (Swan River); not *I. inous* Waterhouse, Proc. Linn. Soc. N. S. Wales, 1903, p. 259.

♂. Above. Forewing dark brown; centrobasal area metallic green. Hindwing dark brown; centrobasal area metallic green; tornal spots irregular, large, black crowned with reddish-orange.

Beneath. Forewing pale-brown; markings broad, brown, edged white; subterminal band broad, brown, edged white. Hindwing pale-brown; markings broad, brown, edged white; tornal spots as above.

♀. Above as in ♂; centrobasal areas metallic blue. Beneath as in ♂.

Loc.—Waroona, Carnarvon.

The above two descriptions will place these two species beyond doubt, which Hewitson's descriptions and figures fail to do.

NOTE ON THE RELATION OF THE DEVONIAN AND CARBONIFEROUS FORMATIONS WEST OF TAMWORTH, N.S.W.

BY L. A. COTTON, B.A., B.Sc., ASSISTANT LECTURER AND DEMONSTRATOR IN GEOLOGY, UNIVERSITY OF SYDNEY, AND A. B. WALKOM, B.Sc., LINNEAN MACLEAY FELLOW OF THE SOCIETY IN GEOLOGY.

(Two text-figures.)

The following notes are the result of observations made by us during a cycling trip from Tamworth to Mudgee, viâ Gunnedah and Coonabarabran, with the object of examining the strata.

The geology of the Tamworth-end of the section examined, has been discussed by Professor David and Mr. E. F. Pittman[*], who have shown the characteristic rocks to be interstratified radiolarian cherts and tuffs, with occasional bands of limestone. They have also shown that, as a result of tectonic movements in the district, the strata have been folded into a sharp anticline between Moonbi and Tamworth, and they have indicated the position of a probable fault, with a throw of 9,000 feet to the east.[†]

Our section (Fig. 2) is a continuation of that given by Professor David and Mr. E. F. Pittman, and extends to a point three miles west of Gunnedah, the section being taken along the road. It is built up from dip and strike observations made, where possible, in the road-cuttings. These are represented on the map. Unfortunately, relatively few of these were obtainable, on account of the extensive development of recent deposits. These consist chiefly of surface-alluvials, and one large bed of river-gravels, at least 60 feet thick, containing pebbles about 3 or 4 inches in diameter, which extends four miles on either side of Somerton.

---

[*] "On the Palæozoic Radiolarian Rocks of New South Wales," Q.J.G.S., Vol. lv., 1899, pp.16-37.

[†] *Op. cit.*, Plate 3.

The section is not detailed on account of the difficulty of obtaining outcrops, and also the short time at our disposal. It is intended to illustrate, in a general way, the lithological character and structural features of the strata.

From Tamworth to within two miles of Carroll Gap (see Fig. 2), the rocks consist of interbedded tuffs and cherts, with one characteristic band of limestone. The tuffs and cherts exhibit considerable variation in their development. In some places, the tuffs appear massive, with very little chert, and in others (particularly the cutting near the 10-mile peg from Tamworth) there is very little associated tuff with the chert. Occasionally, tuffs and cherts are closely interstratified, as at a point about 8½ miles from Tamworth, where six bands of each were observed in a thickness of about 20 feet of strata. The bed of limestone referred to, is about 10 feet thick. It is a black, fine-grained rock, characterised by the presence of small, lath-shaped crystals about 4 mm. by 0·5 mm. Examination under the microscope and treatment with HCl show that they are composed of calcite, but their distribution suggests that they are replacements of some original structure. This was observed in three distinct places, viz., 5·2, 10·7, and 21·4 miles from Tamworth.

The plotting of the dips on the map showed that we were dealing with a series of anticlines and synclines, and the strikes indicated that these were tilted. From the information obtained, we calculated that the axis of tilt is about N.3°W., and the amount of the tilt from 6-7° towards the north. Reference to the section (Fig. 2) will show how these folds harmonise with the anticline east of Tamworth.

The presence of quartz-reefs in the roading cutting 10 miles from Tamworth, observed by Messrs. Harrison and Aurousseau, renders it not unlikely that the Moonbi granite-series underlies this portion of the section.

The most westerly observation of the dip of this series was at a point about two miles east of Carroll Gap. Between this point and Carroll Gap itself, outcrops are obscured by recent alluvial, and at the latter place, there is a bold outcrop of limestone dipping to the

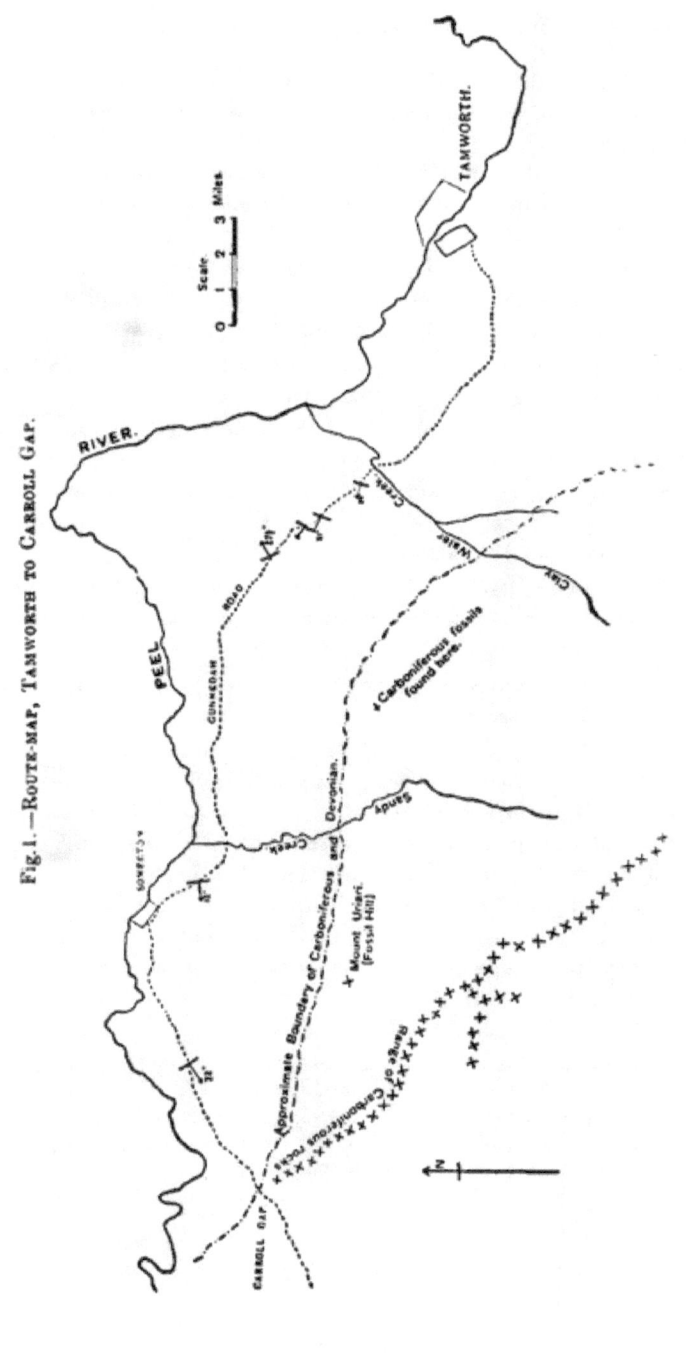

east at about 80°, containing Carboniferous fossils as follows:—
Zaphrentis, Michelinia tenuisepta, Spirifera, Euomphalus, and *Loxonema.*

This is followed, to the west, by a conformable series of tuffs and slates, the dip being in the same direction, and decreasing in amount as we go west.

There is a well-marked physiographic break at this point, probably due to differential erosion.

The sudden discontinuity in the dip and the general appearance of the country lead us to suggest a probable fault to the east of the limestone, letting down the Carboniferous area.

The lithological resemblance of the strata between Tamworth and Carroll Gap to, and the continuity of its folding with the Devonian series of Tamworth, as well as the marked discontinuity with known Carboniferous to the west, leave little doubt but that this series is of Devonian age.

The presence of Carboniferous fossils† at the localities marked on Fig. 1, suggests that the boundary is approximately as represented on that diagram.

The Carboniferous series may be intruded by the porphyrite indicated in the section.

From this point, an alluvial flat extends to a spot about two miles west of Gunnedah, being only interrupted by a ridge of aplitic granite three miles east of that town. At the western edge of this alluvial plain, there occurs a stratified rhyolitic tuff, probably of Carboniferous age, which is overlaid by Permo-Carboniferous Coal-Measures. Further to the west and south, these Coal Measures are capped by Triassic sandstones and claystones, as at Mullaley, where specimens of *Stenopteris* were obtained from a well in the town itself.

---

† The following have been recorded from Mt. Uriari by Mr. W. S. Dun: —*Zaphrentis, Productus semireticulatus, P. longispinus, P.* cf. *Murchisoni, P. undatus, Orthis resupinata, O. australis, Spirifer striata, S. pinguis, Dielasma sacculum, Entolium aviculatum, Aviculopecten* sp., *Euomphalus pentangulatus, Dentalium, Orthoceras* sp.ind.

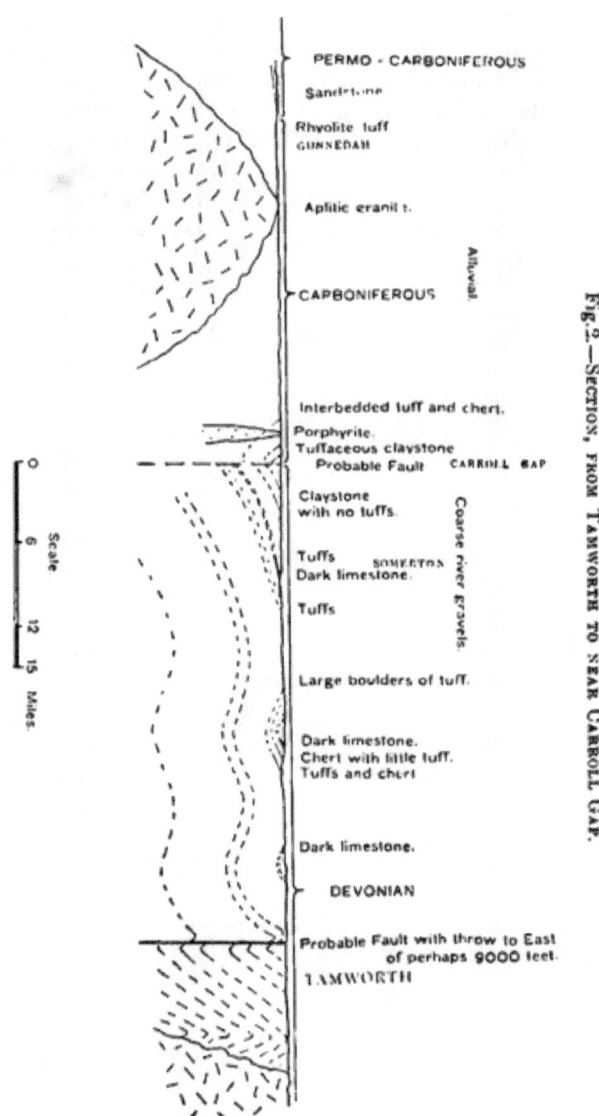

Fig. 2.—Section from Tamworth to near Carroll Gap.

Mr. R. H. Cambage has recently found Carboniferous rocks, consisting of andesite and also cherty shales with *Rhacopteris*, just to the north-west of Currabubula. These shales strike in a north-westerly direction, and dip fairly steeply to the south-west. This point is about 25 miles S.S.E. from Carroll Gap, where Carboniferous rocks occur on the road from Tamworth to Gunnedah. This discovery shows that the whole length of the Peel Range, from Carroll Gap to Currabubula, is probably composed of Carboniferous rocks.

A NEW SPECIES OF *ERIOCHLOA* FROM THE HAWKESBURY RIVER.

By A. A. Hamilton.

[N.O. *Gramineæ*.]

Eriochloa Maidenii, n.sp.

Hawkesbury River(A. A. Hamilton; May, 1912).

A scrambling perennial grass, with slender but rigid decumbent stems, and ascending branches. Stems many-jointed, occasionally rooting. Leaves from under $\frac{1}{2}$ to rarely above 1 inch long, from narrow to broad lanceolate, flat or concave, with a pale thickened margin, the short leaf-sheath and ligula ciliate with long silky hairs; leaves and stems sparingly sprinkled with short hairs, the hairs on all parts of the plant with a bulbous base. Inflorescence reduced to a spike, seldom above 1 inch long, usually shorter, the terminal spike on a peduncle of $\frac{1}{2}$ to $1\frac{1}{2}$ inch, the lateral ones on short branches partly immersed in the leaf-sheaths; rhachis triquetrous; peduncle, rhachis, and pedicels scabrous. Spikelets at the base of the spike paniculate, 2-3 or occasionally 4 in a short raceme; the upper ones solitary, 1 line long, acute, oblong-ovate, not callous at the base; lower pedicels 1 line long, with a tuft of silky hairs at the base; the upper ones shorter, the tuft of hairs diminishing upwards; top of the pedicel cup-shaped, the short stipes of the spikelet in the centre of the depression. Glumes three, two outer empty, nearly equal, with five prominent, parallel nerves, and two shorter, marginal ones, acute, herbaceous, with pale narrow, hyaline margins and apex, pubescent at the base, sparingly so at apex; no rudimentary palea present. Flowering glume coriaceous, obtuse, nearly as long as the outer glumes, with a point or awn $\frac{1}{4}$ line long, exserted. Fruit smooth, its back usually turned from the rhachis. Grain enclosed in the flowering glume and palea (both much involute), free, hardened, glassy, ovoid, not dorsally flattened. Embryo one-third the length of the grain. Hilum basal, punctiform.

A distinct species, which may eventually, in conjunction with other ambiguous species, be incorporated as a separate genus.

In the Fl. Austr.,(vii., p. 459) Bentham, describing the genus *Paspalum*, gives the characters: "Spikelets ... not awned, not callous at the base." In a footnote to the description of the genus *Eriochloa*, Hooker,(Fl. Brit. Ind., vii., p. 20) says: "The thickened base of the spikelet alone distinguishes *Eriochloa* from *Paspalum*." This decision appears to be somewhat arbitrary, as in the present instance the herbaceous seven-nerved outer glumes and the hardened glassy grain, which is not dorsally flattened, are characteristic of *Panicum* rather than *Paspalum*; the inflorescence also, "a character admitted as generic in most Gramineæ,"(Bentham, Fl. Austr., vii., p. 463) approaches *Panicum*, being similar to that of *P. marginatum* R.Br., var. *strictum*, a plant to which it has a superficial resemblance in the field. Most modern authors include, under the genus *Panicum*, only those species which have four glumes, an exception being a form of *P. sanguinale* Linn., in which the small, outer glume is occasionally deficient. In *P. helopus* Trin., we find the awn on the flowering glume as in *Eriochloa*, but the presence of the small outer glume proclaims it a true *Panicum*.

The characters, glumes three, awn on the flowering glume, and the somewhat composite inflorescence, appear to be a sufficient warrant for placing this grass provisionally in the genus *Eriochloa*. Its nearest ally may be found in *E. annulata* Kunth, the inflorescence in some forms of this species being reduced to an interrupted spike.

The Australian species of *Eriochloa* given in the Fl. Austr., are *E. punctata* Hamilt., and *E. annulata* Kunth, with the var. *acrotricha* Benth. Both these species are placed under *E. polystachya* H.B.K., by Hooker, Fl. Brit. Ind.,(vii., 20).

In the Queensland Agricultural Journal (i., 234), Bailey describes a decumbent species of Eriochloa (*E. decumbens* Bail.) from Hammond Island, Torres Straits. He mentions, in a note, that it differs from other Australian species of the genus principally in habit.

This grass was found growing in a gully in the neighbourhood of the Hawkesbury River, in large patches, forming a closely matted undergrowth. Under favourable conditions, it should spread rapidly; and though the stems are somewhat wiry, they carry a fair amount of foliage. It may prove of some value as a winter fodder, as I found it close cropped in August.

The name is proposed with a view to the identification of Mr. J. H. Maiden, Government Botanist of New South Wales, with a Natural Order, concerning which he has furnished so much valuable information.

The type-specimens will be presented to the National Herbarium.

DESCRIPTION AND LIFE-HISTORY OF A NEW SPECIES OF *NANNOPHLEBIA*.

By R. J. Tillyard, M.A., F.E.S.

(Plate lxxiv.)

The genus *Nannophlebia* belongs to Group i. of the *Libellulinæ*, according to the new and excellent classification of Dr. Ris.* It is easily recognised by the following characters:—Small tenderly-built insects of black and yellow pattern; second cubital cross-vein falling near to, but *not right on to*, the proximal angle of the triangle in the forewing, and hence no real "subtriangle" in that wing;† proximal side of triangle in hindwing in line with arculus. Costal side of triangle of forewing broken, that of hindwing regular. Last antenodal cross-vein of forewing complete; superior sector of triangle in forewing placed far from the anal angle of the triangle.

In this genus, Dr. Ris places three distinct forms, which he considers to be all subspecies of the type, *Nannophlebia lorquini* Selys. These he distinguishes as follows:—

1. *N. lorquini lorquini* (*N. lorquini* Selys, 1869). Moluccas.

2. *N. lorquini imitans* (*N. imitans* Ris, 1900). Bismarck Archipelago.

3. *N. lorquini eludens* (*N. eludens* Tillyard, 1908). North Queensland.

The last-named is considered to be the true Australian form of the species; hence Dr. Ris associated with it two females of considerably larger size, and somewhat different markings, recorded from

---

* Coll. Zool. du Baron de Selys-Longchamps, Fasc. ix. Libellulinen, Part i., by Dr. F. Ris, 1909, p 658.

† It is important to point out, however, that this cross-vein is variable in position, and sometimes (especially in the new species about to be described) falls *almost on to* the angle of the triangle. It is, therefore, doubtful whether this is a good character on which to base the genus.

Gayndah (Q.). I also noted the prevalence, at Kuranda, of this larger form of female.

In North Queensland, I found the females of *N. eludens* emerging in January, while the males were also quite fresh, but somewhat more common. I was, therefore, rather surprised at taking, early in December, 1910, a very much torn and battered female of the larger variety at Pallal, near Bingara, in the North-west of New South Wales. It seemed probable that this was a remnant of an earlier brood, or possibly even of a distinct and much earlier species. The problem was solved by me last year, when I found both sexes of the early form fully matured at the end of November, on the Bellinger River (N.S.W.). Comparing them with the types of my *N. eludens*, it was at once evident that they were a new and very distinct species, which I now propose to describe under the name of *Nannophlebia risi* n.sp., in honour of my friend, Dr. F. Ris:—

NANNOPHLEBIA RISI, n.sp. (Plate lxxiv., figs.4,5,7).

♂.*Total length* 33·5, *abdomen* 24, *forewing* 24, *hindwing* 22·5mm.

W i n g s (fig.4): lightly but considerably suffused with pale yellow from base up to nodus. *Pterostigma* 1·8 mm., black, fairly thick, covering one cellule or a little over. *Nodal Indicator* |6, 4·5|. *Membranule* practically nil (the very minutest trace). |5, 5 | H e a d : *eyes* rich green in the living insect (brown when dead), meeting for quite 1·5 mm. *Vertex* tubercled, pale yellow surrounded by black, central *ocellus* large, shining orange; front high, deeply cleft, pale yellow, thickly pitted, and carrying fine black hairs; *clypeus* and *labrum* yellow, *labium* dull yellowish. T h o r a x : *prothorax* very small, black, with a dorsal and two lateral yellow spots; a conspicuous ridge of long brown hairs on collar next thorax. *Meso-* and *metathorax* velvety black marked with lemon-yellow as follows: —a conspicuous dorsal line expanding into a spot, close up to prothorax, about 0·6 mm. across, shaped like a combined "cup and ball"; a pair of wavy humeral bands narrowing and converging slightly towards wing-bases; the latter black, with three yellow spots. *Sides* of thorax yellow, with an intricate pattern of three irregular black bands joining and branching in the manner shown in the plate (Fig. 7). *Notum* black, scuta and scutella yellow. *Legs* black, with yellowish lines on femora and tibiæ. A b d o m e n : 1-2 moderate, 3-6 very pinched, 7-10 much clubbed. *Colour* black marked with yellow as follows:—1, brown, very narrow; 2, a pair of large lateral spots running downwards to genitalia; auricles very small; 3, a pair of large dorsal marks, just touching; 4, a pair of dorsal spots one-third from base, a narrow transverse band two-fifths from apex; 5, dorsal spots one-fifth from base, transverse band about central; 6, dorsal spots close up to base, a pair of elongate central spots touching dorsally; 7, two very small basal spots, a pair of large oval central spots: 8, two round central spots quite separated, with two smaller indistinct spots nearer to base; 9-10, black without spots, yellow lines in sutures (Fig. 5). A p p e n d a g e s: *Superior* 1·5 mm., yellow with black bases and tips; seen from above, straight and pointed; in profile, first three-fifths curving slightly downwards, remainder curving strongly upwards to a very sharp tip; underside with a conspicuous angle carrying minute serrations. *Inferior* 1 mm., yellow, hollowed out above, tip reaching well beyond the angle of the superior (Plate lxxiv., figs. 9, 10)

♀. *Total length* 33, *abdomen* 23·5, *forewing* 26, *hindwing* 24·5 mm. Differs from the male as follows :—*wings* slightly touched with brown all over, and *saffroned at bases in subcostal and submedian spaces only.* (See Ris' "Libellulinen," *loc. cit.*, p.58, fig. 23, Gayndah, which belongs to this species and not to *N. eludens*). *Pterostigma* 2 mm., *nodal indicator* |6-7, 5-6|. Colours duller; abdomen, 1-2 thicker, with lateral |5-6, 5-6| spots large and lunulate; 3-6 not so pinched as in male, 7-10 not so swollen; central spots of 7 large; no spots on 8. *Appendages* dull greyish-black tipped with orange-brown, subcylindrical, the somewhat blunt tips carrying a short black spine (Fig. 13).

Hab.—Northern New South Wales up to North Queensland. Bellinger River, 7♂, 1♀, November-December, 1911. Pallal, 1♀, very old, December, 1910. Gayndah, 2♀ (Coll. Ris and Martin). Mount Tambourine (several specimens in Brisbane Museum). Kuranda, 1♀, January, 1905.

T y p e s : ♂♀. in Coll. Tillyard (Bellinger River, N.S.W.).

The following are the chief differences between the new species and *N. eludens* Tillyard:—*N. risi* is considerably larger (hindwing of ♂ 22·5 as against 18·5 mm. in *N. eludens*); the pterostigma is considerably larger (1·8 against 1·4 mm.); the vertex is pale yellow (brown in *N. eludens*). The thoracic pattern is much bolder and more intricate in *N. risi*, the bands being black, while those of *N. eludens* are brown, and the second and third bands of the sides practically joining in two places so as to isolate a large yellow oval spot, whereas in *N. eludens* these bands are short and separated (Figs. 7-8). The number of yellow spots, and bands on the abdomen is much greater in *N. risi* than in *N. eludens*, there being two yellow areas on each of segments 4-8 in *N. risi* ♂, while *N. eludens* ♂ has one only on 4-6 and none on 7-8 (Figs. 5-6). *The anal appendages of the males of the two species are very different;* those of *N. risi* being long, straight, and parallel when seen from above, while those of *N. eludens* appear short and incurved, almost forcipate: seen in profile, the differences are quite as striking (Plate lxxiv., figs.9-12). The genitalia of segment 2 of the male are not quite similar, the hamule being more prominent in *N. eludens* (Plate lxxiv., Figs. 14-15).

There is, besides, a well-marked difference in flight and habits. *N. risi* flies very swiftly in and out along the edges of the creeks and rivers, while *N. eludens* indulges in fantastic gyrations and evolutions, often rising in a complicated spiral to settle high up on a near-by tree. I did not notice this habit in *N. risi*, though I watched carefully for it. In resting also, *N. eludens* depresses its wings much more than *N. risi* does.

In my opinion, it is impossible to consider these two species as parts of one geographical whole, because *their areas of distribution* overlap, both being found in North Queensland in the same localities. *N. eludens* is on the wing from January to May, while *N. risi* is only represented in December and January by a few old and battered females. I have no doubt that males of *N. risi* could be taken in North Queensland by collecting in September or October, the latter of which is the month during which it appears further south. The supposition that they might be two broods (spring and summer) of a single species also cannot be entertained, even if *N. eludens* were to be found further southwards, because of the very distinct differences already enumerated.

The discovery of this species makes it appear to me more than ever probable that the three forms, now classed as subspecies by Dr. Ris, must be regarded as distinct species. But to settle this point satisfactorily, we require much more material from many localities.

Life-History.—Along the beautiful Bellinger River, the females fly very rapidly, and oviposit by dashing in close to the edge, washing the ova out by brushing the abdomen rapidly on the surface of the water. This action is somewhat similar to that of *Cordulephya* ♀, but is not carried out so furtively. They are very difficult to catch while ovipositing. I knocked one into the water, but it rose quickly and flew away; while the only one I actually caught, had not been ovipositing, and had no eggs inside her.

Although most of the specimens seen were evidently quite mature, I secured two larval skins on the reeds and grass bordering the river. The first was taken about 6 a.m. on October 30th. The temperature was then about 95° Fahr., and dragonflies began to fly actively soon after sunrise; though by 10 a.m.,(the temperature then reaching 104°) all signs of *Odonate* life had vanished. A newly-emerged *Nannophlebia* flew up into the trees from a point about a yard in front of me, and although I could not secure the imago, I soon found the larval skin quite close by. A second skin was found on a grass-stem only a few feet away.

These exuviæ are of great interest, as they throw some light on the phylogenetic relationship of the *Libelluline* with the *Cordulinæ*. Exactly how far this bears out existing theories, it is difficult to say, because it is not easy to decide what larval characters ought properly to be regarded as *Libelluline*, and what as *Corduline*. I propose now to give a careful description of the exuviæ, and then to consider how far it combines the characters of the two subfamilies:—N y m p h ♀. (Plate lxxiv., figs. 1-2): *Total length* 13 mm. Colour almost uniform dull brownish all over, except legs, which are spotted with darker brown. Head small, 1·5 × 3·7 mm., eyes fairly prominent, postocular lobes rounded; antennæ 1·5 mm., seven-jointed. L a b i u m (Fig. 3): *mentum* short and broad, (2·5 × 3·7 mm., when flattened out), median lobe forming a prominent obtuse angle, with a few isolated hairs; *lateral lobes* subtriangular, inner margin and angle slightly rounded, carrying seven very distinct rounded crenations, each separated from the next by an incision *about as deep as the width of the crenation;* each crenation carries two sharp spines, of which the upper is shorter than the lower; these crenations are themselves *very slightly* crenulate, mostly on their upper margins. After the seventh (lowest) crenation, the margin curves round in a single broad curve carrying, firstly, a set of two spines, then a set of five spines close together, of which the first is very small, and, finally, three single spines on the part opposite the median lobe. *End-hook* rather weak, very sharp and narrow, 0·8 mm. Setæ: mental 5, lateral 5, all rather weak. Surface of lateral lobes considerably marked with small black spots. T h o r a x: *prothorax* short and wide, 0·8 × 2·5 mm., with distinct, but not very sharp, anterolateral prominences. *Meso-* and *metathorax* fairly short and smooth, *wing-cases* about 4 mm. long, lying parallel along the back, and reaching about up to end of segment 5 of abdomen. *Legs* of medium length, slender; measurements of femur, tibia and tarsus: fore, 3, 3·4, 1·5; middle, 3·6, 3·8, 1·5; hind, 4·8, 4·5, 1·8 mm. A b d o m e n: oval, 8 × 4 mm , moderately convex beneath, very rounded above, and rising to the dorsal ridge, so that the cross-section appears broadly triquetral. *Lateral spines* only on 8-9, very small; *dorsal spines* on 5-10, nodding; those on 5-6 large, that of 7 flatter and smaller, that of 8 still smaller, while those of 9-10 are close together, very small and depressed. Segment 10 not enfolded by 9, except in so far as the dorsal and lateral spines of 9 project beyond its level (Fig. 2). *Appendages* 0·5 mm., broadly triquetral, with slightly concave sides, tips bluntly pointed; *involucres* of ♀ imaginal appendages very short, lying close in between the larval appendages, the whole forming a truncated triangular pyramid.

Hab.—Bellinger River, at Never-Never (N.S.W.). Emerged October 30th, 1911.

Type: Coll. Tillyard.

A second larval skin, also ♀, is slightly larger than the one described. From the fact that both these larvæ were females, and that battered female imagines have been taken as late as January, it is evident that the males of this species emerge first. It would seem that, at Kuranda, the males of *N. eludens* begin to emerge at a time (January), when only a few battered females of *N. risi* are left, and these few have completed oviposition. The females of *N. eludens* begin to come out a week or two later, and keep on the wing until May. Intercrossing between the two species would, therefore, appear to be quite impossible, apart from structural differences.

Those who are interested in the phylogeny of the *Libellulidæ* will regard the discovery of the larva as of the utmost importance, since it is the first larva of Group i. of the *Libellulinæ* to be recorded. It is generally admitted that the *Libellulinæ* are, on the whole, cænogenetic from a more ancient *Corduline* stock. In so far, then, as Group i. is claimed to be an assemblage of the most archaic remnants of the early *Libellulinæ*, we must look for *Corduline* characters in our newly-found larva. But also, in so far as Group i. may be regarded as *asthenogenetically modified* from the original *Libelluline* stock, we may expect to find very distinct *non-Corduline* characters, which may be similar to those of most *Libelluline* nymphs now existing, or might possibly be peculiar to the genus.

A satisfactory solution of this difficult problem requires a very clear and definite knowledge of what are the truly *Corduline*, and what the truly *Libelluline* characters of present-day nymphs. The two groups are closely allied, and it is difficult to fix upon many distinguishing characteristics. I regard the following as being the most definite Corduline (*i.e.*, archaic) characters of the nymphal forms.

(1) By far the most important, because it is found almost without exception throughout the *Corduliinæ sens. lato*, is the greater

comparative depth of the crenations of the inner margin of the lateral lobes in the nymphal labium. Ranging from a deeply dentate margin in some forms, to the more prevalent crenate form of the *Corduliinæ s. str.*, (in which the depth of the crenate lobe is roughly equal to the width of the depression between them), we find this as the distinguishing mark of the larvæ of this subfamily. The only exceptions are the most cænogenetic forms, such as *Hemicordulia, Tetragoneuria*, etc., which show the more shallow *Libelluline* crenations; while, in the *Libellulinæ*, the only nymph having moderately deep crenations, is that of *Pantala flavescens*. This latter being one of the most recent and highly developed *Libellulinæ*, we must suppose this Corduline character of the labium to be secondarily developed.

It will be seen, at once, that the larva of *Nannophlebia* possesses this *Corduline* character. This is clear evidence of the proximity of Group i. to the *Corduline* stem, and, therefore, of their being archaic, as compared with the general body of the *Libellulinæ*.

(2) Coupled with the above character, but not so distinctive, is the smooth unspotted surface of the lateral lobes, and their fuller and more rounded outline in the *Corduliinæ*, together with a smaller development of spines on the crenations. The tendency of the *Libelluline* labium seems to me to be the development of a broad subtriangular mentum, the compression basally of the lateral lobes to subtriangular form, and a general decrease of the broad curvature of the inner margin. With this comes the increase in the *number* (as distinct from the size) of the crenulations, an often corresponding increase in lateral setæ, and a strong tendency to the production of black spots and warts on the surface of the lobe.

The larger number of setæ is not usually, however, found in any small nymphs, and need not therefore be looked for in *Nannophlebia*. Judged, however, by the general form of the lateral lobe, and by the appearance of black warty spots on it, we must regard the labium as showing distinct *Libelluline* characters.

On the whole, then, the evidence of the labium is that *Nannophlebia* is an archaic *Libelluline* which branched off long ago from the old *Corduline* stock.

(3) The average length of the legs in *Corduline* nymphs (and imagines also) is considerable greater than in the *Libellulinæ*. *Nannophlebia* may be said to have rather long legs for a *Libelluline*, but distinctly shorter than we might expect for a *Corduline* (compare *Cordulephya*). This character may, therefore, be held to agree with the conclusion stated just above.

(4) In *Corduline* nymphs there appears to be a much greater tendency to the retraction of segment 10 of the abdomen, and the enveloping of it by segment 9, (or sometimes even 9 and 10 may be retracted into 8). There are, however, many exceptions to this. Also, the appendages in *Corduline* nymphs are usually somewhat longer than in the *Libellulinæ*, though the difference in some particular cases is not very great. In so far as these characters may be judged to have any value, *Nannophlebia* must be held to be distinctly *Libelluline*.

(5) The general outline of the nymphs of the two groups is somewhat variable, but there is a type that is common to both, *viz.*, the smooth oval body, triangular front, and rounded postocular lobes of the head(compare *Diplacodes, Hemicordulia, Cordulephya*); and to this general type, *Nannophlebia* belongs.

Reviewing the above evidence, I am inclined to conclude as follows:—

Group i. of the *Libellulinæ*, as proposed by Dr. Ris, is justified as an archaic group, probably heterogeneous, but containing all those asthenogenetic remnants that still exist, of the earliest offshoots in a Libelluline direction from the parent(*Corduline*)stem.

We have now to face a further and most interesting problem, which may be stated as follows. Both the *Libellulinæ* and the *Corduliinæ* possess archaic forms which appear to be fairly closely allied; *e.g.*, Group i. of the *Libellulinæ*, *Cordulephya* in the *Corduliinæ*. How far is this resemblance due to real affinity; how far is it due to asthenogenetic convergence? The answer to this contains within it the solution of the vexed problem of the genesis of the *Libelluline* anal loop. If we can prove that *Nannophlebia* and *Cordulephya*, for instance, are really close allies, and not merely alike by convergence, we have a strong ground from which to argue that the present-day broad hindwing and specialised anal loop of the *Libellulinæ* was developed secondarily from a wing in which the original broad *Anisopterous* hindwing had been reduced to approximately equal width with the forewing. If not, we should rather accept a theory of the development of all the present-day loops from a broad-winged but very generalised archaic type, to which *Chlorogomphus* may hold the clue, and regard all the narrow-winged forms, even if proved archaic, to be the result of asthenogenetic convergence. The former theory is strongly held by Dr. Ris, whose opinion, as without doubt that of the most accomplished Odonatologist of the present day, cannot be lightly put aside. To me, however, the latter seems to be by far the more probable.

Let us first of all, therefore, compare both larval and imaginal forms of *Nannophlebia* and *Cordulephya*[*] :—

A. Larvæ:—

(1) *The labia.*—These are very distinct, *Cordulephya* showing high specialisation in several points. Compare *a*, the long narrow gulf-like incisions of the upper part of the inner margin of the lateral lobe in *Cordulephya*, with the normal crenations of *Nannophlebia*; *b*, the much longer end-hook in *Cordulephya*; *c*, the more numerous and more strongly developed setæ, both lateral and mental, in *Cordulephya*; *d*, the larger number of spines (3-4), on the lower (normal) crenations of *Cordulephya*; *e*, the finely speckled or spotted surface of the lateral lobes in *Cordulephya*, with the few but larger and more conspicuous black spots on *Nannophlebia*. One cannot but conclude that *Nannophlebia* is really more closely allied, in its labium, to the main *Eucordulian* stock, than it is to the distinctly aberrant *Cordulephya*.

(2) *The antennæ.*—Though both are seven-jointed, those of *Nannophlebia* are very much shorter than those of *Cordelphya*.

(3) *The legs.*—Those of *Cordulephya* are very much the longer.

(4) *The abdomen.*—In *Cordulephya*, segment 10 is fully recessed into 9; while in *Nannophlebia*, it is normal in position. [The ar-

---

[*] For characters of *Cordulephya*, see Plates xi. and xii., pp.421-2, These Proceedings, Vol.xxxvi., Part 2, 1911.

rangements of dorsal and lateral spines show nothing in common; but I do not regard these as beyond specific value.]

B. Imagines:—

(1) *Colour-scheme.*—Somewhat similar in broad outline; very distinct in detail.

(2) *General build and habits.*—These show considerable similarity, but cannot be held to indicate affinity, as the results of asthenogenetic convergence must necessarily tend to a general resemblance in form and habits.

(3) *Wing-venation.*—Beyond the fact that both are of the narrow-winged type, there is very little similarity in detail. Contrast *a*, the *Corduline* angulated hind-wing of *Cordulephya* ♂ with the rounded *Libelluline* hind-wing of *Nannophlebia* ♂; *b*, the difference in position of second antenodal compared with arculus; *c*, the number of antenodals; *d*, the points of origin and amounts of fusion of the sectors of the arculus; *e*, the positions of the cubital cross-veins; *f*, the points of origin of the superior sector of the triangle; *g*, the position of the hind-wing triangle (compare also *Cordulephya* with *Tetrathemis* or *Hypothemis*, which are closer to it in this character); *h*, the anal loops (*Cordulephya* reduced to two strongly marked large cells in *C. pygmaea*).

If these two wing-forms were really close approximations to an archaic wing-type, I do not think we could expect so much diversity of detail. Assuming, however, that the narrowing of the wing is due to asthenogenesis, the marvel would be, not that they are so close as they are, but that elimination and reduction should fail to produce something even closer (consider, for example, the long but excessively similar set of reduction-forms in the *Agrionidæ*).

(4) *Tibial keel.*—A recognised *Corduline* character. Present in *Cordulephya*; no sign of it in *Nannophlebia*.

The main weight of the above evidence seems to me, however much one may regret the fact, to be strongly against the assumption of a close relationship between *Nannophlebia* and *Cordulephya*. It points rather to the fact that the ancestral *Libellulinæ* branched off from the *Corduliinæ* much further back than we are inclined to suspect, and that, in the resemblance between Group i. of the *Libellulinæ* and such forms as *Cordulephya*, we have only a *partial* solution of the problem. These two are *nearer by asthenogenetic convergence* at the present day *than their ancestors probably were before asthenogenesis began to act upon them*. Nevertheless, those ancestors did possess archaic characters common to the original stock, and it was their failure to improve on the weak points of their venational structure, that caused them to drop behind in the race of progress. The main body of these ancestral forms has long ago perished, but there remain to-day those few "end-twigs" of the old stem, which have survived by adopting asthenogenesis. This line of development must, of necessity, produce forms that are true convergences, in the sense that they now appear more closely related than they would, if we knew their past history in full.

To deal, finally, with the problem of the *Libelluline* anal-loop, we have to state one very strong objection to the theory of its re-development from a narrowed-down type of hind-wing. It is this: those who support this theory will scarcely admit the possibility of the re-formation of the unstressed four-sided "triangle" from a more highly-developed three-sided structure. They say, that, when once so useful a form as the latter had become developed, no species could possibly have gone back to the ancestral form, or it must have perished. But they ask us to believe a far harder thing; *viz.*, that a race with a broad hind-wing, whose anal area was built up roughly on lines similar to *Petalura*, could not only lose this structure (whose *uselessness* they surely would not attempt to prove, in the face of the survival of the *Aeschnine* and *Macromian* loops), but also that, having lost it, they redeveloped a new type of loop afresh. Surely this theory is only supported because of the apparent necessity of insisting on the archaic value of the narrow-winged types. This *Libelluline* loop (like all other loops, but not necessarily on the same plan) developed from the original fairly broad hindwing of the *Anisopterid* stock, which contained *all the material* (in the form of numerous small cells) for the formation of any suitable bracing or strengthening of the wing-area, either on *Aeschnine* or *Libelluline* lines.

I do not contend that it is necessary to assume even that the present-day "quadrilaterals" in the *Libellulidæ*, ever possessed ancestors with a *fully-formed* three-sided triangle. I think, rather, that their ancestors were the laggards in this race for the perfect triangle, and that they attained only a certain measure of success in that direction, without gaining a position of equilibrium. Needham has shown (without emphasising the point) by his excellent diagrams of the gradual formation of the triangle, what an enormous stress must be thrown on to those originally weak crossveins, which are finally called upon to play the part of strong sides to the triangle. Anything less than complete success, in this difficult piece of evolution, must surely have stood self-condemned, and either exists still as an unstable form (e.g., *Synthemis*) or embarked on the backward path of asthenogenesis, in which, since the aim is no longer to produce the ideal flying wing, the reduction back to the weaker form would rapidly proceed.

The argument for the Single-Development Theory of the Anal Loops may be briefly put as follows:—All present-day hind-wings of the *Anisoptera* were developed from an original *anisopterous* type, which had a hind-wing broad enough to contain all the cell-material necessary for present-day developments. By various arrangements of the basal cells and the anal and cubital branch-veins traversing them, *all* the present-day loops (and probably other kinds now lost) were developed. Thus arose, with varying degrees of final success, the *Gomphine, Petalurine, Chlorogomphine, Aeschnine, Macromian,* and *Libelluline* loops, in all their forms and variations. Of these, the most recent and most successful is the *Libelluline* loop, whose origin may probably be sought near to the point from which *Chlorogomphus* sprang, and from which that genus appears to have diverged but little.

Besides these *menogenetic* types, at various points along the evolutionary route, unsuccessful competitors gave up the race, and adopted, as a means for their preservation, the process of *asthenogenesis*, so successfully carried out long before by the main army of *Zygoptera*. The effect of reduction of the wing-venation has been to produce a *superficial* convergence in all these forms, mainly by the return of the triangle to quadrilateral form (though not necessarily from an actual three-sided triangle, which was probably never formed with stability), and by the reduction of the anal area of the hind-wing to a comparatively few cells, *whose arrangement is then bound to show some similarity in all these forms*. But *they all retain clear indications of the stock from which they branched*, e.g., *Hypothemis*, *Tetrathemis*, and *Nannophlebia* are essentially *Libellulinæ*, *Cordulephya* essentially *Corduline*, *Agriogomphus* essentially *Gomphine*. These forms, while based upon ancestral characters that are truly archaic compared with those of the more successful menogenetic forms *most closely allied to them*, but *not necessarily archaic in comparison with other menogenetic forms not closely allied* (e.g., *Chlorogomphus*), are usually quite highly specialised in some other directions, e.g., in flight, larval development, tibial armature, etc.

If this theory be correct, we are still a long way off from discovering the point of origin of the *Libelluline* from the *Corduline* stock. We must, perhaps, confess that this is lost in antiquity. Nevertheless, we may still hope for light on this problem from the discovery of the larva of *Chlorogomphus*, which may very possibly show characters common to both of the groups in question.

One other point is worthy of mention. In the development of his theory of the classification of the *Libellulinæ*, Dr. Ris places together in Group ii. the narrow-winged forms, *Agrionoptera* and *Lathrecista*, with the normal-winged *Orthetrum*. We want, therefore, the larva of one of these narrow-winged genera. If it turns out to be similar to *Orthetrum* (a very distinct type), it will vindicate his classification. If, however, it does not, it will be a serious blow to the evolutionary view expressed for Group ii., and will, I take it, require a reconsideration of the Double-Origin Theory of the *Anisopterid* anal loops. In my view, forms like *Agrionoptera* are not, in any sense, ancestral to *Orthetrum*, but are an asthenogenetic development on a line of their own, converging towards *Orthetrum* (if one may say so, though the convergence has not gone far) by elimination or alteration of characters originally essentially different.

In conclusion, then, the discovery of the nymph of *Nannophlebia* leaves these problems in a most interesting state; for while the new light thrown by it is not to be despised, yet it is not sufficient to solve the problem satisfactorily.

EXPLANATION OF PLATE LXXIV.

Fig. 1.—Exuviæ of *Nannophlebia risi*, n.sp., ♀ (× 4·5).

Fig. 2.—Exuviæ of *Nannophlebia risi*, side view of abdomen (× 4·5).

Fig. 3.—Exuviæ of *Nannophlebia risi*, labium, left side (× 30).

Fig. 4.—*Nannophlebia risi*, n.sp., imago, basal half of wings of male (yellow shading omitted) (× 4·5); *m*, obsolescent membranule.

Fig. 5.—*Nannophlebia risi*, n.sp., imago, ♂, colour-pattern of abdomen (× 4·5).

Fig. 6.—*Nannophlebia eludens* Tillyard, ♂, colour-pattern of abdomen (× 4·5).

Fig. 7.—*Nannophlebia risi*, n.sp., ♂, colour-pattern of side of meso- and metathorax (× 4·5).

Fig. 8.—*Nannophlebia eludens* Tillyard, ♂, colour-pattern of side of meso- and metathorax (× 4·5).

Fig. 9.—*Nannophlebia risi*, n.sp., ♂, appendages, lateral view.

Fig. 10.—*Nannophlebia risi*, n.sp., ♂, appendages, dorsal view.

Fig. 11.—*Nannophlebia eludens* Tillyard, ♂, appendages, lateral view.

Fig. 12.—*Nannophlebia eludens* Tillyard, ♂, appendages, dorsal view.

Fig. 13.—*Nannophlebia risi*, n.sp., ♀, appendages, right side, dorsal view.

Fig. 14.—*Nannophlebia eludens* Tillyard, ♂, genitalia of segment 2, lateral view, ventral side uppermost.

Fig. 15.—*Nannophlebia risi*, n.sp., ♂, genitalia of segment 2, lateral view, ventral side uppermost.

ON SOME TREMATODE PARASITES OF MARSUPIALS AND OF A MONOTREME.

By S. J. JOHNSTON, B.A., D.Sc., DEMONSTRATOR IN BIOLOGY, UNIVERSITY OF SYDNEY.

(Plates lxxv.-lxxvi.)

The small group of Trematodes, here under discussion, comprises two new species of *Harmostomum* from marsupials, and two species of *Mehlisia*, one from a marsupial, also described as new, and one from the platypus, *Ornithorhynchus anatinus* Shaw, described by me in these Proceedings in 1901, under the designation *Distomum ornithorhynchi*(7). The two species of *Harmostomum* are closely related to one another; but, what is more interesting, are also closely related to *H. opisthotrias* Lutz, parasitic in the South American marsupial, *Didelphys aurita*(13); so nearly, in fact, as I shall show in detail later on, that they must be looked upon as derived from a common ancestor; and, in this way, they supply some circumstantial evidence of the phylogenetic relationship of the Australian and the South American marsupials.

HARMOSTOMUM DASYURI, sp.n.

(Plate lxxv., Figs. 1, 5-8.)

Parasitic in the intestine of *Dasyurus viverrinus*, found in the vicinity of Sydney, N.S.W.

Diagnosis.—Small, flattened worms, rounded in front, pointed behind, about 6 mm. long, by 1·25 mm. broad. Integument armed with spines, except on the posterior half of the dorsal surface. Suckers very large, the ventral almost as wide as the body; *ratio of the oral to the ventral sucker,* 2:3. Small prepharynx, well developed pharynx, and short œsophagus present. Intestinal limbs with a forwardly directed loop, thence running back to the extreme posterior end of the body. Excretory vesicle very small in its unpaired part, dividing into two long branches, *giving off numerous vessels.* Gonads oval, *comparatively large,* in the posterior end of the body, the anterior testis with its *long axis transversely, posterior with its long axis longitudinally disposed;* ovary lying between the two testes, with its long axis transversely placed. Genital pore near the anterior edge of the anterior testis. Copulatory organs well developed, but *cirrus-sac* moderate, and not surrounding the vesicula seminalis. Laurer's canal present, but no receptaculum seminis. Uterus in ascending and descending coils, not reaching anteriorly beyond the ventral sucker, nor posteriorly beyond the front of the anterior testis. Yolk-glands lying at the sides of the body, between the ventral sucker and the anterior testis; just reaching inwards beyond the intestinal limbs.

Eggs dark-shelled, oval, flattened on one side, small, 0·0254 × 0·0165 mm.

Type-specimen in the Australian Museum, No. W. 352.

I received eight specimens of this worm, all obtained from one host, from the Bureau of Microbiology, Sydney; of these, two were sectioned, and the others mounted whole. The host, which was sent in to the Bureau by Mr. Thomas Steel, came from Hunter's Hill, a suburb of Sydney. These moderately small worms, 6·33 mm. in average length, and 1·24 mm. in breadth, have a somewhat flattened, elliptical cross-section, remain fairly broad, and are rounded off in front; but, behind the gonads, taper to a point posteriorly. The cuticle is fairly thick, and the ventral surface and the sides are thickly beset with small pointed spines, which gradually become finer posteriorly, but are present right up to the posterior end. On the dorsal surface, however, they practically vanish at the level of the posterior edge of the ventral sucker. Both the suckers are large. The oral sucker is subterminal, with its opening directed ventrally; the average diameter is 0·67 mm. The ventral sucker, lying in the first body-third, is almost as broad as the worm's body, its average diameter being 1·001 mm., so that the ratio of the diameter of the oral sucker to that of the ventral, is 2:3. The pharynx, which is preceded by a short præpharynx, is a large muscular organ, practically circular in ventral view, and having a diameter just one-half that of the oral sucker. There is a short œsophagus, 0·08 mm. long. The intestinal limbs run at first anteriorly, as far as the oral sucker, and then run backwards, in a straight or slightly wavy course, to the extreme posterior end of the body. Looss(8) says, of *H. œquans* Lss., that these forwardly running loops are caused by the contracted state of the body; but I cannot agree with this, in regard to the similar loops found in the two species of *Harmostomum* described in this paper, but regard them as very characteristic and peculiar features of their alimentary canal. My specimens show no signs of unusual contraction, and there seems to be no reason why the slight, but inevitable contraction brought about by ordinary methods of fixing and preserving, should cause this peculiar feature in these worms and their relations, but in no others.

The excretory system is peculiar, and corresponds, in its main features, to that of *H. leptostomum* Olss., described by Looss (9, p. 168). The median, undivided part of the excretory vesicle, opening at the posterior end of the body, is very short, only 0·16 mm. long; but it divides into two branches that run to the level of the oral sucker, and, bending round, course back once more to the posterior end, giving off numerous capillary branches, that end in flame-cells, along their whole length; but the flame-cells are more numerous at the anterior end than elsewhere. A special feature of these vessels, which Looss, in the case of *H. leptostomum* Olss., regards as branches of the vesicle itself rather than ordinary collecting tubes, is that, for part of their course, they possess little patches of cilia projecting into their lumen.

The genital pore is situated on the ventral surface, in the middle line, just in front of the anterior testis. The testes, which are large oval bodies lying in the posterior third of the body, seem to be characteristically placed, the anterior with its long axis transversely or slightly obliquely across the body, while the posterior has its long axis lying directly longitudinally in regard to the body of the worm. They are equal in size, and measure 0·57 mm. × 0·46 mm. The ovary, which lies between them, and is sometimes slightly overlapped by them, is also oval in shape, with its long axis transversely placed. The vasa deferentia come off from the middle of the anterior surface of each testis respectively; that from the posterior skirts round the lateral aspect of the ovary and anterior testis (Fig. 5), and joins its fellow just after it leaves the anterior testis. The tube, formed by their union, shortly enters the vesicula seminalis, which is a coiled tubular body, of comparatively considerable length, not enclosed in the cirrus-sac, but lying free in the parenchyma. The cirrus-sac, a moderately developed muscular sac, surrounding the cirrus with its ejaculatory duct, does not extend inwards beyond the junction of the ejaculatory duct with the vesicula seminalis. The prostate cells lie free in the parenchyma. The cirrus-sac and vagina, which has thick muscular walls, are surrounded by modified parenchyma cells.

The ovary (0.39×0.31 mm.) is smaller than the testes, and lies either median or slightly lateral. Like the testes, it is a smooth oval body. The oviduct leaves it in the middle of its ventral surface (Fig. 6), and runs to its posterior edge; here the ootype is situated, and just in front of this, Laurer's canal takes its origin, and curves round to the dorsal surface, where it opens on the exterior (Fig. 6). There is no receptaculum seminis. The "shell-glands" round the ootype are not well developed. The yolk-reservoir lies close to the ootype. From the ootype, the female duct runs forwards in a slightly coiled course to the level of the genital opening, and this part of it, which is stuffed full of sperms, is the receptaculum seminis uterinum; it then runs, in a series of transversity placed loops in the ventral surface of the body, as far forwards as the middle of the ventral sucker, returning in the dorsal part of the body by a series of complex folds to end at the genital opening. The loops of the uterus laterally lie strictly within the inner boundary of the intestinal limbs.

The yolk-glands consist of numerous, quite small, oval follicles (average size 0.038×0.023 mm.), which lie in the lateral aspect of the body outside the intestinal limbs; in front, they just reach the level of the posterior edge of the ventral sucker, while posteriorly, they do not pass beyond the level of the anterior testes. Their ducts form two conspicuous lines that at first gradually, then more quickly, converge on the yolk-reservoir.

The small dark-shelled eggs (0·0254 × 0·0165 mm.) have the characteristic elliptical shape, flattened on one side, and are very numerous.

HARMOSTOMUM SIMILE, n.sp.

Parasitic in the intestine of the bandicoot, *Perameles obesula*, found in the vicinity of Sydney, N.S.W. (Fig. 2).

Diagnosis. — Small worms, oval in cross-section, rounded in front, pointed behind, about 3 mm. long, by 0·5 mm. broad. Integument spiny on the ventral and lateral surfaces, but smooth on the dorsal surface, *except at the extreme anterior end*. Suckers comparatively large, *ratio of the oral to the ventral sucker*, 3:4. Alimentary and excretory systems as in *H. dasyuri*. Gonads oval: anterior testis *smaller than posterior*, fairly globular in form. Genital pore near the anterior edge of the anterior testis. Cirrus and vagina well developed and muscular, but *cirrus-sac very poorly developed*. Laurer's canal present, but no receptaculum seminis. Uterus and yolk-glands as in *H. dasyuri*. Eggs very small, 0·0219 × 0·0129 mm.

Type-specimen in the Australian Museum, No. W.353.

I have received four specimens of this worm, one from the Bureau of Microbiology, Sydney, and three from my friend, Dr. Harvey Johnston, of the University of Queensland. Two were sectioned, and the others mounted whole.

This is obviously closely related to the foregoing species, pretty closely corresponding in its anatomical structure, but differing from it in its much smaller size, in the relative sizes of the suckers, in being less spiny, in its more weakly developed cirrus-sac, in the anterior testis being smaller than the posterior, and subglobular, and in the size of the eggs, which are smaller in *H. simile*. In the latter, too, the testes are nearer the posterior end, so that there is practically no tail. All four worms were about the same size, the average length being 2·98 mm., breadth 0·52 mm. The diameter of the oral sucker averages 0·273 mm., that of the ventral 0·372 mm. The pharynx, with a diameter of 0·155 mm., is comparatively larger than in *H. dasyuri*. The anterior testis measures 0·218 mm. in average diameter, the posterior 0·272 × 0·239 mm., the ovary 0·227 × 0·187 mm.

These two species are obviously very closely related to *H. opisthotrias*, Lutz, parasitic in a South American marsupial, apparently more closely related to it than to any other species of *Harmostomum*. They differ from it chiefly, as far as one can judge from the descriptions given by Lutz(13), and later by Braun(2) (though Braun probably had to do with another species), in the very different relations in size of the suckers, in the different relative sizes of the testes, in the size of the eggs, and several other very minor points. But these three (or four) species from marsupials agree so closely in so many characteristic features, such as the whole structure of the alimentary tract, and the whole configuration of the genital system, that they should be looked upon as having been derived from common ancestors. These species from marsupials agree together, and differ from the other known species of Harmostomum, as *H. leptostomum* Olss., *H. æquans* Lss., parasitic in mammals; and *H. fuscatum* R., *H. marsupium* Brn., *H. centrodes* Brn., *H. mordens* Brn., *H. caudale* R., parasitic in birds, in the fact that neither the coils of the uterus, nor the yolk-glands extend anteriorly beyond the ventral sucker.

A second species of worm from *Dasyurus viverrinus*, and that parasitic in the duodenum of the platypus, I have found it necessary to refer to a new genus.

M E H L I S I A,* gen. nov.

Fasciolid trematodes of moderate size, elongated and narrow, leaf-like, thick; widest just behind the ventral sucker, with a constriction in front of this (Fig. 3). Integument spiny, cuticle thick. Suckers large, near together. Præpharynx, pharynx, no œsophagus, intestinal limbs extending to near posterior end. Excretory vesicle with main stem reaching testis, and dividing into four longitudinal branches that form an anastomosing network in anterior end of body, opening into a sinus surrounding oral sucker; a similar sinus round ventral sucker; ciliated vessels and supplementary vessels present. Genital pore near midline, in front of ventral sucker. Copulatory organs present. Testes large and

* Named from the gland of Mehlis, which is of very large size.

elongated, in middle of body; ovary in front of testes to one side of the middle line. Laurer's canal present; no receptaculum seminis. "Shell-gland" very large. Uterus short. Yolk-glands extensive, laterally placed in front of the testes; behind the posterior testes spreading under the whole surface of the body. Eggs very large. In the intestine of lower mammals.

MEHLISIA ACUMINATA, sp.n.

(Figures 3, 9, 10.)

Parasitic in the intestine of the marsupial "cat," *Dasyurus viverrinus.*

Diagnosis.—Size moderate; form elongate, narrow leaf-shaped, *tapering to a sharp point behind.* Integument spiny; cuticle thick. Suckers very large, near together; *ratio of oral to ventral,* 1:2. Præpharynx, pharynx, no œsophagus, simple intestinal limbs, reaching the posterior end. Excretory system of vessels and sinuses as in the genus. Copulatory organs present. Genital opening just in front of ventral sucker. Testes one behind the other in the middle of the body; ovary in front of the testes on one side of the middle line, much smaller than the testes. Laurer's canal present, but no receptaculum seminis. "Shell-gland" very large. Uterus short, restricted to the middle field between the ovary and ventral sucker and intestinal limbs. Yolk-glands extending from the posterior edge of the ventral sucker to the posterior end, at first laterally placed, behind the posterior testis spreading over the whole surface of the body. Eggs very large, 0·134 × 0·079 mm., few in number.

Type-specimen in the Australian Museum, No. W.355.

I have received about 40 specimens of this trematode, some from Dr. J. P. Hill, of the University of London, and formerly of the University of Sydney, some from Dr. Harvey Johnston, of the University of Queensland, and some from the Bureau of Microbiology, Sydney, all taken from the intestine of the marsupial "cat," *Dasyurus viverrinus,* collected in various parts of New South Wales. In shape, these worms are elongated and narrow, leaf-like, flattened dorsoventrally, but the flatness varies considerably, and in preserved specimens the shape in transverse sections is almost invariably somewhat flattened oval. They are widest just behind the ventral sucker, rounded in front, but gradually tapering to a long point behind; there is a slight constriction near the ventral sucker, just in front of the widest part of the body. The average size is 11·2 mm., long, by 2·34 mm. wide.

The cuticle is thick and tough, beset with numerous sharp-pointed spines, closely set in the anterior region of the body, but gradually becoming sparse and scattered towards the posterior extremity. In the body-wall, the longitudinal muscles are arranged in columns separated from one another by connective tissue cells (Fig. 9).

The suckers are very large; the oral spherical, with its aperture ventrally placed near the anterior end; the ventral, placed close to the oral, is also spherical, nearly as wide as the body, and deeply implanted in it. The average diameters are, oral 0·66 mm., ventral 1·32 mm.; ratio of oral to ventral, 1:2. The relative size is very constant, being practically the same in every specimen measured.

The pharynx, much smaller than the oral sucker, joins it through a præpharynx of length rather less than its own. There is practically no œsophagus, and the intestinal limbs run out to the sides of the body, and then proceed, in a pretty straight course, to end a little distance in front of the posterior extremity. They are quite simple in form, showing no signs of lateral cæca.

The excretory system of vessels is very richly developed, and exhibits some very marked peculiarities. The main stem of the vesicle, which opens by a small pore at the extreme posterior end, is a long wide tube reaching up to the level of the posterior testis, where it divides into four longitudinal branches that run forwards to the anterior end of the body. Both from the main stem and its four branches, a series of short lateral branches proceed towards the surface, and break up into a number of branches that lie in the parenchyma among the yolk-cells, many of them reaching the inner aspect of the cuticle. In this respect, as in others to be pointed out below, they resemble the condition found in *Mesaulus grandis* R.,(Braun, 5). The four longitudinal vessels, given off from the stem of the vesicle, end in front in an anastomosing network of vessels, which is connected, by a fairly large opening (Fig. 10) on each side, with a large sinus surrounding the oral sucker. A similar sinus also surrounds the ventral sucker. Similar sinuses surrounding the suckers have been found by Braun (2, 5) in *Mesaulus grandis* R., and in *Echinostoma incrassatum*, Dies., but their connection with the excretory system was not observed (5, p. 27). All these vessels, including the network and the sinuses, are lined in the same way by a nucleated syncytium. Given off from them are smaller intracellular tubes that end in flame-cells. The latter are more numerous at the anterior end of the body.

Opening into the sinus that surrounds the oral sucker, I find a pair of tubes of quite different character. The walls are thicker, and elongated patches of cilia (Fig. 9) project into the lumen. The intervals between these groups of cilia are small, so that the tube is ciliated in the greater part of its length. These two tubes run backwards, one on each side, to a level some distance behind the testes, where each passes into a tube lined by columnar nucleated cells, but bearing no cilia. These latter tubes, which I have marked "supplementary tubes" in Fig. 9, run forwards, parallel to their ciliated companions, and backwards to the posterior end of the body where they bend round, and are continued forwards again for some distance. At about the level where they disappear, a second forwardly running branch is given off from the parent supplementary tube, and this second branch reaches a level somewhat in front of the junction of the supplementary tube with the ciliated tube. The supplementary tube and its branches gradually become smaller and thinner-walled, and finally end in a system of intercellular spaces lying in the parenchyma. The function of all these tubes and sinuses is, no doubt, respiratory as well as excretory, and the fluid in their cavities is kept in circulation by the ciliated tubes.

The genital pore is situated on the ventral surface, near the middle line, just in front of the ventral sucker. The gonads lie close together, occupying about the middle third of the body-length. The testes, which lie in the middle line, one behind the other, are very large, 1·69 mm. long by 0·59 mm. broad, roughly crescentic or S-shaped, with an irregular, indented outline. The ovary is rounded or oval in shape, with a smooth outline, much smaller than the testes, close in front of the anterior, and a little to one side (the right) of the middle line. The ducts of the testes run forwards, laterally placed, one on each side of the uterus, then dorsal to the ventral sucker; they join at the base of the cirrus-sac, and immediately enter the S-shaped vesicula seminalis. The cirrus-sac is a muscular-walled, pear-shaped body of considerable size; the prostate cells lie in its parenchyma surrounding the proximal part of the ejaculatory duct, into which their fine ducts open. The oviduct leaves the ovary on its dorsal aspect, and soon gives off Laurer's canal, which, after a short curved course, opens on the dorsal surface near the middle line. Just distal to its junction with Laurer's canal, the oviduct expands into the ootype, and here the duct of the yolk-reservoir opens into it. The next portion of the female duct is frequently filled with sperms, and is the receptaculum seminis uterinum. The "shell-gland" or gland of Mehlis, is a large mass of elongated cells with fine ducts opening into the ootype. Not only the ootype, but also the yolk-reservoir and Laurer's canal lie embedded in this mass of gland-cells. There is no receptaculum seminis. The uterus, which is comparatively very short, lies in the middle field of the body between the ovary and the ventral sucker, being disposed in several transversely placed coils, which do not reach laterally the intestinal limbs. The final part of its course, lying dorsal to the ventral sucker, is fairly straight. The vagina or metraterm has its muscular walls only moderately developed.

The follicles of the yolk-glands are small (0·069 × 0·056 mm.), and exceedingly numerous. They form compact masses, lying, at first, at the sides of the body, but, at the level of the posterior testis, they begin to spread over to the middle, and behind the testes they fill up the whole field, forming a complete layer under the surface of the body (Fig. 3). Anteriorly, they do not extend beyond the posterior edge of the ventral sucker. There is a longitudinal yolk-duct on each side, lying near the outer side of the intestinal limbs, receiving numerous tributaries from the follicles as it passes (Fig. 9). The anterior and posterior parts of these ducts meet at the level of the anterior edge of the anterior testis, and, from the point of junction on each side, a transverse duct proceeds to meet its fellow of the other side, in the mass of the shell-gland.

The elliptical eggs are light-yellow in colour, very large(0.134×0.079 mm.), and comparatively few in number.

MEHLISIA ORNITHORHYNCHI mihi.

(Figs. 4 and 11.)

Parasitic in the duodenum of the platypus, *Ornithorhynchus anatinus*.

Diagnosis.—Elongated worms, tapering somewhat, but rounded off at each end. Integument spiny, spines larger than in *M. acuminata*. Suckers large, near together; *ratio of oral to ventral*, 2:3. Præpharynx, pharynx, no œsophagus, simple intestinal limbs extending to the posterior end. Excretory system of vessels and sinuses as in the genus. Copulatory organs present. Testes elongated, lobulated, *obliquely placed* in the middle line, one behind the other. Ovary, uterus, shell-gland, Laurer's canal and receptaculum seminis as in *M. acuminata*. Vitelline glands as in *M. acuminata* in regard to their extent, but consisting of *larger follicles*. Eggs 0.13×0.069 mm., few in number.

Type-specimen in the Australian Museum, No. W. 354.

I have already published an account of this species, in the Proceedings of this Society (7), where a figure of the worm is given. In that figure, the structures marked *d.s.g.*, should be the Laurer's canal. Fig. 4 in this paper is a corrected presentment of the female organs. The general anatomy, and especially the excretory system, are very similar to the descriptions given for *M. acuminata*. It differs from that species principally in the shape of the body, in its smaller size, in the larger size of its spines, in the ratio of the suckers, in the oblique position and more elongated form of the testes, and in the larger and less numerous follicles of the yolk-glands.

Relationship.—These two species seem to me to be related, on the one hand to the Fasciolinæ, and, on the other, to the Echinostominæ and Psilostominæ. They should be looked upon, I think, as members of a sub-family Mehlisiinæ, with, for the present, the characters of the genus, intermediate in position between those groups. They differ from the Fasciolinæ in their form and size, in the simpler form of the gonads and intestinal limbs, for the most part, and especially in the character of their excretory apparatus; while they differ from the Psilostominæ in the absence of a receptaculum seminis, the very large size of the gland of Mehlis, the larger and more complex form of the testes, in the form of the excretory system in some respects, and in the more extended disposition of the yolk-glands. They find their nearest relatives, perhaps, in such forms as *Cotylotretus rugosus* Odhn., (14), and *Mesaulus grandis* R.(5). In determining the phylogenetic relationships of Trematodes, it should be borne in mind that they were parasitic in the early ancestors of the vertebrates, and, owing to the conditions under which their lives are passed, have been much less subjected to evolutionary changes in form than their hosts, so that we should rather expect to find the nearest relatives of trematode parasites of primitive mammals amongst such groups as the Echinostominæ and Psilostominæ parasitic in birds and reptiles.

LITERATURE.

1. BRAUN, M.—"Ueber *Clinostomum* Leidy." Zool. Anz., xxii., 1899.
2. ———.—"Zur Kenntniss der Trematoden der Säugethiere." Zool. Jahrb. (Syst.), xiv., 1901.
3. ———.—"Zur Verständigung über die Gültigkeit einiger Namen von Fascioliden-Gattungen." Zool. Anz., xxiv., 1901.
4. ———.—"Die Arten der Gattung *Clinostomum* Leidy." Zool. Jahrb.(Syst.), xiv., 1901.
5. ———.—"Fascioliden der Vögel." Zool. Jahrb.(Syst.), xvi., 1902.
6. COHN, L.—"Zwei neue Distomen." Centralb. Bakt., xxxii., 1902
7. JOHNSTON, S. J.—"On a new Species of Distomum from the Platypus." Proc. Linn. Soc. N. S. Wales, 1901.
8. LOOSS.—"Weitere Beiträge zur Kenntniss der Trematoden-Fauna Ægyptens, etc." Zool. Jahrb.(Syst.), xii., 899.

9. Looss.—"Die Distomen unserer Fische u. Frosche." Bibliotheca Zoologica, Heft 16, 1896.
10. ———— "Nachträgliche Bemerkungen zu den Namen," etc. Zool. Anz., xxiii., 1900.
11. Lühe.—" Ueber Heminriden." Zool. Anz., xxiv., 1901.
12. ———— " Zur Kenntniss einiger Distomen." Zool. Anz., xxii., 1899.
13. Lutz, A.—" Distoma opisthotrias, ein neuer Parasit der Beutelratte." Revista do Museu Paulista, 1895.
14. Odhner, T.—"Trematoden aus Reptilien." Ofver. Vet. Akad. Forh., Stockholm, lix., 1902.
15. Pratt.—" Synopsis of North American Invertebrates, xii." American Naturalist, xxxvi., 1901.
16. Stiles & Hassall.—" An Inventory of the Genera and Subgenera of the Trematode family Fasciolidæ." Arch. d. Parasitologie, i., 1898.

EXPLANATION OF THE PLATES.

Figures 1-3 are drawings of whole-mounts, made with the help of the camera lucida. Figure 4 is a diagram compiled from a series of transverse sections. These drawings were made by Mr. F. W. Atkins, of the Sydney Technical College. Figures 5-11 are untouched up photographs of sections.

Reference letters.

$C.s.$, cirrus-sac—$C.r.$, ciliated vessel of the excretory system—$Ej.d.$, ejaculatory duct—$E.$, excretory vessel—$E.s_1.$, excretory sinus round the oral sucker—$E.s_2.$, excretory sinus round the ventral sucker—$G.p.$, genital pore—$G.c.$, genital chamber—$Int.$, intestinal limbs—$L.c.$, Laurer's canal—$L.y.d.$, longitudinal yolk-duct—$M.l.$, longitudinal muscle—$M.c.$, circular muscle—$O.$, ovary—$O.c.s.$, opening of ciliated vessel into oral sucker sinus—$O.e.v.$, opening of excretory vessels into the sinus—$O.d.$, Oviduct—$Oot.$, ootype—$P.$, penis—$Ph.$, pharynx—$P.Ph.$, præpharynx—$Pr.$, prostate—$R.s.$, receptaculum seminis—$R.s.u.$, receptaculum seminis uterinum—$S.g.$, " shell-gland "—$S.v.$, supplementary vessel—$T.$, testis—$T.y.d.$, transverse yolk-duct—$Ut.$, uterus—$Ut.a.$, ascending loop of uterus—$Ut.d.$, descending loop of uterus—$Vag.$, vagina—$V.d.$, vas deferens—$V.s.$, vesicula seminalis—$Y.d.$, yolk-duct—$Y.g.$, yolk-glands—$Y.r.$, yolk-reservoir.

Fig. 1.—*Harmostomum dasyuri*, from the intestine of the marsupial "cat," *Dasyurus viverrinus*.
Fig. 2.—*Harmostomum simile*, from the intestine of *Perameles obesula*.
Fig. 3.—*Mehlisia acuminata*, from the intestine of *Dasyurus viverrinus*
Fig. 4.—Diagram of the female organ of *Mehlisia ornithorhynchi*.
Fig. 5.—Horizontal longitudinal section through the posterior end of *H. dasyuri*; (× 45).

Fig. 6.—Transverse section of *H. dasyuri* through ovary, oviduct, and Laurer's canal;(× 110).
Fig. 7.—T.S., *H. dasyuri* (× 180).
Fig. 8.—T.S., *H. dasyuri*;(× 90).
Fig. 9.—T.S., *Mehlisia acuminata*, showing ciliated vessel and supplementary vessel of the excretory system;(× 160).
Fig. 10.—T.S., *M. acuminata*, showing the sinus round the sucker, as well as a number of vessels of the network, together with their opening into the sinus;(× 40).
Fig. 11.—T.S., *M. ornithorhynchi*, showing the arrangement of the muscle layers, the very large shell-gland, etc. ;(× 55).

SPECIAL GENERAL MEETING.
November 27th, 1912.

Mr. W. W. Froggatt, F.L.S., President, in the Chair.

Business: To consider certain proposed alterations in, or additions to, Rules xiv., xvi., xvii., xix.-xxi., xxiii., xxiv., xxvi., xxvii., and lxiii.

Rule xiv., line 3—*Omit the words* by ballot.

Rule xvi. *For the words* five weeks at least prior to the Annual General Meeting—*substitute* held in December.

Rule xvii. *For the words* twenty-one clear days before the Annual General Meeting—*substitute* before the last day of December.

Rule xix. *For the words* nine days at least before the Annual General Meeting for submission to a Council Meeting held one week prior to the Annual General Meeting—*substitute* on or before the twenty-first day of January.

Rule xx. Omit.

Rule xxi., lines 5-6—*Omit the word* balloting: *and for the words* Council at this Meeting—*substitute* Secretary.

Line 7. *Add the words* in alphabetical order.

Last line, *after the word* Auditor—*add* A copy of such lists shall be sent to each member of the Society by posting the same to his ordinary address before the last day of January.

Rule xxiii. Substitute new Rule xxiii.

Rule xxiv. Substitute new Rule xxiv., and new Rule xxiv. bis.

Rule xxvi.—*For the words* months of December and—*substitute* month of.

Rule xxvii., last line—*For the words* unless the Council shall otherwise direct—*substitute* if the Council shall so direct.

Rule lxiii., lines 2-3, and 6-7. *For the words* the majority – *substitute* a majority of three-fourths.

Mr. W. S. Dun moved, and Mr. R. H. Cambage seconded the motion, that the alterations as proposed be adopted.

Mr. A. F. Basset Hull moved the following amendments (seconded by Dr. H. L. Kesteven, and supported by Mr. W. J. Clunies Ross):—

Rule xvi. *Omit all the words after* Meeting *in line* 4.
„ xvii. *Omit* lists, *insert* list.
„ xviii. Omit the Rule.
„ xix. *Omit* Independent *in line* 1.
„ xxii. Omit the Rule.

On being put to the Meeting, the amendments were lost.

The original motion was then put and carried.

SPECIAL GENERAL MEETING.
December 18th, 1912.

Mr. W. W. Froggatt, F.L.S., President, in the Chair.

Business: To confirm the amendments in, and additions to the Rules, passed at the Special General Meeting held on 27th November, 1912.

Mr. W. S. Dun moved, and Mr. R. H. Cambage seconded the motion: that the amendments in, and additions to the Rules, passed at the Special General Meeting held on 27th November, 1912, be confirmed.

On being put to the Meeting, the motion was carried.

DONATIONS AND EXCHANGES.

Received during the period November 30th, 1911, to November 27th, 1912.

(From the respective Societies, etc., unless otherwise mentioned.)

Adelaide.

DEPARTMENT OF AGRICULTURE OF SOUTH AUSTRALIA
  Bulletin No.74[The Poultry Tick. By D. F. Laurie, Government Poultry Expert and Lecturer](1912).

DEPARTMENT OF MINES : GEOLOGICAL SURVEY OF SOUTH AUSTRALIA—
  Review of Mining Operations in the State of South Australia during the Half-years ended December 31st, 1911 and June 30th, 1912, Nos. 15-16(1912).
  Report No. i. The Yelta and Parramatta Mines. By L. Keith Ward, Government Geologist, and R. Lockhart Jack, Assistant Geologist, (1912).

EDUCATION DEPARTMENT OF SOUTH AUSTRALIA—
  An Introduction to the Study of S. Australian Orchids. By R. S. Rodgers, M.A., M.D. Second edition. Published by the Department(8vo. Adelaide, 1911).

PUBLIC LIBRARY, MUSEUM, ETC., OF SOUTH AUSTRALIA—
  Report of the Board of Governors for 1910-11(1912).

ROYAL SOCIETY OF SOUTH AUSTRALIA—
  Transactions and Proceedings, and Report. xxxv.(1911).

WOODS AND FORESTS DEPARTMENT OF SOUTH AUSTRALIA—
  Annual Progress Report upon State Forest Administration for the year 1910-11(1911). By W. Gill, F.L.S., F.R.H.S., Conservator of Forests.

Albany, N.Y.
NEW YORK STATE LIBRARY
Sixty-third Annual Report of the New York State Museum. 1909(in four volumes; 1911).

Amsterdam.
KONINKLIJKE AKADEMIE VAN WETENSCHAPPEN—
Jaarboek, 1910(1911).
Proceedings of the Section of Sciences. xiii.(1910-11).
Verhandelingen. xvi. 4-5(1910).
Verslag van de Gewone Vergaderingen. xix.(1910-11).

Ann Arbor.
UNIVERSITY OF MICHIGAN—
Thirteenth Report of the Michigan Academy of Science. March-April, 1911(1911).

Antwerp.
SOCIETE ROYALE DE GEOGRAPHIE D'ANVERS—
Bulletin. xxxiv., 3-4(1911).

Auckland.
AUCKLAND INSTITUTE AND MUSEUM—
Annual Report. 1911-12(1912).
Transactions of the New Zealand Institute. 191 (191).

Baltimore.
JOHNS HOPKINS UNIVERSITY—
Hospital Bulletin. xxii., 246, 249-250; xxiii., 251-260(1911-12).
University Circulars. 1911, 3-10(1911).

MARYLAND GEOLOGICAL SURVEY—
General Reports. Vol. ix.(1911).
Report on Geology and Palæontology of Maryland : Lower Cretaceous(1911).
Report on Prince George's County : with two maps in portfolio(1911).

Basle.
NATURFORSCHENDE GESELLSCHAFT IN BASEL.—
Verhandlungen. xxii.(1911).

Berkeley, Cal.
  UNIVERSITY OF CALIFORNIA—
    Publications. Botany, iv., 12-15(1912).
                  Geology. Bulletin. vi.,13-19; vii.,1-5(1911-12).
                  Pathology. ii., 4-8(1912).
                  Physiology. iv., 8-16 (1912).
                  Zoology. vii., 10; viii., 3, 8-9; ix., 1-8; x., 1-8(1911-12).
    Reprint: "Commencement Address," by B. I. Wheeler [Univ. Cal. Chronicle, xi., 3].

Berlin.
  DEUTSCHE ENTOMOLOGISCHE GESELLSCHAFT ZU BERLIN—
    Deutsche Entomologische Zeitschrift, 1911, 6; 1912, 1-5(1911-12).
  ENTOMOLOGISCHER VEREIN ZU BERLIN—
    Berliner Entomologische Zeitschrift, lvi., 3-4(1912).
  GESELLSCHAFT F. ERDKUNDE ZU BERLIN—
    Zeitschrift. 1911, 8-10; 1912, 1-7(1911-12).

Berne.
  NATURFORSCHENDE GESELLSCHAFT IN BERN—
    Mitteilungen aus dem Jahre, 1911(1912).
  SOCIETE HELVETIQUE DES SCIENCES NATURELLES
    Actes, 94me. Session, 1911(2 vols: ?1912).

Birmingham.
  BIRMINGHAM NATURAL HISTORY AND PHILOSOPHICAL SOCIETY
    List, 1912; Annual Report for 1911(1912).
    Proceedings, xii., 5(1912).

Bonn.
  NATURHISTORISCHER VEREIN IN BONN—
    Sitzungsberichte. 1910, 2; 1911, 1(1911-12).
    Verhandlungen. lxvii., 2; lxviii., 1(1911-12).

Boston.
  AMERICAN ACADEMY OF ARTS AND SCIENCES—
    Proceedings, xlvi., 25; xlvii., 4-15; xlviii., 1(1911-12).

Boston Society of Natural History
Memoirs. vii.(1912).
Proceedings. xxxiv., 9-12(1910-11).

Bremen.
Naturwissenschaftlicher Verein
Abhandlungen. xxi., 1(1912)

Brisbane.
Colonial Botanist's Department—
Six Separates: "Contributions to the Flora of Queensland" [Queensland Agricultural Journal, March, April, June, August, November, December, 1911].
Department of Agriculture and Stock
Queensland Agricultural Journal, xxvii., 6; xxviii., 1-6; xxix., 1-5(1911-12).
Geological Survey of Queensland—
Publications. Nos. 235(Records, No. 3), 237 (1911-12).
Royal Society of Queensland—
Proceedings. xxiii., 2(1912).

Brooklyn.
Brooklyn Institute of Arts and Sciences—
Science Bulletin. i., No. 17 (1910).

Brussels.
Académie Royale de Belgique—
Annuaire. 78ᵐᵉ. Année(1912).
Bulletin de la Classe des Sciences. 1911, 8-12; 1912, 1-7 (1911-12).
Societe Entomologique de Belgique—
Annales. lv.(1911).
Mémoires. xix.(1912).
Societe Royale Botanique de Belgique—
Bulletin. xlviii., 1911(1911-12).

Budapest.
Museum Nationale Hungaricum—
Annales. ix., 2; x., 1(1911-12).

Buenos Aires.
  MUSEO NACIONAL DE BUENOS AIRES—
    Anales. Serie iii. Tomo xiv.-xv.(1911-12).

Buffalo, U.S.A.
  BUFFALO SOCIETY OF NATURAL SCIENCES—
    Bulletin. x., 1(1910).

Caen.
  SOCIETE LINNEENNE DE NORMANDIE—
    Bulletin. 6°Série. iii.(1911).
    Mémoires. xxiv., 1(1911).

Calcutta.
  GEOLOGICAL SURVEY OF INDIA—
    Records. xlii., 2(1912).
  INDIAN MUSEUM—
    Records. iv., 8-9; vi., 4-5(1911).

Cambridge, England.
  CAMBRIDGE PHILOSOPHICAL SOCIETY—
    List of Fellows, etc., 1912(1912).
    Proceedings. xvi., 3-8(1911-12).
    Transactions, xxi., 15-18; xxii., 1(1911-12).

Cambridge, Mass.
  MUSEUM OF COMPARATIVE ZOOLOGY AT HARVARD COLLEGE—
    Annual Report of the Curator for 1910-11(1911).
    Bulletin. liii., 6-9; liv., 7-15; lv., 1(1911-12).

Cape Town.
  DEPARTMENT OF AGRICULTURE, CAPE OF GOOD HOPE—
    Fifteenth Annual Report of the Geological Commission, 1910(1911).
    Geological Commission: Geological Map of the Colony of the Cape of Good Hope., Sheets 19 and 26(1912).
  SOUTH AFRICAN MUSEUM—
    Annals. vii., 5; ix., 2; x., 2-3; xi., 2(1911-12).
  ROYAL SOCIETY OF SOUTH AFRICA—
    Transactions. ii., 3-4 (1912).

Chicago.
CHICAGO ACADEMY OF SCIENCES
Bulletin, iii., 4-5(1910-11). Special Publication, No.3(1911).
FIELD MUSEUM OF NATURAL HISTORY—
Geological Series. iii., 9(1911).
Report Series, iv., 2(1912).

Christchurch, N.Z.
PHILOSOPHICAL INSTITUTE OF CANTERBURY—
Transactions and Proceedings of the New Zealand Institute, xliv., 1911(1912).

Christiania.
KONGELIGE NORSKE FREDERIKS UNIVERSITET
Archiv for Mathematik og Videnskab. xxvii.-xxxi.(1905-10).

Cincinnati, Ohio.
LLOYD LIBRARY—
Bibliographical Contributions. Nos. 3-6(1911-12).
Bulletin. Nos. 16-20(1911-12).
Synopsis of the Section Ovinus of Polyporus. By C. G. Lloyd(1911).

Colombo, Ceylon.
COLOMBO MUSEUM—
Administration Reports, 1910-11. Part iv., Education and Science(in two parts).
Spolia Zeylanica. viii., 29-30(1911-12).

Columbus, Ohio
BIOLOGICAL CLUB OF THE OHIO STATE UNIVERSITY
Ohio Naturalist. xii., 1-8(1911-12).

Copenhagen.
ACADEMIE ROYALE DES SCIENCES ET DES LETTRES DE DANEMARK—
Bulletin. 1911, 4-6; 1912, 1-3(1911-12).

KJOBENHAVNS UNIVERSITETS ZOOLOGISKE MUSEUM
Danmark-Ekspeditionen til Grönlands Nordöstkyst, 1906-08.
Bind iii., 14; v., 8-9, 11-12(1911-12).
"The Danish Ingolf-Expedition." v., 2(1912).

NATURHISTORISKE FORENING I KJOBENHAVN—
   Videnskabelige Meddelelser for Aaret 1911, lxiii.,(1912).

Decatur, Ill.
AMERICAN MICROSCOPICAL SOCIETY—
   Transactions. xxx.,3-4; xxxi.,1(1911-12).

Dublin.
ROYAL DUBLIN SOCIETY—
   Economic Proceedings. ii., 3-4(1911).
   Scientific Proceedings. New Series. xiii., 11-23(1911-12).
ROYAL IRISH ACADEMY—
   Index to Serial Publications, 1786-1906(1912).
   Proceedings. Section B. xxix., 7-9; xxx., 1-2; xxxi., 2, 10-13, 16-20, 23, 24, 26-31, 35, 36, 40, 41, 43, 44, 46, 53, 56-60, 63, 65(1911-12).

Durham.
UNIVERSITY OF DURHAM PHILOSOPHICAL SOCIETY—
   Proceedings. iii.,4-5; iv.,1-4(1910-12).

Edinburgh.
ROYAL SOCIETY OF EDINBURGH—
   Proceedings. xxxi., 5, T.p., etc.; xxxii., 1-3(1912).
   Transactions. xlviii., 1(1912).

Florence.
SOCIETA ENTOMOLOGICA ITALIANA—
   Bulletino. xlii.,1910(1910).

Frankfurt am Main.
SENCKENBERGISCHE NATURFORSCHENDE GESELLSCHAFT-
   Abhandlungen. xxix., 4; xxxiv., 1-2(1911).
   Bericht, 42, 1911, 1-4(1911).

Freiburg i Br.
NATURFORSCHENDE GESELLSCHAFT ZU FREIBURG I. BR.
   Berichte, xix., 1-2(1911-12).

Garrison, N.Y.
AMERICAN NATURALIST. xlv., Nos.539-540; xlvi., Nos.541-550 (1911-12).

Geneva.
SOCIÉTÉ DE PHYSIQUE ET D'HISTOIRE NATURELLE DE GENÈVE—
Compte Rendu, xxviii., 1911(8vo., 1912).
Mémoires. xxxvii., 3(4to., 1912).

Grahamstown, S. Africa.
ALBANY MUSEUM
Records. ii., 4(1912).

Granville, Ohio.
DENISON UNIVERSITY SCIENTIFIC ASSOCIATION
Bulletin of the Scientific Laboratories. Vols. xvi., pp. 347-423; xvii., pp. 1-20(1911-12).

Graz.
NATURWISSENSCHAFTLICHER VEREIN F. STEIERMARK
Mitteilungen. xlviii., 1911(1912).

Haarlem.
SOCIÉTÉ HOLLANDAISE DES SCIENCES—
Archives Néerlandaises. Série iii. A.i., 3-4(1912).

Hague.
NEDERLANDSCHE ENTOMOLOGISCHE VEREENIGING—
Entomologische Berichten. Deel iii., 61-66(1911-12).
Tijdschrift voor Entomologie. lv., 1-3(1912).

Halifax.
NOVA SCOTIAN INSTITUTE OF SCIENCE—
Proceedings and Transactions, xii.,3; xiii.,1(1912).

Hamilton, Canada.
HAMILTON ASSOCIATION—
Journal and Proceedings, Nos. xxiv.-xxvi., 1908-10(1908-10).

Helder.
NEDERLANDSCHE DIERKUNDIGE VEREENIGING—
Tijdschrift. 2de.Serie. xii.,2(1911).

Helsingfors.
SOCIETAS SCIENTIARIUM FENNICA—
Acta. xxxviii., 4, 5; xl., 6, Minnestal; xli., 2-7(1911-12).

Bidrag till Kännedom, 69, 70(1-2), 71 (1-2), 72 (3), 73 (2), (1911-12).
Erdmagnetische Untersuchungen. Band i., Teil i., 1910(1911).
Meteorologisches Jahrbuch für Finlande. Beilage zum Jahrg., 1904, 1905; Band v., 1905; Band vi., 1906; Band x., Teil 2, 1910(1911-12).
Oefersigt. liii., 1910-11, Afd. A, Afd. C(1911).
Tables Générales des Publications, 1838-1910(1912).

SOCIETAS PRO FAUNA ET FLORA FENNICA—
Acta. xxxiii.-xxxv., No.1(1909-11).
Meddelanden. xxxvi.-xxxvii.(1910-11).

Hobart.
DEPARTMENT OF MINES—
Progress of the Mineral Industry of Tasmania for the Quarters ending 30th September and 31st December, 1911; 31st March and 30th June, 1911(1911-12).
Geological Survey Bulletins. Nos. 10-12 (1911-12).
Geological Survey Report, No.2(1911).
Report of the Secretary of Mines for the Years 1910, 1911 (1911-12).

ROYAL SOCIETY OF TASMANIA—
Annual Report for 1911(n.d.).
Papers and Proceedings, 1911(n.d.).

Honolulu, T.H.
BERNICE PAUAHI BISHOP MUSEUM—
Memoirs, iii., Text and Plates(1911).
Occasional Papers. iv., 5, Tp., etc.; v., 1-2(1911-12).

COLLEGE OF HAWAII
Publications: Bulletin No.1(1911).

Indianapolis, Ind.
INDIANA ACADEMY OF SCIENCE—
Proceedings. 1910(1911).

Jena.
MEDICINISCH-NATURWISSENSCHAFTLICHE GESELLSCHAFT—
Jenaische Zeitschrift. xlvii., 4; xlviii., 1-3(1911-12).

Lansing, Mich.
   MICHIGAN ACADEMY OF SCIENCE—
   Thirteenth Report(1911).

   MICHIGAN STATE AGRICULTURAL COLLEGE EXPERIMENT STATION.
   Division of Bacteriology and Hygiene—Technical Bulletin. Nos. 8-10—Report of the Bacteriologist, 1911(1911). *From Dr. C. Marshall.*

Leipsic.
   ZOOLOGISCHER ANZEIGER. xxxviii.,18-26; xxxix.,1-26; xl.,1-11 (1911-12). *From the Publishers.*

Liege.
   SOCIETE GEOLOGIQUE DE BELGIQUE—
   Annales. xxxvii., 4; xxxviii., 1-3(1911).

London.
   BOARD OF AGRICULTURE AND FISHERIES—
   Annual Report of Proceedings under the Salmon and Fresh-water Fisheries Act for the Year 1910(1911).
   Journal of the Board of Agriculture. xviii., 8-12, and Supplement No. 7; xix., 1-7 and Supplement Nos. 8-9(1911-12).
   Leaflets: Nos.241, 251, 258-263(1911-12).

   ENTOMOLOGICAL SOCIETY—
   Transactions. 1911(1911-12).

   GEOLOGICAL SOCIETY—
   Geological Literature added to the Society's Library during the year ended December 31st, 1910(1911).
   List, April, 1912(1912).
   Quarterly Journal. lxvii., 3-4; lxviii., 1-3(1911-12).

   LINNEAN SOCIETY—
   Journal. *Botany.* xxxix., 274, T.p., etc.; xl., 276-278; xli., 279(1911-12). *Zoology.* xxxi.,208; xxxii.,212-13(1911-12).
   List of the Society. 1911-12(1911).
   Proceedings, 123rd Session, 1910-11(1911).
   Transactions. Second Series. *Botany.* vii., 16-18(1912).—*Zoology.* xi., 8-10; xiv., 2-4; xv., 1(1912).

ROYAL BOTANIC GARDENS, KEW—
 Bulletin of Miscellaneous Information, 1911(1911).
 Hooker's Icones Plantarum. Fourth Series. x., 3(1911).
 From the Bentham Trustees.
ROYAL MICROSCOPICAL SOCIETY—
 Journal. 1911,6; 1912,1-4(1911-12).
ROYAL SOCIETY—
 Philosophical Transactions. Series B.ccii., 287-293; cciii., 294-295(1911-12).
 Proceedings. Series B. lxxxiv., 572-575; lxxxv., 576-582 (1911-12).
ZOOLOGICAL SOCIETY—
 Abstract of Proceedings. Nos. 100-111(1911-12).
 List of Fellows, May, 1912(1912).
 Proceedings. 1911, 4; 1912, 1-3(1911-12).
 Transactions. xx., 1-2(1912).

Lyons.
SOCIETE BOTANIQUE DE LYON—
 Annales. xxxv.-xxxvi., 1910-11(1911).

Madison, Wis.
WISCONSIN ACADEMY OF SCIENCES, &c.—
 Transactions. xvi., Part ii., Nos.1-6(1909-10).

Madrid.
REAL SOCIEDAD ESPANOLA DE HISTORIA NATURAL—
 Boletin. xi., 8-10; xii., 1-7(1911-12).
 Memorias. vii., 1-3; viii., 1-2(1911-12).

Manchester.
MANCHESTER LITERARY AND PHILOSOPHICAL SOCIETY—
 Memoirs and Proceedings. lv.,3; lvi.,1-2(1911-12).
UNIVERSITY OF MANCHESTER: MANCHESTER MUSEUM—
 Publications of the Manchester Museum. No. 72(1911).

Manila, P.I.
BUREAU OF SCIENCE OF THE GOVERNMENT OF THE PHILIPPINE ISLANDS—
 Philippine Journal of Science. A.(Chemical and Geological Sciences and the Industries). vi., 4-6; vii., 1-2, and Memo-

rial Number(1911-12). B.(Medical Sciences). vi.,4-6; vii., 1-2(1911-12). —C.(Botany). vi.,5-6; vii.,1-4(1911-12). —D. (Ethnology, Anthropology, and General Biology). vi.,5-6; vii.f1-3(1911-12).

Tenth Annual Report of the Bureau of Science, 1910-11 (1912).

Bureau of Science, &c.: Division of Geology and Mines
Geologic Reconnaissance Map of Mindanao(?1912).

Department of the Interior: Bureau of Forestry
Annual Report of the Director, 1910-11(1911).

Marseilles.

Faculté des Sciences de Marseille—
Annales. xviii., xx., et Supplément(1909-12).

Massachusetts.

Tufts College—
Tufts College Studies. Scientific Series. iii.,2(1912).

Melbourne.

Australasian Journal of Pharmacy—
Vols. xxvi., 312; xxvii., 313-317, 319-322(1911-12). *From the Publisher.*

Royal Australasian Ornithologists' Union—
Bulletin No. 3(1912).
"The Emu." xi., 3-4; xii., 1-2(1912).

Commonwealth of Australia: Minister of Trade and Customs—
Fisheries: Zoological Results of the Fishing Experiments carried out by the F.I.S. "Endeavour," 1909-10(H. C. Dannevig, Commonwealth Director of Fisheries). Parts i.-iii.(1911-12).

Commonwealth Bureau of Census and Statistics—
Official Year-Book of the Commonwealth of Australia. No. 5, 1901-11(1912).

Department of Agriculture of Victoria—
Journal. ix., 11-12; x., 1-11(1911-12).

FIELD NATURALISTS' CLUB OF VICTORIA—
   Victorian Naturalist. xxviii., 7-12; xxix., 1-7(1911-12).
NATIONAL MUSEUM—
   Memoirs. No.4(1912).
PUBLIC LIBRARY, MUSEUMS, &c., OF VICTORIA—
   Report of the Trustees for 1911(1912).
ROYAL GEOGRAPHICAL SOCIETY OF AUSTRALASIA : VICTORIAN
      BRANCH—
   Victorian Geographical Journal. xxviii.,1910-11(1911).
ROYAL SOCIETY OF VICTORIA—
   Proceedings. New Series. xxiv., 2; xxv., 1(1912).
UNIVERSITY OF MELBOURNE—
   Calendar. 1912(1911).

Mexico.
INSTITUTO GEOLOGICO DE MEXICO—
   Boletin. Num. 28(1911).
   Parergones. iii., 9-10(1911).

Modena.
LA NUOVA NOTARISIA—*From the Editor, Dr. G. B. De Toni.*
   Serie xxiii. Gennaio, Aprile, Luglio, Ottobre, 1912(1912).

Monaco.
MUSEE OCEANOGRAPHIQUE DE MONACO—
   Bulletin. viii., 218-219, T.p.etc.; ix., 220-246(1911-12).

Montreal.
ROYAL SOCIETY OF CANADA—
   Proceedings and Transactions. Third Series. v.,1911(1912).

Moscow.
SOCIETE IMPERIALE DES NATURALISTES—
   Bulletin. Année 1910,4(1911).

Munich.
KONIGLICHE BAYERISCHE AKADEMIE DER WISSENSCHAFTEN
   Abhandlungen der Math.-physikal. Classe. xxv., 6-8(1911-12).
   Supplement Band ii., 5-7(1911-12).

Sitzungsberichte der Math.-physikal. Classe. 1911, 1-3; 1912, 1(1911-12).

Nantes.
SOCIETE DES SCIENCES NATURELLES DE L'OUEST DE LA FRANCE—
Bulletin. 2me.Série. x.,4; 3me.Série. i.,1-4(1910-11).

Naples.
ZOOLOGISCHE STATION ZU NEAPEL—
Mittheilungen. xx., 3(1912).

MUSEO ZOOLOGICO DELLA R. UNIVERSITA DI NAPOLI—
Annuario(Nuova Serie). iii.,13-27,T.p.,&c.(1912).

New Haven, Conn.
CONNECTICUT ACADEMY
Transactions. xvi., pp. 117-245; xvii., pp. 1-139, 141-211(1910-12).

New York.
AMERICAN GEOGRAPHICAL SOCIETY—
Bulletin. xliii., 11-12; xliv., 1-9(1911-12).

AMERICAN MUSEUM OF NATURAL HISTORY—
Annual Report [Forty-third] for the Year 1911(1912).
Bulletin. xxx.(1911).

NEW YORK ACADEMY OF SCIENCES—
Annals. xx.,3; xxi.pp 87-263, T.p.,&c.(1910-12).

Ottawa.
GEOLOGICAL SURVEY OF CANADA—
Publications: Memoirs, Nos. 9E, 16E, 15P, 24E, 27, 28 [Nos. 1130, 1150, 1113, 1204, 1211, 1213](1911-12)—Geological Maps 13A, 14A, Province of Nova Scotia [Nos. 1133,1134] (1910-11).

Oxford.
RADCLIFFE LIBRARY, OXFORD UNIVERSITY MUSEUM—
Catalogue of Books added during 1911(1912).

Palo Alto, Cal.
LELAND STANFORD JUNIOR UNIVERSITY—
Publications. University Series. Nos. 5-6(1911).

Paris.
  Journal de Conchyliologie. lix.,1-4, lx.,1(1911-12).
  Museum d'Histoire Naturelle—
    Bulletin. Année 1910, 6-7; 1911, 1-6(1910-11).
    Nouvelles Archives. 5me.Série. ii.,1-2; iii.,1-2(1910-11).
  Société Entomologique de France—
    Annales. lxxvii., 1(1908); lxxx., 1-4; lxxxi., 1(1911-12).
    Bulletin, 1907, 1908, 1909, 1910, 1911, 1912, Nos. 1-14(1907-1912).
    Faune des Coléoptères du Basin de la Seine. iv.,1,Scarabeidæ (1911).
  Société Zoologique de France—
    Bulletin. xxxv.-xxxvi.(1910-11).
    Mémoires. xxiii.(1910).

Pavia.
  Istituto Botanico dell'Universita di Pavia—
    Atti. ii. Serie. Vol. ix.(1911).

Perth, W.A.
  Geological Survey of West Australia—
    Annual Progress Report for the Year 1911(1912).
    Topographical Map of Meekatharra(1911).
  Government Statistician, West Australia—
    Monthly Statistical Abstract. 1911, Nos. 137-138; 1912, Nos. 139-148(1911-12).
  Natural History and Science Society of W.A.—
    Journal. iii.,1-2(1910-11).
  West Australian Museum and Art Gallery—
    Records. i.,2(1912).

Philadelphia.
  Academy of Natural Sciences—
    Proceedings. lxii., 2; lxiii., 2-3; lxiv., 1(1910-12).
  American Philosophical Society—
    Proceedings. l., 199-202, T.p.&c.; li., 204(1911-12).
    Transactions. N.S. xxii., 1(1911).

University of Pennsylvania—
  Contributions from the Botanical Laboratory. iii., 3(1911).
  Contributions from the Zoological Laboratory for 1911, xvii. (1912).
Zoological Society of Philadelphia—
  Fortieth Annual Report of the Board of Directors, April, 1912(1912).

Pietermaritzburg.
Natal Government Museum—
  Annals. ii., 3(1912).

Plymouth.
Marine Biological Association of the United Kingdom—
  Journal. N.S. ix.,2-3(1911-12).

Portici.
Laboratorio di Zoologia Generale e Agraria della R. Scuola Superiore d'Agricoltura in Portici—
  Bollettino. vi.(1912).

Prague.
Societas Entomologica Bohemiæ—
  Acta. viii.,2-4; ix.,1-2(1911-12).

Pusa, India.
Agricultural Research Institute—
  Memoirs of the Department of Agriculture in India. *Botanical Series.* iv., 3-6(1912). *Entomological Series,* ii., 9; iv., 1-3(1912)—Report of the Agricultural Research Institute, 1910-11(1912)—Report on the Progress of Agriculture in India for 1910-11(1912).

Richmond, N.S.W.
Hawkesbury Agricultural College—
  H. A. C. Journal. ix., 1-3, 5-11 (1911-12).

Rio de Janeiro.
Museo Nacional do Rio de Janeiro—
  Archivos. xiii.-xv.(1905-09).

Rock Island, Ill.
AUGUSTANA COLLEGE—
Augustana Library Publications. No.7(1910).

St. Louis.
MISSOURI BOTANICAL GARDEN—
Twenty-second Annual Report, 1911(1911).

St. Petersburg.
ACADEMIE IMPERIALE DES SCIENCES—
Annuaire du Musée Zoologique. 1910, xv., 3; 1911, xvi., 3 (1910-11).
Bulletin. 6^eSérie. 1911, 14-18; 1912, 1-13(1911-12).
Faune de la Russie et des Pays Limitrophes—Aves, Vol. i., Pt.1; Hydroidea, i.; Marsipobranchii et Pisces, i.(1911).
Schedæ ad Herbarium Rossicæ. No.vii.(1911).
Travaux du Musée Botanique. Nos.8-9(1911-12).

COMITE GEOLOGIQUE (INSTITUT DES MINES)—
Bulletins. xxx., 1-5(1911-1911).
Mémoires. Nouvelle Série. Livraisons 61, 67, 71, 73(1911).

RUSSISCH-KAISERLICHE MINERALOGISCHE GESELLSCHAFT—
Verhandlungen. Zweite Serie. xlvii.(1909).

SOCIETAS ENTOMOLOGICA ROSSICA—
Horæ Entomologicæ. xl., 1-2(1911).
Revue Russe d'Entomologie. xi., 3-4; xii., 1(1911-12).

San Francisco.
CALIFORNIA ACADEMY OF NATURAL SCIENCES—
Proceedings. Fourth Series. i., pp. 289-430; iii., pp. 73-186 (1911-12).

Santiago de Chile.
MUSEO NACIONAL DE CHILE—
Boletin. ii., 2(1910).

Sendai, Japan.
TOHOKU IMPERIAL UNIVERSITY—
Science Reports, i.,1(1912).

Stockholm
  ENTOMOLOGISKA FORENINGEN I STOCKHOLM—
    Alfabetiskt Register, Arganogaran 11-30, 1890-1909(1911).
    Entomologisk Tidskrift. xxxii., 1-4 (1911).
  KONGL. SVENSKA VETENSKAPS-AKADEMIE—
    Arkiv f. *Botanik*. x., 2-4(1911).—*Kemi*. iv., 2(1911)
      Mathematik, Astronomi och Fysik. vi., 4; vii., 1-2(1911).
    Arsbok, 1911(1911).
    Handlingar, N.F. xlvi., 4-11, T.p.&c.: xlvii., 1(1911).
    Les Prix Nobel en 1909, en 1910(1910-11).
    Meddelanden från K. Vetenskapsakademiens Nobelinstitut.
      ii., 1(1909-11).
  ZOOTOMISCHER INSTITUT DER UNIVERSITAET ZU STOCKHOLM—
    Arbeiten. Band viii.(1912).

Stuttgart.
  VEREIN F. VATERLAENDISCHE NATURKUNDE IN WUERTTEMBERG—
    Jahreshefte. lxvii. Jahrgang nebst eine Beilage(1911).

Sydney, N.S.W.
  AUSTRALIAN MUSEUM—
    Annual Report, 1910-11(1911).
    Memoir iv., 16(1911).
    Miscellaneous Series. No. vii.,(1912).
    Records. viii., 3; ix., 1(1912).
    Special Catalogue No. i. iii., 4-5, T.p.&c.(1912).
  BOTANIC GARDENS AND DOMAINS, SYDNEY—
    Annual Report for 1910(1911).
    Critical Revision of the Genus *Eucalyptus*. ii., 4-6(1912).
      By J. H. Maiden, Government Botanist, &c.
  BUREAU OF STATISTICS—
    Official Year-Book of New South Wales, 1911(1912).
  CHIEF SECRETARY'S DEPARTMENT: FISHERIES BRANCH—
    Two Pamphlets, by D. G. Stead, F.L.S.: "On the Need of
      more Uniformity in the Vernacular Names of Australian

Edible Fishes," and "The Future of Commercial Marine Fishing in New South Wales" (8vo., Sydney, 1911).

DEPARTMENT OF AGRICULTURE, N.S.W.—
Agricultural Gazette of New South Wales. xxii.,12; xxiii., 1-11(1911-12).
Science Bulletin. Nos. 1, 2, 8(1912).

DEPARTMENT OF AGRICULTURE, FOREST BRANCH, N.S.W.—
Forest Flora of New South Wales. By J. H. Maiden, Government Botanist, &c. v., 6-9(1911-12).
Report of the Forestry Branch for the Year ended 30th June, 1911(1912).
Report of the Proceedings of the Interstate Conference on Forestry, Sydney, November, 1911(1912).

DEPARTMENT OF MINES—
Annual Report of the Department of Mines for 1911(1912).
"Coal Resources of New South Wales." By E. F. Pittman, Government Geologist(1912).
Mineral Resources. Nos.15-16(1911-12).

DEPARTMENT OF PUBLIC INSTRUCTION—
Public Instruction Gazette of New South Wales, v.,2-12; vi.,1-10 and Supplement [Bird League No.](1911-12).

DEPARTMENT OF PUBLIC INSTRUCTION: TEACHER'S COLLEGE—
Records of the Education Society. Nos.11-13(1911-12).
Teachers' College Calendar, 1912(1912).

DEPARTMENT OF PUBLIC INSTRUCTION TECHNICAL EDUCATION BRANCH—
Annual Report, 1910(1911).
Technical Gazette of New South Wales, ii.,1-3(1912).

GOVERNMENT BUREAU OF MICROBIOLOGY—
Second Report, 1910-11(1912).

HARRINGTON'S PHOTOGRAPHIC JOURNAL. xx.,235; xxi.,236-239, 241-246(1911-12).

INSTITUTION OF SURVEYORS, N.S.W.—
"The Surveyor." xxiv.,11-12; xxv.,1-10(1911-12).

николай South Wales Naturalists' Club—
"Australian Naturalist." ii.,9-12(1912).

Royal Anthropological Society of Australasia—
"Science of Man" N.S. xiii.,8-11(1911-12).

Royal Society of New South Wales—
Journal and Proceedings. xlv.,2-4(1912).

University of Sydney—
Calendar, 1912(1912).

Tokyo.

College of Science, Imperial University of Tokyo—
Journal. xxix.,2; xxx.,1-2; xxxi.; xxxii.,1-7(1911-12).

Tokyo Zoological Society—
Annotationes Zoologicæ Japonenses. viii.,1(1912).

Toronto.

Canadian Institute—
Transactions. ix.,2(1912).

Trondhjem.

Kongelige Norske Videnskapers Selskap—
Fortegnlse over Selskapets Skrifter, 1760-1910(1912).
Skrifter, 1910, 1911(1911-12).

Tunis.

Institut Pasteur de Tunis—
Archives. 1911,4; 1912,1-3(1911-12).

Turin.

Museo di Zoologia, &c., della R. Universita di Torino—
Bolletino. xxvi., Nos.634-644(1911).

Upsal.

Kongl. Universitets-Bibliotheket i Upsal—
Bref och Skrifvelser af och till Carl von Linné med Understöd af Svenska Staten utgifna af Upsala Universitet. Första Afdl. Del vi.(1912).—Bulletin of the Geological Institution of the University of Upsala. Vol. xi.(1912)—Results of the Swedish Zoological Expedition to Egypt and the White Nile. Part iv.(1911).

Vienna.
K. K. NATURHISTORISCHES HOFMUSEUM IN WIEN
Annalen. xxv.,1-4; xxvi.,1-2(1911-12).

K. K. ZOOLOGISCH-BOTANISCHE GESELLSCHAFT
Verhandlungen. lxi.,7-10; lxii.,1-4(1911-12).

Washington, D.C.
BUREAU OF AMERICAN ETHNOLOGY —
Annual Report, xxvii., 1905-06(1911).
Bulletin. Nos.44, 51(1911).

CARNEGIE INSTITUTION OF WASHINGTON
Department of Experimental Evolution : Annual Report of the Director, 1911[Reprint from Year Book No. x.].
Publications, Nos.143-144(1911).

SMITHSONIAN INSTITUTION —
Annual Report of the Board of Regents for the Year ending June 30th, 1910(1911).

U. S. DEPARTMENT OF AGRICULTURE—
Bureau of Animal Industry: Bulletin, Nos.39, Parts xxxiii., xxxiv., xxxvi., 127, 130, 132, 137, 138, 141, 193, 196(1911-12). Twenty-sixth and Twenty-seventh Annual Reports, 1909, 1910(1911-12).
Bureau of Biological Survey: Bulletin, Nos. 36, 38, 41(1910-12).—Circular, Nos.81,84(1911).—North American Fauna, No.34(1911).
Bureau of Chemistry: Bulletin, Nos. 145(revd.), 149(1912). Circular, Nos. 75, 78(1911-12).
Bureau of Entomology: Bulletin, Nos.75 Pt.iii., Contents of No.80, Index to No.91, 95 Pts.iv.-vi., 96 Pts.iv.-v., 97 Pts. iv., vi., vii., 98, 100, 102, 108, 109 Pts. iv.-vi., 112, 115 Pt.i., 116 Pt.i.(1908-12). Circular, Nos.143-161(1912).— Technical Series, Nos.19 Pts.iv.-v., 20 Pt.v., 22, 23 Pts.i.-ii., 24, 25 Pt.i.(1912).
Bureau of Plant Industry: Bulletin, Nos.196, 201, 230, 235 (1910-12).—Circular, Nos.76, 80, 85(1911).
Bureau of Soils: Bulletin, Nos. 68, 71, 84(1911-12).

Division of Publications: Circular, Nos.11-18(1911).
Document No.305(1912).
Farmers' Bulletin, Nos.421, 423, 428, 456, 476, 483, 487, 492, 500, 503(1910-12).
Forest Service: Bulletin, Nos.83, 86, 89, 91, 92, 103(1910-11). - Circular, Nos.23(5th revn.), 179(1910-11).
Office of Experiment Stations: Bulletin, 231, 238(1910-11).—Circular, No.106(1911).—Experiment Station Record, Vol. xxiii., 6-8; xxiv., 1-8; xxv., 1-6; xxvi., 1(1910-12).
Office of Public Roads: Bulletin, No.37(1911).
Office of the Secretary: Circular, No.38(1911).—Report of the Secretary, 1910(1910).
Year-Book, 1911(1912).

U. S. GEOLOGICAL SURVEY—
Bulletin. Nos.431, 449-452, 454-464, 467-469, 472-483, 486-490, 495(1911).
Mineral Resources, 1909, Parts i.-ii.(1911).
Monograph. lii.(1911).
Professional Papers. Nos.70, 73, 75(1911).
Water Supply and Irrigation Papers. Nos.256, 261, 263, 265-269, 272-277(1911).

U. S. NATIONAL MUSEUM—
Annual Report for the Year ending June 30th, 1911(1912).
Bulletin. Nos.50 Pt.v., 76, 77(1911).
Contributions from the U. S. National Herbarium. xiii.,10-12; xiv.,3; xvi.1(1911-12).
Proceedings. xxxix. xl.(1911).

WASHINGTON ACADEMY OF SCIENCES—
Proceedings. xiii.(1911).

Wellington, N.Z.
DEPARTMENT OF EDUCATION—
"New Zealand Plants and their Story." By L. Cockayne, Ph.D., F.L.S,(8vo. Wellington, 1910).— "Geology of New Zealand." By P. Marshall, D.Sc., M.A.(8vo. Wellington, 1912).

DEPARTMENT OF MINES: GEOLOGICAL SURVEY OF NEW ZEALAND.
Bulletin. New Series. Nos.8-13(1909-11).
Third, Fourth, and Fifth Annual Reports [New Series] (1909-11).

PRIVATE DONORS.

ANDERSON, W., F.R.S.E., F.G.S., Cape Town—One Separate: "On the Occurrence of skeletal Dinosaurian Remains in a Series of Sandstones and Shales, at the Stypstee Drift, Compies River, &c.(April, 1912).

DANES, Dr. J. V., Czech University, Prague—Four Separates: (a) "Physiography of some Limestone Areas in Queensland" [Proc. R. Soc. Queensland, xxiii., 1910]; (b) "Geographical and Politicoeconomical Problems of the Commonwealth of Australia"[Bulletin of the Bohemian Geog. Soc. 1910]; (c) "On the Physiography of Northeastern Australia"[Proc. Roy. Bohemian Soc. Scis., 1911]; (d) "Absence de traces glaciaires dans la Californie méridionale [La Géographie, Bull. Soc. Géog., Paris, xix., 1909].

FROGGATT, W.W., F.L.S., Sydney—Five Entomological Separates from the Agricultural Gazette of New South Wales, 1911-12 [Miscellaneous Publications, Nos. 1428, 1523, 1537, 1544, 1554].- One Pamphlet[Bulletin No.3, Dept. Agric. N. S. Wales, 1911].

GILRUTH, J. A., D.V.Sc., F.R.S.E., Darwin: One Separate: "The Introduction and Spread of the Cattle-Tick, and of the associated Disease, Tick-fever in Australia"[Proc. R. Soc. Victoria, xxv.(N.S), 1912].

———— ———— and Sweet, Georgina, D.Sc.—One Separate: "Further Observations on Onchocerca Gibsoni, the Cause of Worm-nodules in Cattle"[Proc. R. Soc. Victoria, xxv. (N.S.), 1912].

HALLIGAN, G. H., F.G.S., Sydney—Three Separates (in one), with Discussion on the Papers: "The Bar-Harbours of New South Wales," by G. H. Halligan; "Sand-Movements at Newcastle Entrance, N.S.W.," by C. W. King; "Fremantle Harbour Works, W.A.," by C. S. R. Palmer [Proc. Inst. Civil Engineers, Session 1910-11].

LAWRENCE, Sir E. DURNING, Bt., London—One Pamphlet: "The Shakespeare Myth"[8vo. London, 1912].

MARSHALL, Dr. C., Ann Arbor, U.S.A. One Reprint: "Society of American Bacteriologists, December, 1911" [Science, xxxv., March, 1912].

OOBORN, Prof. T. G., B.Sc., University of Adelaide Five Separates: (1) "The Scab Diseases of Potatoes" [Ann. Rept. and Proc. Manchester Microscop. Soc., 1909]; (2-3) "Dowels of some Egyptian Coffins of the xii.th Dynasty," and "A Note on the submerged Forest at Llanaber, Barmouth" [Mem. and Proc. Manchester Lit. Phil. Soc. liii., and lvi., 1909, 1912]; (4) "Spongospora subterranea (Wallroth) Johnson" [Ann. Bot., xxv., April, 1911]; (5) "Preliminary Observations on the Mildew of Grey Cloth(Journ. Economic Biology, vii., June, 1912].

OSBORN, Mrs. T. G., M.Sc.(née Miss E. M. Kershaw, M.Sc.), Adelaide Two Separates: (1-2) "A Fossil Solenostelic Fern," and "Structure and Development of the Ovule of Bowenia spectabilis" [Ann. Bot. xxiv., and xxvi., October, 1910, July, 1912].

[Printed off 10th July, 1913.]

INDEX.
(1912.)
(a) GENERAL INDEX.

Aboriginal remains, exhibited, 236.
—————— traditions about the Nambucca River, 236.
Acarids from a bull's hide, exhibited, 591.
Acorn, with four cotyledons, exhibited, 492.
Action of Fat-Solvents upon Sewage-sick Soils, 238.
Address of the President (W. W. Froggatt), March 27th, 1912, 1.
Agrionidae, on some new and rare Australian, 404.
Algae, Australian Marine, Supplementary List of, 157.
Allandale, N.S.W., glendonites from exhibited, 493.
Alstonville, N.S.W., tubers of Eupomatia from, exhibited, 558.
Amycterides, Revision of, Part ii., 83.
Anemone, abnormal flower of, exhibited, 557.
Anisoptera, Australian, Descriptions of New Species, 572.
Announcements, 136, 235, 282, 390, 590, 652.
Apple, Fibrovascular System of Quince Fruit compared with that of, 689.
Apples, Bitter Pit of, 10.
Apricot tree, remarks on the effect of burning on, 136.
Aru Island, two new Species of Ichneumonidae from, 217.
Aurousseau, Marcel, elected a Member, 235.
Australasian Association for the Advancement of Science, announcement, 390, 652.
Australia, Sphagna of, 383.
—————— Supplementary list of Marine Algae of, 157.

Australian Agrionidae, new and rare, 404.
—————— Anisoptera, Descriptions of new, 572.
—————— Bees, i., 594.
—————— *Cicadidae*, Synonymical Notes on, 600.
—————— *Curculonidae*, Subfam. Cryptorhynchides, Revision of, Part ix., 602.
—————— Flora, Hydrocyanic Acid in plants of the, 220.
—————— Frogs, Trematode Parasites of, 285.
—————— *Lycaenidae*, Notes on, Part v., 698.
—————— Species of the genus *Crocisa*, 594.

Bacteriologist, Macleay, to the Society, Résumé of year's work, 3.
Baker (R. T.). On two unrecorded Myrtaceous Plants from New South Wales, 585.
—————— Re-elected to the Council, 43.
—————— See Exhibits.
Balance Sheet, 1911, 44.
Barraba to Nandewar Mountains and Boggabri, flora of, 622.
Bees, Australian, of the genus *Crocisa*, 594.
——, A Collection of, from Tasmania, 596.
Bell, N.S.W., rare Acacia from, exhibited, 591.
Bernier Island, W.A., rare Cicadas from, exhibited, 394.
Betche (E.), and Maiden (J. H.). Notes from the Botanic Gardens, No. 17, 244.
Bickford (E. I.). *See* Exhibits.

Bitter Pit of Apples, reference to, 10.
Blackall Range, Q., trap-door nests of spiders from, exhibited, 496.
Blackburn (Dr. C. B.). Letter of thanks for sympathy from, 282.
———— (Rev. T.). Notice of his decease, 235.
Blacktown, a western Grass from, introduced with stock, exhibited, 559.
Boggabri, flora. *See* Barraba to Nandewar Mountains and Boggabri, flora of, 622.
Bog-moss, used for packing Trout-ova, exhibited, 283.
Botanic Gardens, Sydney, Notes from, No. 17, 244.
————————————Water-rat from, exhibited, 493.
Breakwell (E.). Elected a Member, 136.
Brewster (Miss A. A.). Elected a Member, 282.
Brotherus (V. F.) and Watts (Rev. W. W.). The Mosses of the Yarrangobilly Caves District, N.S.W., 363.
Buprestidae, Descriptions of new Species of, 497.
Burbury (F. E.). Elected a Member, 652.
Burragorang, flora. *See* Camden to Burragorang flora, 617.
Burrinjuck, N.S.W., Mistletoes from, exhibited, 137.
Butterflies, aberrant, exhibited, 558.
———————— rare, exhibited, *Cyclopides croites* from W.A., 236— *Euploea corinna* from Sydney to Port Darwin, 494.

Cadell (Miss M.). Elected a Member, 652.
"Caltrops," weed introduced by stock-trains, exhibited, 558.
Cambage (R. H.). Notes on the Native Flora of New South Wales: Supplementary Lists to Part viii., Camden to Burragorang and Mount Werong, 617.
————————. Part ix., Barraba to Nandewar Mountains and Boggabri, 622.
Camden to Burragorang and Mt. Werong, flora of, 541.
Cameron (P.). Descriptions of two new Species of *Ichneumonidae* from the Island of Aru, 217.
————————. On a Collection of Parasitic Hymenoptera (chiefly bred), made by Mr. W. W. Froggatt in New South Wales, with Descriptions of new Genera and Species, Part iii., 172.
Campbell (J. H.). Hon. Treasurer's Financial Statement, 43.
————————. Re-elected Hon Treasurer, 136.
Carboniferous and Devonian Formations west of Tamworth, Note on the Relation of, 703.
Carne (J. E.). Notice of his Visit to New Guinea, 10.
Carter (H. J.). Descriptions of some new species of Coleoptera, 480.
————————. Notes on the Genus *Stigmodera*, with Descriptions of eleven new Species, and of other *Buprestidae*, 497.
Cayzer (A.). Elected a Member, 136.
Central Pacific Ocean, *Molacanthus* from, 553.
Chapman (H. G.). Observations on the effect of burning on an apricot-tree, 136.
————————. *See* Exhibits.
Cheel (E.). *See* Exhibits.
Chemistry of *Doryphora sassafras*, 139.
Chenopod, causing fibre-balls in sheep, exhibited, 394.
Cicada injurious to fruit- and forest-trees, exhibited, 654.
Cicadas from Bernier Island, and Perth, W.A., exhibited, 394.
Cicadidae, Synonymical Notes on recently described, 600.
Cleland (J. B.). Elected to the Council, 235.
————————. Note on the Scent of the Grass *Eragrostis leptostachya*, 391.
————————. *See* Exhibits.
Cockatoo, Great Black Palm, hard seeds eaten by, exhibited, 493.

INDEX.

Cockerell (T. D. A.). A small Collection of Bees from Tasmania, 596.

——————. Australian Bees, i., A new *Crocisa*, with a List of the Australian Species of the Genus, 594.

Coleoptera, Descriptions of some new, 480.

——————, *Buprestidae*, Notes on and Descriptions of, 497.

Collarenebri, N.S.W., trap-door nests of spiders from, exhibited, 496.

Colo, Specimens of "Kangaroo Grass" from, exhibited, 393.

Constitution of the Gastropod Protoconch, etc., 49.

Contributions to our Knowledge of Soil-Fertility, No. v., 238; No. vi., 655.

Cooktown, rare dragon-fly from, exhibited, 590.

Copepod, a new Endoparasitic: Morphology and Development, 673.

Cotton (L. A.) and Walkom (A.B.). Note on the Relation of the Devonian and Carboniferous Formations west of Tamworth, N.S.W., 703.

Council, Elections to, 43, 235.

Cox (Dr. J. C.). Message of sympathy to, in illness, 492,—Letter of thanks from, 556—Notice of his decease, 593.

Crocisa, Description of a new, 594.

——————, List of the Australian Species of, 594.

Cryptorhynchides, Revision of the Subfamily, Part xi., 602.

Cudgen, Tweed River, a grass, *Paspalum galmarra*, from, exhibited, 394.

Curculionidae, Australian Revision of, Part xi., 602.

Cyperaceae from Northern Territory, exhibited, 495.

Darling River, fruits of *Owenia acidula* from, exhibited, 137.

Darwinia taxifolia var., exhibited, 393.

Date Palm, fungus on, exhibited, 592

Deane (H.), retirement from the Council, 235.

Description and Figures of three Specimens of *Molacanthus* from the Pacific Ocean, 553.

——————Life-History of a new Species of *Nannophlebia*, 712.

——————of a new Species of Eucalypt from Parramatta, 568.

Descriptions of new Genera and Species of Parasitic Hymenoptera, 172.

—————— of new Species of Australian Anisoptera, 572.

—————— of new Species of Coleoptera, 480, 497.

——————of new Species of *Ichneumonidae*, 217.

Development and Morphology of a new Endoparasitic Copepod, 673.

Devonian and Carboniferous Formations west of Tamworth, Notes on the Relation of, 703.

Diptera, larval, from the windpipes of Kangaroos, exhibited, 560.

Distant (W.L.). Synonymical Notes on some recently described Australian *Cicadidae*, 600.

Distribution of Hydrocyanic Acid in the Australian Flora, 220.

Dogs and Hydatid Cysts, Remarks on an exhibit, 493.

D'Ombrain (E. A.). *See* Exhibits.

Donations and Exchanges, Notice of, 48, 136, 235, 282, 390, 492, 556, 590, 652.

——————for the year 1911-12. 743.

Doryphora sassafras, Chemistry of, 139.

Dragon-fly (*Austrocordulia refracta*), rare, exhibited, 590.

Du Boulay (W.). Elected a Member, 282.

Duck, abnormally coloured egg of, exhibited, 390.

Edwards (E. S.). Elected a Member, 136.

Egg of Duck, abnormally coloured, exhibited, 390.

iv.   INDEX.

Eggs and Skin of Petrels, exhibited, 48.
Elections: Auditor, 43—Council, 43, 235—Hon. Treasurer, 136—Linnean Macleay Fellows, 1912-13, 5—New Members, 136, 235, 282, 390, 492, 556,652—President, 43—Vice-Presidents, 136.
Eragrostis leptostachya, Note on the Scent of, 391.
Eragrostis spp., exhibited, 392.
Eriochloa, a new Species of, from the Hawkesbury River, 709.
Eucalypts of Parramatta, with Description of a new Species, 561.
Eupomatia Bennettii, drawing of the tubers of, exhibited, 558.
Exhibits:—
  Baker (R. T.). Sections of buttress of a Fig-tree, 557.
  Bickford (E. I.). West Australian Pitcher-plant, 654.
  Chapman (H.G.). Mosquito larvæ in sea-water, 237.
  Cheel (E.). Mistletoes from Burrinjuck, N.S.W.; *Rosa turbinata*, and *Grevillea asplenifolia* var. *Shepherdiana*, 137—Fungus on River She-oak, 236—Grasses (*Eragrostis* spp.), Kangaroo Grass, *Darwinia taxifolia* var. *grandiflora*, pods of *Stizolobium* spp., 393—Grasses, various, 494—Sweetbriar infested with Rose-rust; Rust-smitten Grasses; Viviparous Fescue Grass; Kangaroo Grass showing two distinct forms, 592—Grasses infested with Smuts; Bulbous Meadow Grass, 654.
  —————, for Mr. D. G. Stead. Bog-moss used for packing Trout-ova, 283.
  Cleland (J. B.). Manna from *Kunzea* sp., 283—Hydatid Cysts, to show how they are devoured by dogs without injury, 493—Acarids on a bull's hide; *Lomatia* leaves for export, 591.
  D'Ombrain (E. A.). Seeds eaten by Great Black Palm Cockatoo, 493.

Exhibits:—
  Dun (W. S.) [For A. B. Walkom]. Glendonites from the Lower Marine Series, 493.
  Fletcher (J. J.). Spine-tailed Swift struck by lightning, 138.
  Froggatt (J. L.). Fungus emitting iodoform-like odour, 557.
  ————— (W. W.). Rare West Australian Mole-cricket; two rare Cicadas from Bernier Island, and Perth, W.A., 394—Mealy Bug from South Australia; trapdoor nests of spiders, 496—Dipterous larvæ from windpipes of Kangaroos, 560—Australian and Tasmanian Bees, 592—Cicada destructive to fruit and forest trees, 654.
  ————— [For W. B. Gurney]. European Lecanid Scale on Grape-vines, 592.
  Gurney (W.B.). European Lecanid Scale on Grape-vines, 592.
  Hall (C.). Abnormal flower of *Anemone coronaria*, 557.
  Hamilton (A. A.). A new grass from the Hawkesbury River; three species of *Erigeron*, 495. Caltrops weed; a variable grass (*Panicum crus-galli*); drawing of the tubers of *Eupomatia Bennetti*; specimens of two species of *Pimelea*, 558—Three interesting plants (*Medicago hispida*, var. *inermis*, *Acacia obtusata*, *Cotula reptans*), 591.
  Hamilton (A. G.). Photograph of the large Green Frog, 591.
  Hull (A. F. B.). Skin and Egg of Allied Petrel; eggs of Fleshy-footed Petrel, 48.
  McCulloch (A. R.). Land-crab from Murray Island, 136—Water Rat killed in the Botanic Gardens 493.
  Mackinnon (E.). Six parasitic Fungi, 592.
  Stead (D. G.). Embryos and fry of the Salmon Catfish, 48—Aboriginal remains from a Shell-deposit, Macleay River; Oyster-shells from a deposit

Exhibits:—
  at Nambucca River, 236—Bog-moss used for packing Trout-ova, 283—Photographs of a Southern Ribbon-Fish, 492—Oyster and Cockle Shells from a deposit at Macleay River, 556.
  Steel (T.). Fleshy corolla-tubes of the Mohwa, 235—An abnormally coloured egg of a Muscovy Duck, 390—Acorn with four Cotyledons, 492.
  Tillyard (R. J.). Photographs of a seedling of the W. A. Christmas-Tree, 137—A rare dragon-fly and its larval skin, 590.
  Turner (F.). A grass (*Panicum glabrum*), with a note confirming his determination, 48—Fruits of *Owenia acidula*, 137—Fruits of *Nitraria Schoberi*; *Solanum petrophilum*, a suspected poisonous plant; Grasses from New Caledonia, 283—Grasses from the Northern Territory; a grass from Cudgen, Tweed River; a Chenopod with hairy fruiting perianths causing fibre-balls, 393—Grasses and Cyperaceous plants from the Northern Territory, 495—A western grass from Blacktown, 559.
  Walkom (A. B.). Glendonites from the Lower Marine Series, 493.
  Waterhouse (G. A.). A rare butterfly (*Cyclopides croites*), 236—Butterfly (*Euploea corinna*) from E., N.E., and N. Australia, 494—A series of aberrant Rhopalocera, 558.

Fat-solvents, action of, upon sewage-sick soils, 238.
Federal Government and Science, 9.
Fellow, Linnean Macleay, Résumé of the year's work, 5.
Fellowships, Linnean Macleay: Announcements respecting, 590, 652 —Elections to, 5.

Ferguson (E.W.). Revision of the *Amycterides*. Part ii. *Talaurinus*, 83.
Ferns of Lord Howe Island, 395.
Fibre-balls in Sheep, reputed to be due to a Chenopod, 394.
Fibrovascular System of the Quince-fruit, compared with that of the Apple, 689.
Fig-Tree, sections of buttress of, exhibited, 557.
Figures and Description of three specimens of *Molacanthus*, 553.
Fishes. See Exhibits (D.G.Stead).
Fletcher (J. J.). See Exhibits.
Flinders Chase, Kangaroo Island, reservation of, 7.
Flora, Australian, distribution of hydrocyanic acid in plants of the, 220.
Frog, Green, photograph of, exhibited, 591.
Froggatt (J. L.). See Exhibits.
—————— (W. W.). Collection of Parasitic Hymenoptera made by, described, 172.
—————— Presidential Address, March 27th, 1912.
—————— Re-elected President, 43.
——————. See Exhibits.
Frogs, Australian, some Trematode Parasites of, 285.
Fungi. See Exhibits (E. Cheel, J. L. Froggatt, E. Mackinnon).
Fungus, emitting iodoform-like odour, exhibited, 557.

Garland (J.R.). Re-elected a Vice-President, 136.
Gastropod Protoconch, Constitution, etc., 49.
Genera, New, of Parasitic Hymenoptera, 172.
Genus *Stigmodera*, Notes on the, 497.
Girault (A. A.). Elected a Member, 652.
Glendonites, from Lower Marine Series, exhibited, 493.
Glyceria fordeana, exhibited, 559.
Goldfinch (G.M.). Elected a Member, 492.
Grace (W. H.). Elected a Member, 235.

Grape-vine, Lecanid Scale on, exhibited, 592.
Grass, Bulbous Meadow, exhibited, 654.
———— from Hawkesbury River, exhibited, 495.
———— Note on the scent of a, 391.
———— Viviparous Fescue, exhibited, 592.
Grasses from New Caledonia, exhibited, 283.
———— from Northern Territory, exhibited, 393, 495.
———— Rust-smitten, exhibited, 592.
————. See Exhibits (E. Cheel; A. A. Hamilton; F. Turner).
———— Smut-smitten, exhibited, 653.
Grevillea asplenifolia, var. *Shepherdiana*, exhibited, 137.

Hall (C.). See Exhibits.
————. The Eucalypts of Parramatta, with Description of a new Species, 561.
Hallmann (E. F.). Appointment to a Linnean Macleay Fellowship, 5.
Hamilton (A. A.). A new Species of Eriochloa [Gramineae] from the Hawkesbury River, 709.
————————————. See Exhibits.
Hamilton (A. G.). See Exhibits.
Hawkesbury River, Acarids on bull's hide from, 591.
————————. A new grass from, 495.
————————. *Darwinia taxifolia* var. *grandiflora*, from, 393.
Hedley (C.). Elected a Vice-President, 136—Re-elected to the Council, 43.
————————.On some Land-Shells collected in Queensland by Mr. S. W. Jackson, 253.
————————and Hull (A. F. B.). The *Polyplacophora* of Lord Howe and Norfolk Islands, 271.
Hooker, Lady. Expression of sympathy with, 43.
———————(Sir J. D.). Obituary notice of, 7.

Howson (F.). Elected a Member, 235.
Hull (A. F. B.). See Exhibits.
————————and Hedley (C.). The *Polyplacophora* of Lord Howe and Norfolk Islands, 271.
Hydatid cysts, how manipulated by dogs, 493.
Hydrocyanic acid in Plants, Part i.,Distribution in the Australian Flora, 220.
Hymenoptera, Parasitic, descriptions of new genera and species, 172.

Ichneumonidae, descriptions of two new species from the Island of Aru, 217.
Inactivity of the Soil-Protozoa,655.
India, fleshy corollas of Mohwa from, exhibited, 235.
Irby (L. G.). Elected a Member, 136.
Island of Aru, descriptions of two new species of *Ichneumonidae*, from, 217.

Jackson (S. W.). Land-Shells collected in Queensland by, described, 253—Trap-door nests of spiders collected by, exhibited, 496.
Jellore Creek, fungus on River Sheoak from, exhibited, 236.
————, Mount, Kangaroo Grass from, exhibited, 393.
Johnston (S. J.). On some Trematode Parasites of Australian Frogs, 285.
————. On some Trematode Parasites of Marsupials, and of a Monotreme, 727.

Kangaroo Grass, exhibited,393,592.
Kangaroo Island, Flinders Chase reservation, 7.
Kangaroos, dipterous larvae from windpipes of, exhibited, 560.
Kembla Grange, *Rosa turbinata* from, exhibited, 137.
Kesteven (H. L.). A new endoparasitic Copepod: Morphology and Development, 673.

Kesteven (H. L.). Elected a Member, 235.

——————. Remarks on mirage-effects visible in Hyde Park, 590.

——————. The Constitution of the Gastropod Protoconch: its value as a taxonomic feature and the significance of some of its forms, 49.

Kunzea sp., manna from, exhibited, 283.

Kurrajong, mistleto on, exhibited, 137.

Land-crab from Murray Island, exhibited, 136.

Land-shells collected in Queensland, 253.

Lea (A. M.). Revision of the Australian *Curculionidae* belonging to the Subfamily *Cryptorhynchides*, Part xi., 602.

Leaves of *Lomatia*, exhibited, 591.

List of Australian Bees of the Genus *Crocisa*, 594.

List, Supplementary, of the Marine Algæ of Australia, 157.

Lomatia leaves, exhibited, 591.

Lord Howe Island, Ferns of, 395.

——————, Petrels, skin and eggs of, exhibited, 48.

——————*Polyplacophora* of, 271-281.

Lovell (T.H.). Elected a Member, 556.

Lower Marine Series, Glendonites from, exhibited, 493.

Lucas (A. H. S.). Re-elected to Council, 43—Re-elected a Vice-President, 136.

——————. Supplementary List of the Marine Algæ of Australia, 157.

Lycaenidae, Notes on Australian, Part v., 698.

McAlpine (D.). Appointment to investigate Bitter Pit of Apples, 10.

——————, The Fibro-vascular System of the Quince Fruit, compared with that of the Apple, 689.

McCulloch (A. R.). A Description and Figures of three specimens of *Molacanthus* from the Central Pacific Ocean, 553.

——————. Notice of motion, 237.

——————. *See* Exhibits.

Mackinnon (E.). *See* Exhibits.

Macleay River, oyster and cockle shells, from a deposit at, exhibited, 236, 556.

Maiden (J. H.), and Betche (E.). Notes from the Botanic Gardens, Sydney, No. 17, 244.

Manna from *Kunzea* sp., exhibited, 283.

Marsupials, Trematode Parasites of,

Masters (G.). Notice of his decease, 282.

——————(Mrs. G.). Letter of thanks for sympathy, from, 390.

Mathews (G. M.). Elected a Member, 390.

Mealy Bug from South Australia, exhibited, 496.

Meetings, Special General, 590, 741, 742.

Milton, N.S.W., Ribbon-fish from, exhibited, 492.

Mirage-effects visible in Hyde Park, 590.

Mistletoes from Burrinjuck, N.S.W., exhibited, 137.

Mohwa, fleshy corolla-tubes of, exhibited, 235.

Molacanthus, Description and Figures of, from Central Pacific Ocean, 553.

Mole-cricket from Perth, W.A., exhibited, 394.

Monotreme, Trematode Parasite of a, 727.

Mosquito-larvæ in sea-water, exhibited, 237.

Mosses of the Yarrangobilly Caves District, N.S.W., 363.

Murray Island, land-crab from, exhibited, 136.

Myrtaceous Plants from New South Wales, on two unrecorded, 585.

Nambucca River, oyster-shells from a deposit at, exhibited, 236 —aboriginal tradition about the, 236.

Nandewar Mountains, flora. See Barraba to Nandewar Mountains and Boggabri, flora of, 622.

Nannophlebia, Description and Life-History of a new Species of, 712.

Nattai River, *Grevillea asplenifolia* var., from, exhibited, 137.

New Caledonia, grasses from, exhibited, 283.

New South Wales, Notes on Native Flora of, Part viii., continued, 617—Part ix., 622.

————, Parasitic Hymenoptera, descriptions of new genera and species, 172.

————, two unrecorded Myrtaceous Plants from, 585.

Nitraria Schoberi, fruits of, exhibited, 283.

Norfolk Island, *Polyplacophora* of, 271.

North (D.S.). Elected a Member, 556.

Northern Territory, *Cyperaceae* from, exhibited, 495—Grasses from, exhibited, 392, 393, 495, 496—Visit of scientific men to, 9.

Note on the Relation of the Devonian and Carboniferous Formations west of Tamworth, N.S.W., 703.

———— on the scent of the grass, *Eragrostis leptostachya*, 391.

Notes from the Botanic Gardens, Sydney, No. 17, 244.

———— on Australian Lycaenidae, Part v., 698.

———— on the Genus *Stigmodera*, with Descriptions of eleven new Species, and of other Buprestidae, 497.

———— on the Native Flora of New South Wales, Part viii., continued, 617—Part ix., 622.

————, Synonymical, on some recently described Australian *Cicadidae*, 600.

O'Callaghan (M. A.). Elected a Member, 556.

Oestrus larvæ from kangaroos, exhibited, 560.

Owenia acidula, fruits of, exhibited, 137.

Oyster-shells, from deposits at Nambucca and Macleay Rivers, exhibited, 236, 556.

Palmer (L. F.). Elected a Member, 136.

Panicum crus-galli, a variable grass, exhibited, 558.

Papers, proposed time-limit to, 237, 284.

Parasites, dipterous, of kangaroos, exhibited, 560.

———— Trematode, of Australian Frogs, 285—of Marsupials and of a Monotreme, 727.

Parasitic Hymenoptera, on a Collection of, made by Mr. W. W. Froggatt, 172.

Parramatta, Eucalypts of, 561.

Peick (A. H. W.). Elected a Member, 492.

Perth, W. A., rare Cicada from, exhibited, 394.

Petrels, Allied and Fleshy-footed, skin and eggs of, exhibited, 48.

Petrie (J. M.). Hydrocyanic acid in Plants, Part i., Its Distribution in the Australian Flora, 220.

————. Re-appointment to a Linnean Macleay Fellowship, 5— Résumé of year's work, 5.

————. The Chemistry of *Doryphora sassafras*, 139.

Pimelea, two species, of, exhibited, 558.

Pine, Red, mistleto on, exhibited, 137.

Pitcher-plant, West Australian, exhibited, 654.

Plankton of the Sydney Water Supply, 512.

Plant, suspected poisonous, exhibited, 283.

Plants, exotic, from seeds introduced in ballast, exhibited, 652.

————, Hydrocyanic acid in, 220.

————, inland, from seeds brought by stock, exhibited, 559.

————, two unrecorded, Myrtaceous, 585.

Playfair (G. I.). Plankton of the Sydney Water-Supply, 512.

Polyplacophora of Lord Howe and Norfolk Islands, 271.
Prickly Pear problem, 11.
Protoconch, Constitution of the Gastropod: its Value as a Taxonomic Feature and the Significance of some of its Forms, 49.
Protozoa of Soil, inactivity of,655.

Queensland, on some Land-Shells collected by Mr. S. W. Jackson in, 253.
Quince Fruit, Fibro-vascular System of, compared with that of the Apple, 689.

Rayment (F. H.). Re-elected Auditor, 43.
Revision of the Amycterides, Part ii., *Talaurinus*, 83.
——————Australian *Curculionidae*, belonging to the Subfamily *Cryptorhynchides*, Part xi., 602.
Rhopalocera, aberrant, exhibited, 558.
Ribbon-Fish, photo. of Southern, exhibited, 492.
Rock-Cod, stranded in recent storms, 390.
Roeburne district, W.A., deleterious Chenopod from, exhibited, 394.
Rosa turbinata, exhibited, 137.
Rules, Special Meeting to consider amendment of, 590.

Salmon Catfish, developmental stages of, exhibited, 48.
Sea-water, mosquito-larvæ in, exhibited, 237.
Seeds eaten by Great Black Palm Cockatoo, exhibited, 493.
Sewage-sick Soils, action of Fat-solvents upon, 238.
Shell-deposits at Macleay River, 236, 556—at Nambucca River, 236.
Shells from Shell-deposits,exhibited, 236, 556.
She-oak, fungus on, exhibited, 236.
Smith (R.). Elected a Member, 136.
——— (R. Greig). Contributions to our Knowledge of Soil-Fertility: No. v., The Action of Fat-solvents upon Sewage-sick Soils, 238—No. vi., The inactivity of the Soil-Protozoa, 655.
——— ———. Résumé of the year's work of the Macleay Bacteriologist to the Society, 3.
Snapper stranded in recent storms, 390.
Soil-Fertility,Contributions to our Knowledge of, No. v., 238—No. vi., 655.
———Protozoa, the inactivity of, 655.
Soils, action of Fat-solvents upon sewage-sick, 238.
Solanum petrophilum, a suspected poisonous plant, exhibited, 283.
South Australian Mealy Bug, exhibited, 496.
Species, New, of: Australian Anisoptera, 572—Coleoptera, 480, 497—*Crocisa*, 594—*Eriochloa*, 709—*Eucalyptus*, 568—*Ichneumonidae*, 217—*Nannophlebia*, 712—Parasitic Hymenoptera, 172.
Spencer (R. H.). Elected a Member, 136.
Sphagna of Australia and Tasmania, 383.
Spiders, trapdoor-nests of,exhibited, 496.
Stead (D. G.). Remarks on the effects of storms on reef-frequenting organisms, 390.
——————. *See* Exhibits.
Steel (T.). Re-elected a Vice-President, 136—Re-elected to the Council, 43.
——————. *See* Exhibits.
Stigmodera, Notes on the Genus, with Descriptions of eleven new Species, 497.
Stizolobium spp., pods exhibited, 393.
Storms, remarks on the effects of, on reef-frequenting organisms, 390.
Sweetbriar, rust-smitten, exhibited, 591.
Swift, Spine-tailed, struck by lightning, exhibited, 138.

Sydney Botanic Gardens, Notes from the, No. 17, 244.
Sydney Water-supply, Plankton of, 512.

Talaurinus: Revision of the *Amycterides*, Part ii., 83.
Tasmania, a small collection of Bees from, 596.
————, Sphagna of, 383.
Thomson (J. A.). Elected a Member, 390.
Tillyard (R. J.). Description and Life-history of a new Species of *Nannophlebia*, 712.
———— ————. On some Australian *Anisoptera*, with Descriptions of new Species, 572.
———— ————. On some new and rare Australian Agrionidae, 404.
———— ————. *See* Exhibits.
Trematode Parasites of Australian Frogs, 285—of Marsupials and of a Monotreme, 727.
Trout-ova, bog-moss packing for, exhibited, 283.
Turner (F.). *See* Exhibits.

Ulmarra, Clarence River, ova of Salmon Cat-fish from, exhibited, 48.

Walgett, dipterous larvæ in Kangaroos, from, exhibited, 560.
Walkom (A. B.). Appointment to a Linnean Macleay Fellowship, 5.

Walkom (A. B.) and Cotton (L. A.). Note on the Relation of the Devonian and Carboniferous Formations west of Tamworth, N.S.W., 703.
Ward (J. B.). Elected a Member, 390.
Warren, N.S.W., suspected poison-plant, from, exhibited, 283.
Waterhouse (G. A.). Elected to the Council, 43.
————————. Notes on Australian *Lycaenidae*, Part v., 698.
————————*See* Exhibits.
Water-rat from the Botanical Gardens, exhibited, 493.
Watts (Rev. W. W.). Elected a Member, 492.
———— ————. The Ferns of Lord Howe Island, 395.
———— ————. The Sphagna of Australia and Tasmania, 383.
————————and Brotherus (V. F.). The Mosses of the Yarrangobilly Caves District, N.S.W., 363.
Werong, Mount, flora. *See* Camden to Burragorang and Mount Werong, flora of, 617.
West Australian Christmas-tree, photo. of seedling exhibited, 137.
————————Pitcher-plant, exhibited, 654.
————————rare butterfly, exhibited, 237.

Yarrangobilly Caves District, Mosses of, 363.

(b) BIOLOGICAL INDEX.

Names in italics are synonyms.

The generic names only of the " List of Marine Algæ"(pp.157-171) are indexed herein.

	Page.
Acacia armata	626, 628, 636, 644
Baileyana	566
conferta	245
Cunninghamii	645, 648
dealbata	566, 629, 636, 645
decora	644, 648
decurrens	204, 225, 566
var. mollis	617
discolor	225
elata	225
floribunda	225
gonocarpa	252
hakeoides	644
homalophylla	645
implexa	645
juniperina	225
lanigera	628
leptophleba	251
linifolia	225
longifolia	225
lunata	629
melanoxylon	629, 636
neriifolia	628, 636, 644
obtusata	591, 629
Oswaldi	645
oxycedrus	225
pendula	645, 650
podalyriæfolia	566
pycnantha	566
rubida	629, 636
Ruppii	244
salicina	644
suaveolens	225
tetragonocarpa	252
triptera	644
viscidula	629
Acæna ovina	618
sanguisorbæ	618, 619
Acalles	603
Acallopais rudis	603
sculpturatus	603
Acanthaceæ	646
Acanthochites	271
approximans	276, 281
costatus	276
grano-striatus	276
leuconotus	275, 281
Acanthocladium	380
extenuatum	380

	Page.
Acanthopleura	272
Acetabularia	168
Achnanthes microcephala	515
Aciagrion	449, 472
fragilis	409, 472, 478, 479
hisopa	472
Ackama Muelleri, var. hirsuta	246
Acrocladium	379
chlamydophyllum	379
Acropeltis elata	161
Actinotus helianthi	227, 617
minor	227
Adelium angulicolle	488
Coxi	486
flavicorne	487
geminatum	487
Adiantum æthiopicum	396, 631, 648
hispidulum	395, 619, 648
Adriana tomentosa	618, 627, 647
Aeschninæ	579
Agarista glycine	212
Agrimonia eupatoria	225
sanguisorbæ	225
Agriocnemis	424, 443, 445, 446, 448, 453, 456, 461, 462, 468
argentea	409, 461, 477
exsudans	409, 461, 462, 477
hyacinthus	409, 453, 457, 459, 462, 477
materna	461
minima	460
pruinescens	453
pygmæa	459
rubricauda	409, 459, 462, 476, 477
splendida	409, 456
rubris	437
Agriogomphus	725
Agrion	407, 409, 423, 424, 429, 441, 443, 444, 445, 446, 447, 448, 449, 451, 462, 465, 468, 476, 478
lyelli	409, 449, 462, 468, 476, 478, 479
punctum	450
Agrionidæ	404, 405, 406, 407, 421, 429, 455, 456, 473, 474, 722
Agrionoptera	725

	PAGE.
Agropyrum scabrum	653
Agrotis sp.	214
Ajuga australis	627, 630, 646
Alatidotasia	602, 614
rubriventris	614
Alectrion (Nassa)	63
Alloneura	431, 432, 441
analis	441
coelestina	431, 432
dorsalis	441
solitaria	408, 431, 432, 442
solitaris	431
Alpheus	66, 81
heterocheles	65
Alphitonia excelsa	614, 648, 649
Alsophila australis	233, 621, 631, 642
var. *nigrescens*	397
robusta	397, 398
Alstonia constricta	228, 646
Alternanthera triandra	647
Amarantaceae	647
Amaryllideae	232, 618, 620, 631
Amblystegium	377
(Euamblystegium) Novæ-Valesiæ	377
serpenti	377
Amblystoma punctatum	356
Amœba limax	661, 662, 668, 669
Amorphota ephestiæ	187
Ampagia	602, 603, 605, 607, 609, 612
alata	603, 604, 605
cognata	604, 607
erinacea	603, 604, 605, 606, 607
femoralis	603, 604, 605
montivaga	603, 604, 605
rudis	603
squamigera	607
Ampagiosoma	602, 611
convexum	612
Amperea spartioides	231
Amphidium cyathicarpum	382
Amphipogon strictus	620
Amphiroa	163, 164
Amphistomum spinulosum	303, 305
subclavatum	286, 355
Amycterides	83
Amycterus	86
morbillosus	103
Amydala	602, 607
abdominalis	608
Anabæna	514, 534
Anadyomene	167

	PAGE.
Anagallis arvensis	620, 646
Andrena infima	599
Andropogon affinis	631, 648
annulatus	283
australis	619, 620
pertusus	283
sericeus	648
Anemone coronaria	557
Angophora cordifolia	226, 566
intermedia	566, 629, 645, 648
lanceolata	226, 566
subvelutina	566, 626, 629
Anguillaria dioica	631, 647
Anguillula fluviatilis	546
Anisoptera	572, 724
Anthela (Darala)denticulata	185, 186
Antheræa simplex	184
Anthericum elegantissimum	234
Anthistiria arguens	393
australis	393
ciliata	393
ciliata	618, 631, 648
frondosa	393
imberbis	393, 653
membranacea	496
Anthochites	271
Anthonomus grandis	12
Anthrocephalus carpocapsæ	201
pomonellæ	200, 201
Anurea cochlearis	515
Aotus sp.	619
Apanteles sp.	214
tasmanica	196
Aphelinæ	215
Aphelini	215
Aphidæ	51
Aphidiinæ	197
Apjohnia	167
Apocyneæ	228, 646
Apophyllum anomalum	643
Ar. triangularis	515
Araliaceæ	227, 629
Araucaria Cunninghamii	263
Archæolithothamnion	162
Aressida	209
annulicornis	207, 208, 209
nigricornis	208, 209
Argasidæ	26
Argemone mexicana	643
Argia	444, 445, 446, 448, 457
Argiocnemis	448
rubescens	409, 454, 478

INDEX.

Argiolestes, 406, 407, 420, 423, 429
   alpinus, 408, 414, 417, 421, 474
   amabilis .. 408, 415, 421, 474
   aureus..408, 415, 417, 421, 474
   fontanus .. 408, 414, 419, 421, 440, 474
   griseus, 408, 410, 420, 421, 474
     r. albescens 414
     r. eboraeus .. 408, 412, 413
     r. intermedius 408, 412
     r. tenuis.. .. .. .. 408, 412
   icteromelas, 408, 410, 413, 419
     r. amabilis 438
     r. nobilis .. 408, 410, 413, 420, 421, 438, 447
   minimus, 408,415, 420, 421, 474
Aristolochiaceæ.. 146
Aroideæ.. 232
Arthrocardia.. 164
Arthropodium strictum .. 627, 647
Arundo Phragmites.. .. 631, 648
Arunta *flava*.. 600
   interclusa 600
Asarum.. 146
Asclepiadaceæ 228
Asperula oligantha, 627, 629, 645
Aspidiotus perniciosus.. .. 34, 35
Aspidium *aculeatum* 631
   aculeatum *var.* Moorei .. 399
   apicale 402
   decompositum 618
   molle.. 396
Asplenium adiantoides.. 395
   bulbiferum 398, 399
     var. Howeanum 399
   falcatum.. 395
   flabellifolium .. 233, 618, 631
   lucidum 395
   melanochlamys.. 396
   pteridioides .. 397, 398, 399
   Robinsonii 395
Asterolasia correifolia.. .. 631, 633, 634
   var. mollis 634
   var. Muelleri .. 628, 631, 632, 633, 634, 635, 636, 639
   mollis 634
   Muelleri.. 628
Astiotrema 318
Astralium fimbriatum 73
   imperiale.. 74
   tentoriforme 74
Astrotricha longifolia.. 227
Atherosperma ... 139, 143, 146, 151, 155

Atherosperma moschatum,139, 143, 151, 154, 155, 229
Atheya Zachariasi... 538
Atriplex hastata 652
Aulacomniaceæ.. 372
Austroæschna anacantha ... 584
   aspersa 584
   forcipata.. .. .. .. 572, 581
   costalis 584
   multipunctata...572, 579, 580, 584
   parvistigma 572, 579, 580, 581, 584
   severini 581
Austroagrion 409, 449, 466
   coeruleum.. .. .. 409, 467, 478
   cyane 409, 450, 456, 467, 478, 479
Austroenemis.. 409, 448, 456, 457
   splendida...409, 424, 456, 457, 462, 477
Austrocordulia refracta 590
Austrogomphus arenarius ... 577
   armiger 572, 577, 584
   doddi 572, 575, 584
   manifestus... ... 572, 576, 584
Austrolestes ... 408, 421, 422, 423, 424
   alleni 408, 425, 427, 474
   analis 424, 426, 453, 474
   annulosus 474
   aridus... ... 408, 427, 428, 474
   cingulatus 422, 424, 473
   colensonis 427
   insularis ... 408, 425, 453, 474
   io 474
   leda 424, 427, 428, 474
   paludosus ...408, 425, 427, 474
   psyche 425, 473
   tenuissimus ... 408, 425, 426, 427, 474
Austrosticta ... 432, 434, 435, 442
   fieldi...408, 434, 435, 442, 475, 476
Austrotriton... ... ... 62, 69
   radialis 62
Avena barbata 653
   fatua... 654
Aviculopecten sp. 706
Avrainvillea... 170

Bacillariaceæ 514
Bacillarieæ 534

	Page
Bacillus mycoides	656
prodigiosus	656
subtilis	656, 659, 664
vulgatus	656, 659, 664
Bacterium coli	659, 664
fluorescens	659, 664
putidum	656, 664, 665
Baeckea crenulata	226
densifolia	617
diffusa	226
linifolia	226
Banksia ericifolia	230
integrifolia	231
latifolia	231
marginata	231
serrata	231
spinulosa	230
Barbula chlorotricha	368
pseudo-pilifera	368, 381
var. scabrinervis	368
torquata	368
Bartramia erecta	373
Mossmanniana	373
papillata	371, 373
Bartramiaceæ	373, 382
Bartramidula Hampei	373
Bassia latifolia	235
Bauera rubioides	225
Beilschmiedia	146
Belenois java teutonia	559
Berberidaceæ	153
Beyeria viscosa	647, 648
Bidens tripartitus	227
Bignoniaceæ	229, 630, 646
Billardiera scandens	619, 628
Bittium	63
Bixineæ	222
Blastophye	161
Blechnum capense	397, 631
cartilagineum	233, 618
discolor	620, 631
serrulatum	233
Boerhaavia diffusa	229, 647
Boragineæ	618, 646
Bornetella	168
Boronia Barkeriana	223
ledifolia	223
pinnata	223
Bosmina longirostris *var. cornuta*	515
rapi	190
Bossiæa heterophylla	225, 619
prostrata	618

	Page
Bossiæa scolopendria	225
Brachycœliidæ	296
Brachycœliinæ	296, 329, 336, 337, 338, 339, 340, 341
Brachycœlium	336, 338, 341
crassicolle	336, 337, 338, 339, 349, 350
hospitale	349, 350
Brachycome graminea	645
multifida	629
scapiformis	619
Brachyloma daphnoides	630
Brachysaccus	289, 290, 291, 296, 304, 316, 320
anartius	296, 316, 317, 319, 320, 352, 353, 359, 361
symmetrus	296, 319, 320, 352, 359
Brachytheciaceæ	380
Brachythecium paradoxum	380
plumosum	380, 381
pseudo-plumosum	380
rivulare	381
rutabulum	380, 381
salebrosum	380
Bracon australicus	193
levisulcatus	194
pilitarsis	193
Braconidæ	193, 214
Braconinæ	193
Brandesia	349
Breutelia affinis	374, 381
commutata	374, 382
divaricata	382
pendula	375, 381
Breynia oblongifolia	231, 617, 647
Bromus arenarius	648
Bryaceæ	371
Bryopsidaceæ	168
Bryopsis	168
Bryum abruptinervium	371
austro-affine	372
altisetum	371
bimum	372
blandum	368, 372
cæspiticium	372
lævigatum	372
oblongifolium	372
pohliæopsis	367, 372
pyrothecium	367, 372
Sullivani	372, 382
ventricosum	372

INDEX.

	Page
Bubaris	116
Buckinghamia celsissima	230
Bufonidæ	289
Bulbine bulbosa	620, 631, 647
semibarbata	631, 647
Bulbochæte setigera	513
Burchardia umbellata	620
Bursaria spinosa	222, 619, 644, 648
Cadellia pentastylis	244
Cæsia parviflora	620
Calama expressa	189
Caleana major	620
Caliagrion	409, 448, 468, 469
billinghursti	409, 462, 468, 477, 478
Callandra	14
Callicoma serratifolia	225
Callimone	210
graminis	209, 210, 211
reticulatus	210
Callipsygma	170
Callistemon lanceolatus	226, 618
linearis	226, 617
Callitris calcarata	137, 618, 627, 630, 647
glauca	647
robusta	647, 648
sp.	231
Callomelitta picta	596, 599
Calopterygidæ	404, 405, 406, 407
Calopteryginæ	464
Calopteryx maculata	464
Calothrix	513
confervicola	513, 533
Calotis lappulacea	645
microphylla	645
Calythrix tetragona	629, 645
Campanulaceæ	228, 619, 627, 630, 646
Camploplegini	187
Campoplex calamæ	189
Camptochæte deflexa	382
gracilis	375
Camptorrhinus	602, 614
dorsalis	615
var. inornatus	616
Campylium decussatum	367, 379
relaxum	379
stellatum	378
subrelaxum	366, 371, 379
Campylopus introflexus	367, 381

	Page
Candalides	699
absimilis	699
gilberti	699
heathi	699
hyacintha	699
simplexa	699
xanthospilos	699
Candollea serrulata	619, 630
Candolleaceæ	630
Canthium oleifolium	645, 648
Capparideæ	643
Capparis Mitchelli	643
Caprifoliaceæ	227
Capsella bursa-pastoris	643
Cardisoma carnifex	136
Carduus pycnocephalus	646
Carex appressa	631, 648
Gaudichaudiana	648
inversa	631, 648
Carpocapsa pomonella	37, 179, 201
Carpopeltis	161
Carumbium populifolium	231
Caryophylleæ	628, 644
Cassia australis	644
eremophila	644
Cassinia aculeata	227, 619, 629
aurea	617, 618
sp.	629, 646
Cassis	77
Cassytha glabella	229, 618
paniculata	229
Casuarina Cambagei	647, 650
Cunninghamiana	236, 627, 645, 647, 650
lepidophloia	647
Luehmanni	647, 650
sp.	203, 206
suberosa	231
Casuarineæ	231, 627, 647
Caulerpa	169, 170
Caulerpaceæ	169
Caustis flexuosa	232
pentandra	232
Celastrineæ	644
Celastrus Cunninghamii	644
Centaurea melitensis	645
Cephalogonimus americanus	350, 457
lenoiri	350
Cephalotus follicularis	654
Ceratitis capitata	14, 40
Ceratium	539
hirundinella	515, 539
Ceratodon purpureus	366

xvi   INDEX.

	PAGE.
Ceratopetalum apetalum	225
gummiferum	225
Ceriagrion	445, 449, 465, 479
glabrum	469, 471
Cerithiopsis acuminatus	67
halligani	67
Cetochilus	54
Chætomorpha	166
Chætosphæridium	520
globosum	520
rar. microscopicum	520
Chætura caudacuta	138
Chalcididæ	199, 214
Chalcidinæ	199
Chalcis tegularis	199
Chalcotænia australasiæ	481
bi-impressa	480
elongata	481
Cheilanthes tenuifolia	402, 631, 648, 649
Cheilosporum	164
Chenolea carnosa	394
Chenopodiaceæ	229, 647
Chiloglottis diphylla	592
Chiton	271
canaliculatus	278
corypheus	277, 281
discolor	278
funereus	279, 281
howensis	278, 281
Chitonidæ	271
Chlamydomonas intermedia	548
sp.	548
Chloanthes stoechadis	229
Chloris barbata rar. decora	393
decora	393
divaricata	393
truncata	648
Chloritis aridorum	257, 258, 269
cognata	257, 258
rar. præcursoris	257, 269
inflecta	256, 269
jacksoni	256, 269
Chlorocladus australasicus	168
Chlorodesmis	170
Chlorogomphus	721, 724, 725
Chlorophyceæ	157, 165, 514, 516
Chodatella	520, 521, 522
citriformis	521, 522
longiseta	521, 522
subsalsa	521, 524
Chondracanthidæ	686
Chondracanthus	684, 685, 686
Chondrococcus	162

	PAGE.
Choretrum lateriflorum	231
spicatum	618
Chrysopogon parviflorus	391
Cicada convergens	601
Cinnamomum	146
camphora	146
Oliveri	139, 154
Citriobatus multiflorus	222
Citrus australis	223
Cladophora	166, 167
Cladophoraceæ	166
Cladorchinæ	296, 302
Clematis aristata	222, 643
glycinoides	222, 628
microphylla	222, 643, 648
Cleonymidæ	207
Cleonyminæ	207
Clinostomum	738
Cliona sp.	557
Cluthaira	211
agaristæ	211
Codiaceæ	170
Codiophyllum	160
Codium	171
Codonocarpus australis	647
Colocasia antiquorum	232
macrorrhiza	232
Colpoda cucullus	655, 657, 659, 660, 661, 666, 672
Columbella australis	67
Comesperma ericinum	222, 618, 619
retusum	619
sylvestre	628
volubile	222
Commelyna cyanea	617
Commelynaceæ	617
Compositæ	227, 233, 248, 617, 618, 619, 627, 629, 645
Confervoideæ	165
Coniferæ	231, 618, 627, 630, 647
Conospermum angustifolium	230
taxifolium	620
Conulus	263
Convolvulaceæ	249, 646
Convolvulus marginatus	646
Copheus spicatus	546
Coprosma hirtella	629, 641
Corallina	164
Corallinaceæ	157, 162
Coralliophila	63
lischkeana	69
Cordulephya	716, 720, 721, 722, 723, 725
pygmæa	722

	Page.
Corduliinæ .. 572, 591, 716, 720,723	
Correa speciosa 619, 628, 644	
Cosmarium.. 528	
alpestre.. .. .. 529, 530	
anisochondrum *var.* confusum.. .. .. 529, 549	
binum 530	
var. australiensis 530	
var. fontense 530, 549	
capitulum *var.* detritum, 515, 528, 549	
contractum *var.* ellipsoideum.. 528	
var. subellipticum, 529, 549	
var. subfoveatum .. 528, 549	
ellipsoideum.. 528	
var. intermedium 515	
var. minor.. 515	
foveatum.. 528	
incrassatum.. 528	
Meneghinii 529	
var. Regnellii 529, 549	
phaseolus γ achondrum .. 528	
Regnellii.. 529	
subspeciosum β validus .. 530	
subtumidum 528, 529	
subturgidum 530	
turgidum.. 530	
var. alpestre.. 529	
var. subrotundatum .. 530	
Cothurnia amphorella.. 548	
Cotula australis 645	
reptans 591	
Cotylotretus rugosus 738	
Craspedia Richea.. .. .. 629, 645	
Crassulaceæ 226, 629, 645	
Cratodecatoma 205	
ruficeps 206	
Crematogaster 211	
Crinia signifera 289, 290	
Crinum flaccidum 232	
Crocisa *albomaculata* 595	
albopicta.. 595	
beatissima 595	
cæruleifrons.. 595	
darwini 595	
lamprosoma.. 595	
lugubris 595	
macleayi 595	
nitidula 595	
novæ-hollandiæ.. 595	
quadrimaculata 595	

	Page.
Crocisa quartinæ 595	
rotundata 595	
tincta.. 595	
turneri 595	
waroonensis 594, 595	
Croton phebalioides.. 231	
Crowea saligna 223	
Cruciferæ 643	
Crucigenia 517	
tetrapedia.. .. .. .. 516, 517	
Cryptandra amara 224, 628	
Cryptinæ.. .. .. 175, 217	
Cryptini 180	
Cryptocarya triplinervis 229	
Cryptonemia 161	
Cryptonemineæ 157, 159	
Cryptoplax 280	
Cryptorhynchides 602	
Cryptorhynchus ephippiger .. 615	
femoralis 603, 604	
Cucumis myriocarpus 645	
Cucurbitaceæ.. 645	
Culex vigilax 237	
Cupania anacardioides.. 224	
semiglauca 224	
tomentella 224	
Cupido simplexa 699	
Curculionidæ 602	
Curis olivacea.. 510	
viridi-cyanea 511	
Cyathea brevipinna 397	
Macarthuri 397	
Cycadeæ 231, 251, 630	
Cyclochila laticosta 600	
virens 600	
Cyclophorus confluens.. 395	
serpens 620	
Cyclopides croites 236	
Cyclops 54, 684, 686	
Cyclotella 536, 537, 538	
comta *var.* quadrijuncta 537	
Meneghiniana .. 515, 536, 537	
var. Kutzingiana 537	
var. major 537	
var. minutissima,515,536,537	
var. stelligera, 515, 536, 537	
var. stellulifera.. 537	
Schrœteri 538	
Cylindracheta (Cylindrodes)	
Campbelli.. 394	
Kochii 394	
Cylindrocystis minutissima .. 528	
Cylindrodes 294	

	PAGE.
Cymatium 56, 70, 73, 76, 79	
abboti.. .. .. 74, 75, 82	
bassi	78
columnarium	79
cutaceum	77
parkinsonianum, 60, 74, 75, 78, 79, 82	
petulans 78, 79	
pumilio 78, 79	
quoyi	79
radiale 67, 75	
spengleri	78
textile..	75
tortirostris 60, 74, 75, 82	
tritonis 76, 78, 79	
woodsi.. .. .. 69, 75	
Cymatium (Septa) rubicunda..	78
Cymatium (Triton) woodsi ..	67
Cymbidium canaliculatum ..	647
suave	231
Cynipidæ..	199
Cynodon convergens	393
incompletus..	5
Cynoglossum australe, 618,646,648	
Cyperaceæ .. 232, 249, 496, 619, 620, 627, 631, 648	
Cyperus concinnus 496, 648	
difformis..	496
ferax	349
fulvus.. .. .. .. 496, 648, 649	
gracilis	648
pygmæus..	496
rotundus..	496
sanguineo-fuscus	620
squarrosus..	496
vaginatus 627, 648	
Cysticercus tenuicollis..	493
Cystignathidæ	289
Cytospora leucostoma..	592
Dactylococcopsis..	520
montana..	520
raphidioides	520
Dacus oleæ	14
tryoni 14, 35, 199	
Daldinia concentrica	236
Dampiera Brownii..	227
sp...	630
Danis apollonius..	698
apollonius	698
Macleayi	698
salamandri	698
syrius..	698
taygetus	698

	PAGE.
Danthonia *longifolia*	619
penicillata	648
var. longifolia	619
var. semiannularis.. ..	620
semiannularis	620
Daphnandra.. .. .. 151, 152	
aromatica	152
micrantha	152
repandula	152
Darala 185, 186	
Darwinia fascicularis	226
taxifolia..	226
var. grandiflora..	393
Dasya 157, 158, 159	
Dasycladiaceæ	168
Dasycladus	168
Dasyeæ..	157
Dasyphlœa	161
Dasyurus viverrinus, 727, 732, 733, 739	
Daucus brachiatus..	645
Davallia dubia	402
Davidsonia pruriens	225
Daviesia brevifolia..	224
corymbosa	224
latifolia..	628
ulicina..	628
Decatoma..	206
Decatomini 205, 206	
Demodex folliculorum *var*. bovis..	591
Dendrobium speciosum ..	231
Dentalium sp...	706
Derbesia	168
Derbesiaceæ..	168
Dermatolithon	163
Desm. pseudostreptonema ..	513
Swartzii	513
Desmia..	162
Desmidiaceæ.. .. .. .. 514, 526	
Desmodium varians	618
Deyeuxia Forsteri	648
Diachasma carpocapsæ	198
Dianella cærulea..	620
revoluta, 232, 619, 620, 631, 647	
tasmanica	619
Dicherotropis..	89
cavirostris	90
Dameli	90
Dichodontium Wattsii..	366
Dichotomum elegans	519
Dicksonia antarctica	233
nephrodioides	397
Dicranaceæ	366

INDEX.

Dicranella sp. 366, 372
Dicranoloma subpungens... .. 367
  Sullivani 367, 372
Dicrocœliinæ .. 338, 339, 340, 341
Dictyosphæria 167
Didelphys aurita 727
Dielasma sacculum... 706
Digitaria debilis.. ... ... 494, 495
  sanguinalis... 495
  tenuiflora 494, 495
Dilleniaceæ, 222, 619, 626, 628, 643
Dillwynia ericifolia *var.* phy-
  licoides.. 628
  floribunda 225
Dinobryon.. ... ... 515, 516
  elegantissimum 547
  sertularia... 515
    var. cylindricum 516
    var. divergens 515, 516
    var. Schauinslandii .. 516
Diphlebia .. 404, 406, 407, 423, 429
Diplachne loliiformis 250
  Peacockii... 250
Diplacodes... 720
Diplodiscus, 289, 290, 291, 296, 304,
                                349, 350
  megalochrus,296, 302, 308, 352,
                             353, 359, 360
  microchrus .. 296, 307, 352, 360
  subclavatus, 286, 307, 308, 309
  temperatus 308, 349, 353
Diploglottis Cunninghamii .. 224
Dipodium punctatum.. ... 617, 620
Discaria australis 628
Distichium capillaceum 366
Distoma cygnoides 356
  opisthotrias... 739
Distomum.. 287
  arcanum 356
  clavigerum 286, 287
  confusum.. 287
  crassicolle 286, 356
  cygnoides .. 286, 287, 353, 357
  cylindraceum .. 285, 286, 355
  endolobum 286
  lancea 358
  medians 286, 287
  mutabile 338
  ornithorynchi 727
  ovocaudatum 286
  pristiophori.. 347
  rastellus.. 286
  retusum 286
  sociale,331,332,334, 337, 338,339
  sp. 738

Distomum variegatum, 286, 287,
                             357, 358
  vitellilobum.. 286
Ditrichum affine.. 382
Diuris maculata.. 630
Docidium.. ... ... 526, 527
  asperum.. 527
  trabecula *var.* Delpontei, 526,
                                   549
Dodonæa boroniæfolia.. ... 644
  tenuifolia 644
  triquetra... 224
  viscosa... ... ... 224, 628, 644
    var. attenuata 628
    var. spathulata 644
Dolichosaccus, 289, 290, 295, 296,
  304, 308, 315, 316, 318, 320,
  345, 348, 349
  diamesus .. 296, 314, 353, 359
  ischyrus .. 296, 313, 315, 352,
                             359, 361
  trypherus .. 296, 309, 314, 315,
                   346, 352, 359, 360, 361
Doodia aspera 402, 631
Doratifera.. 176
  vulnerans 183
Doryanthes excelsa.. 232
Doryetini 195
Doryphora, 139, 143, 146, 151, 152,
                             153, 154, 156
  sassafras, 5, 139, 154, 155, 229
Dracophyllum secundum 228
Drepanocladus brachiatus .. 378
  fluitans *var.* falcatus.. ...378
Drepanocladus (Warnstorfia)
  strictifolius.. 378
Drimys aromatica 222
  dipetala 222
Drosera binata 226
  peltata 226
  spathulata 226
Droseraceæ 226
Dryopteris decomposita 618
  var. nephrodioides 397
  parasitica 396
  punctata 402
Duboisia 5
  myoporoides.. 229
Dumontiaceæ.. 161

Echinocarpus australis 223
Echinococcus veterinorum .. 493
Echinostoma incrassatum .. 735
Echinostominæ.. 738

	PAGE
Echthromorpha	173, 185
intricatoria	185
Ectropothecium (Cupressina) condensatum	379
Ehrharta calycina *var.* versicolor	494
Elachertinæ	211
Elachertini	211
Elachertus	211
Elæocarpus cyaneus	223
Encalypta tasmanica	369
Encalyptaceæ	369
Encyrtidæ	212
Endodonta	264
albanensis	265
austera	266, 270
cinnamea	267, 270
funerea	265
inloidea	266
var. curtisiana	264, 265, 270
recava	267, 270
vinitincta	268
Enteromorpha	165, 166
Entolium aviculatum	706
Entomostraca	514
Eohippus	60
Epacrideæ	228, 248, 617, 630, 646
Epacris Bawbawiensis	248
breviflora	248
heteronema	248
longiflora	228
obtusifolia	228
pulchella	228
purpurascens	228
Stuartii	248
Ephestia kuhniella	14, 188
Epilobium glabellum	618, 619
Epinephelus dæmelii	390
Epiphlœa	160
Eragrostis Brownii	392
elongata	392
leptostachya	391, 393
neo-mexicana	392
pectinacea	392
pilosa	284, 391
plana	392
speciosa	250
trichophylla	250
Erechthites mixta	619
Eremophila longifolia	646
maculata	229
Mitchelli	646
Eremosphæra viridis	524
Eriachne agrostidea	393

	PAGE
Eriachne pallida	653
sp.	653
Erigeron *albidus*	495
bonariensis	495
canadensis	495
linifolius	495
Eriochloa	710
annulata	710
var. acrotricha	710
decumbens	710
Maidenii	495, 709
polystachya	710
punctata	710
Eriostemon	633
buxifolius	223
difformis	644
lanceolatus	223
Erodium cicutarium	628
cygnorum	644
Eryngium rostratum var. paludosum	645
Erythræa australis	646
Erythromma	447
Erythromorpha gnathon	219
trideus	219
wallacei	218
Eucalyptus acmenioides	562, 564, 565, 566, 567
albens	626, 629, 638, 645, 648, 650
Andrewsi	629, 640
Bancrofti	629, 641
Baueri	567
Boormani	563, 567
Bosistoana	563, 564, 565, 567
Bridgesiana	627, 629, 645
Cambagei	629, 640
capitellata	563, 564, 586
citriodora	566
coccifera	637
coriacea	586, 629, 637
corymbosa	562, 564, 566, 567
crebra	561, 563, 564, 565, 567, 645, 650
dealbata	570, 645, 648, 650
dives	586, 629, 638, 639, 610
eugenioides	561, 562, 563, 564, 565, 567
eximia	565, 567
Fletcheri	567
globulus	566, 570, 636
Gunnii	637
var. rubida	629
hæmastoma	562, 563, 564, 565, 567, 568

INDEX.

Eucalyptus hemiphloia, 561, 562, 563, 564, 565, 566, 567
- lævopinea ... 586
- Laseroni ... 585, 589
- longifolia, 561, 562, 564, 565, 567
- macrorrhyncha ... 626, 629
- maculata ... 563, 567
- melanophloia ... 626, 627, 645, 648, 650
- melliodora ... 626, 629, 645, 650
- nigra ... 567
- nova-anglica ... 629, 640
- paniculata ... 562, 563, 564, 565, 566, 567
- Parramattensis ... 567, 568, 571
- patentinervis ... 567
- pilularis ... 562, 564, 565, 567
- piperita ... 564, 565, 567
- *polyanthemos* ... 567
- populifolia ... 645, 650
- punctata, 562, 564, 565, 567, 568
- resinifera, 561, 562, 563, 564, 565, 567, 569
- robusta ... 564, 565, 567
- rostrata ... 645, 650
- rubida ... 629
- saligna, 562, 564, 565, 566, 567
- Seeana ... 570
- siderophloia, 562, 563, 564, 565, 567
- sideroxylon ... 563, 567
- squamosa ... 567, 570
- stellulata ... 586, 587
- *Stuartiana* ... 627
- tereticornis, 561, 562, 563, 564, 565, 566, 567, 569, 626, 629, 645, 650
  - var. *brevifolia* ... 629, 641
  - var. lanceolata ... 570
- umbra ... 564, 567

Eucœlinæ ... 199
Eu-corallina ... 164
Eudoxichiton ... 272
Eu-florideæ ... 157
Eugenia Luchmanni ... 226
- Smithii ... 226
Eulima ... 71
Eulimella ... 71
Euomphalus pentangulatus ... 706
- sp. ... 706
Eupelminæ ... 212
Eupelmis antipoda ... 213
- testaceiventris ... 212

Euphorbia Drummondii ... 647
- peplus ... 233
Euphorbiaceæ ... 231, 233, 617, 618, 620, 627, 630, 647
Euphrasia Brownii ... 630
Euplectrus agaristæ ... 212
- australiensis ... 212
Euplœa *angasi* ... 494
- boisduvali ... 494
- corinna ... 494
- euclus ... 494
- lewini ... 494
- sylvester ... 559
Eupomatia Bennettii ... 558
- laurina ... 558
Euryeus cressida ... 559
Euryglossa walkeriana ... 599
Eurytoma ... 202
- tasmanica ... 203
Eurytominæ ... 202
Eustrephus Brownii ... 232
- latifolius ... 631, 647
Euthyrrhinus meditabundus ... 181, 198, 207
Evodia micrococca ... 223
Exocarpus aphylla ... 647
- cupressiformis, 231, 630, 647, 649
- stricta ... 630
Exoneura bicolor ... 599

Fabronia australis ... 376
Fabroniaceæ ... 376
Fasciola ranæ ... 286
.*Fasciola ranae* ... 286
- *salamandrae* ... 354
- *subclavata* ... 285
Fasciolidæ ... 296, 304, 739
Fasciolinæ ... 738
Festuca bromoides ... 648
- duriuscula ... 592
Ficus macrophylla ... 231, 557
- rubiginosa, 231, 392, 647, 648, 650
Filices, 233, 251, 618, 619, 620, 631, 648
Fimbristylis velata ... 496
Fisherella ambigua ... 533
Fissidens leptocladus ... 367
- lilliputano-incurvus ... 367
- rigidulus ... 367
Fissidentaceæ ... 367

	PAGE.
Fissurella	74
Flagellaria indica	232
Flammulina corticicola	264, 270
delta	263
Florideæ	157
Fretum	260
Froggattoides	601
typicus	601
Froggattoids	601
Fucoideæ	157
Funaria aristata	381
hygrometrica	371
tasmanica	371
Funaria (Entosthodon) sp.	371
Funariaceæ	371
Fusus bifrons	67, 68
var. paucicostata	67
Galeichthys australis	48
thalassinus	48
Galenia secunda	652, 653
Galleria mellonella	191, 192
Gambrus Stokesii	180
Ganeo	350
Gastrodia sesamoides	620
Geijera parviflora	223, 644, 648
Gentianeæ	620, 646
Geraniaceæ	223, 618, 619, 628, 644
Geranium dissectum	618, 619
var. potentilloides	628
Gleichenia circinata	233
dicarpa	233
flabellata	233
Gleocystis	548
Glossidium	312
Glossodia major	231
minor	231
Glyceria fordeana	559, 560
Glycine clandestina	618, 628
Glyphthelmins quieta	349
Gnaphalium japonicum,	617, 629, 646
purpureum	619
Golenkinia	525
radiata	525
var. australis	525, 549
var. paucispina	525, 549
Gomphinæ	423, 575
Gompholobium Huegelii	619
var. leptophyllum	628
latifolium	224
minus	224, 619
Gomphonema parvulum	515

	PAGE.
Gonatozygon	326, 527
Kinahani	526, 527
var. Kjellmanni	526
var. monotænium	526
var. Ralfsii	526
var. tenuissimum	526, 549
Kjellmanni	526, 549
Ralfsii	526
Gonolithon	163
Goodenia barbata	618
bellidifolia	618, 619
decurrens	617
geniculata	630
glauca	646
heterophylla	227, 618
ovata	646
Goodeniaceæ,	227, 617, 618, 619, 627, 630, 646
Gorgodera,	289, 290, 291, 292, 325, 326, 328, 329, 349
amplicava	329
australiensis,	296, 325, 329, 352, 353, 359, 361, 362
cygnoides	326, 327, 329
Gorgoderidæ	296
Gorgoderina	349
Gorgoderinæ	296, 304, 349
Gramineæ,	234, 250, 618, 619, 620, 631, 648, 712
Grammitis rutaefolia	648
Graphiola phœnicis	592
Grateloupia	160
Grateloupiaceæ	159
Gratiola peruviana	620
Grevillea acanthifolia	230
asplenifolia *var.* Shepherdiana	137
buxifolia	230
linearis	230
oleoides	230
punicea	230
sericea	230
sphacelata	230
Grimmia apocarpa	369, 370, 381
f. submutica	369, 381
campestris	370
cygnicollis	370
leiocarpa	370
leucophaea	370
mutica	369
pulvinata *var.* obtusa	370
Grimmiaceæ	369
Gymnodinium	545
cornifax	545

INDEX.

	Page
Gymodinium fuscum	545
var. cornifax	545
neglectum	545
uliginosum	545
Gymnostomum calcareum	367
Hæmadorum planifolium	620
Hakea acicularis	230
dactyloides	230
elliptica	230
eriantha	630
gibbosa	230
leucoptera	648
microcarpa	630
pugioniformis	230
saligna	230
trifurcata	230
Halfordia drupifera	223
Halictus burkei	599
cognatus	599
familiaris	599
globosus	599
lanarius	597, 599
lanuginosus	597
limatus	599
mitchelli	599
orbatus	599
repraesentans	599
tasmaniæ	599
warburtoni	599
Halimeda	171
Halipegus	292
dubius	349
longispina	349
occidualis	349
ovocaudatus	286, 349
Halodictyon	159
Halorageæ	226, 617, 629, 645
Haloragis elata	645, 648
salsoloides	226
sp.	629
tenerioides	617
Halticella stokesi	201
Halymenia	159, 160
Hanowia	159
Haplodasya	159
Haplometra cylindracea	285
Haplometrinæ	296
Hardenbergia monophylla, 626, 628, 644, 648	
Harmostomum	727, 729, 732
æquans	729, 732
caudale	732
centrodes	732

	Page
Harmostomum dasyuri, 727, 731, 739, 740	
fuscatum	732
leptostomum	729, 732
marsupium	732
mordens	732
opisthotrias	727, 732
simile	731, 739
Hecabolini	195
Hecabolus quadricolor	195
Hedwigia albicans	375, 381
Hedwigiaceæ	375
Hedwigidium imberbe	375, 381
Hedycarya Cunninghami	620
Heleocharis acuta	496
sp.	232
Helichrysum apiculatum, 627, 629, 646	
bracteatum	619, 629
collinum	618
diosmifolium	227
elatum	227, 619
ledifolium	248
obcordatum	629, 646, 648
rosmarinifolium	248
semipapposum, 618, 619, 629, 646	
sp.	646
Helicophanta	254, 255
Helipterum anthemoides, 627, 629, 646	
dimorpholepis	629, 646
incanum	629
Helix *annulus*	261
corticicola	264
coxenae	255
crotali	260
dunkiensis	255
funiculata	256
impexa	260
inconspicua	260
iuloidea	264, 265
leucocheilus	259
mariæ	259
marine	259
nicomede	255
pliculosa	256
russelli	264
rustica	260
subrugata	260
villaris	260, 261
yatalensis	259
yorkensis	261
Helix (Conulus) *turriculata*	263
Hemicordulia	719, 720

	PAGE
Hemileia	40
Hemiphlebia	407, 424, 443, 448, 462, 464
mirabilis	409, 463, 478, 479
Hemiteles	214
Hemitelia Moorei	397
Henicopsaltria sp.	394
Heptamerocera	199
loncheæ	199
Heresiarchinæ	173
Hesperornis	60
Heterocotylea	296, 297
Heterodendron oleæfolium	644, 648
Heteropogon insignis	393
Heterosiphonia	158, 159
Hibbertia acicularis	628
Billardieri	619
diffusa	222
linearis	626, 628
var. obtusifolia	643
serpyllifolia	621, 628
volubilis	222
Hibiscus Sturtii	644
Histiopteris	402
Hookeriaceæ	376
Hoploderma	340, 341
Hordeum murinum	648
Hovea linearis	628, 644
longifolia	644
Howittia trilocularis	223
Hoya carnosa	228
Humea elegans	227
Hyal. mucosa	514
Hydrocotyle geraniifolia	617, 618
hirta	627, 629
Hydromys chrysogaster var. leucogaster	493
Hyla aurea	150, 154, 289, 291, 302, 310, 317, 321, 324, 326, 329, 345, 352
citropus	289, 291, 336, 352, 362
cœrulea	289, 290, 314, 319, 330, 331, 352, 591
dentata	289, 291
ewingii	289, 291, 307, 335, 352
freycineti	289, 291, 315, 342, 353
lesueurii	289, 291, 297, 353
peronii	289, 290
phyllochroa	289, 290, 291, 297, 352
sp.	151, 156
Hylidæ	289

	PAGE
Hymenanthera dentata	618
Hymenophyllum marginatum	251
minimum	397, 402
multifidum	397
pumilum	397
tunbridgense	233, 402
Hymenoptera	172, 214
Hymenosporum flavum	222
Hypericineæ	617, 618, 628, 644
Hypericum gramineum	617, 618, 628, 644
Hyperolia marmorata	289, 290
Hypnaceæ	377
Hypochrysops euclides	698
Hypolepis tenuifolia	395, 396, 631
Hypopterygiaceæ	376
Hypopterygium Muelleri	376
Hypothemis	722, 725
Hypoxis hygrometrica	618, 631
Ialmenus icilius	701, 702
inous	702
inous	701, 702
Ichnanthus pallens	393
Ichneumonidæ	172, 214, 217
Ichneumonini	174
Ichthyornis	60
Idocordulina	591
Idotasia	602, 603, 608, 612
æqualis	609, 610
albidosparsa	609, 611
evanida	609, 610
læta	609, 610
montivaga	605
salubris	611
squamigera	607
Illicium	146
Indigofera australis	225, 628, 644
var. platypoda	628
var. signata	644
Infusoria	514, 546
Ionidium filiforme	628
Irideæ	232, 620, 631
Isachne myosotis	393
Ischnochiton	271, 272
crispus	275
intermedius	274, 281
longicymba	275
Ischnura	424, 444, 445, 446, 448, 449, 453, 462
aurora	447, 474
delicata	474
fragilis	472

INDEX. xxv.

Ischnura heterosticta, 109, 451, 452,
    453, 462, 476, 477
  v. tasmanica 409, 451
  pruinescens, 409, 453, 477, 479
  senegalensis 451, 453
  torresiana, 409, 451, 452, 453,
    462, 477
Iscilema mitchelli 496
Isogamae 165
Isopogon anethifolius 230
  ceratophyllus 230
Isopterygium amblyocarpum 380
Isosticta 432, 435, 438, 442
  banksi.. 408, 433, 434, 475, 476
  simplex, 408, 432, 434, 437, 440,
    442, 475
  spinipes 432, 442
Isotoma axillaris 646, 648
Ive 54, 673, 685, 686
  balanoglossi 675, 685
Ixodidae.. 26

Jacksonia sp. 224
Jania.. 164
Jasmineae 228, 630, 646
Jasminum suavissimum 646
Juncaceae .. 32, 619, 620, 631, 648
Juncus Fockei 619, 620
  homalocaulus 631
  pallidus 619, 620, 648
  pauciflorus.. .. 619, 631, 648
  planifolius 619, 620
  prismatocarpus.. 619
  sp.. 620
  vaginatus 232
Junonia vellida 559
Jussiaea repens 645
Justicia procumbens 646

Kochia microphylla 647, 648
  pyramidata 229
Kunzea capitata.. 226
  opposita 629
  pomifera 619
  sp.. .. .. 283, 619, 621
Labiatae .. 229, 620, 627, 630, 646
Lagerheimia .. 520, 521, 522, 547
  ciliata.. .. .. .. 521, 524, 549
    var. acuminata, 522, 523,524,
      525, 549
    var. amphitricha .. 522, 549
    var. comosa.. .. .. 525, 549
    var. coronata 522, 549
    var. cristata.. .. .. 525, 549

Lagerheimia ciliata *var*. gene-
    vensis 522, 549
  var. globosa.. .. .. 524, 549
  var. gracilis .. 521, 523, 549
  var. inermis.. .. .. 523, 549
  var. inflata 522, 549
  var. splendens 547
  var. striolata 525, 549
  var. subglobosa 523
  var. subsalsa 524, 549
  Genevensis.. 521, 522, 523, 525
Lambertia formosa.. 230
Lantana Camara.. 233
Laportea moroides 231
Larrakeeya 601
  pallida.. 601
Lasiopetalum ferrugineum .. 223
Lataurinus 84
  rugiceps 90
Lathrecista 725
Lauraceae 139, 146, 156, 229
Laurelia Novae-Zealandiae.. .. 152
Laurus sassafras 155
Lecanium berberis 592
Lecithodendrium.. 336
  crassicolle 337, 338
Leguminosae, 224, 233, 234, 244,251,
    617, 618, 619, 626, 628, 644
Lembeja *australis* 601
  brunneosa 601
Lembophyllaceae 375
Lembophyllum divulsum 375
Lemmermannia emarginata.. 517
Lentibularineae 620
Lepidium pseudo-ruderale .. 643
Lepidodendron australe 625
Lepidoderma albohirtum 13
Lepidopleurus 271
  badius.. 273
  catenatus 273, 281
  norfolcensis 273, 281
Lepidosperma concavum 232
  laterale 631, 648, 649
Lepodermatinae, 296, 304, 308, 316
Leptobryum pyriforme,364,371,372
Leptocarpus tenax 232
Leptodon Smithii 375
Leptomeria acida 231
Leptopteris Moorei 397
Leptorrhynchus squamatus .. 627,
    629, 646
Leptospermum arachnoideum 226
  flavescens 226, 629
  scoparium 226, 629
  stellatum.. 629

INDEX.

	Page		Page
Leptothecia Gaudichaudii	372	Lisseurytoma	202
Lernæa	685, 686	violaceitincta	202
branchialis	677	Lissopimpla	185
Leskeaceæ	376	10-*notata*	185
Lestes, 406, 407, 410, 421, 422, 423,		*haemorrhoidalis*	185
428, 429, 441, 443,445,462,474		semipunctata	185
aridus	427	Litharthron	164
barbara	422	Lithophyllum	163
cingulatus	408, 421, 422	Lithothamnion	162
colensonis	465	Litsea dealbata	229
paludosus	427	Littorina	70, 71
sponsa	427	Lobelia gracilis	228
tenuissimus	426	pedunculata	619, 646
viridis	421, 422	sp.	630
Lestoidea, 407, 408, 428, 429,475,476		Logania floribunda	228
conjuncta	408, 428, 475, 476	Loganiaceæ	228, 620
Letterstedtia	166	Lolium rigidum *var.* rottbœ-	
Leucania semipunctata	185	lioides	592
Leucaspis japonica	216	spp.	592
Leucoloma Sieberi	381	Lomaria *capensis*	397, 631
Leucopogon amplexicaulis	228	discolor	233, 620, 631
attenuatus	630	Lomatia ilicifolia	630, 641
ericoides	228	longifolia	230
esquamatus	228	silaifolia	230
lanceolatus	228	sp.	591
microphyllus	228	Lonchæa splendida	199
virgatus	228	Loranthaceæ	227, 645
Libellulidæ	718, 724	Loranthus Bidwilli	137
Libellulinæ, 712, 716, 718, 719, 720,		celastroides	227
721, 722, 723, 725		linophyllus	645
Libertia paniculata	631	pendulus	645
Liliaceæ, 232, 234, 619, 620, 627,631,		sp.	645, 648
647		Lorica	272
Limacodes sp.	176	Lotorium	70
Limax	677	bassi	71
Limnæa stagnalis	50	pumilio	78
Limnanthemum crenatum, 620, 646		Lotus australis	225
Limnodynastes dorsalis, 289, 290,		corniculatus	225
314, 352		edulis	234
peronii, 289, 302, 310, 317, 321,		Loxogenes arcanum	349
324, 325, 326, 329, 352		Loxonema sp.	706
sp.	150, 151, 156	Lucifer	684, 686
tasmaniensis,289, 290, 307, 352		Luzula campestris	631
Lindia torulosa	546	*Lycaena elaborata*	700
Lindsaya linearis	233, 620	*Lycaenesthes tasmanicus*	700
microphylla	233	Lycænidæ	698
Lineæ	223, 233, 644	Lycopodiaceæ	232
Lingula	51	Lycopodium densum	232
Linum gallicum	233	Lyonsia eucalyptifolia	646
marginale	223, 644		
Liotia	73	Macadamia integrifolia	230
Lipolexis rapæ	197	ternifolia	230
Lissanthe sapida	617	Macromia terpsichore	584
strigosa	228, 630	*viridescens*	584

	Page
Macrozamia flexuosa	231
heteromera	630
Moorei	251
spiralis	231
Magnoliaceæ	146, 222
Malacocotylea	287, 288, 296, 303
Mallomonas litomesa	547, 548
Plosslii	548
splendens	547, 548
Malva nicænsis	652
Malvaceæ	223, 619, 626, 628, 644
Mangelia lutraria	67
Marattia fraxinea	396
var. salicina	396
salicina	396
Marlattiella	215
aleyrodesii	215
prima	216
Marsdenia suaveolens	228
Marsilea Drummondii	648
Marsileaceæ	648
Mastophora	163
Mathilda decorata	67
Medicago hispida var. inermis	591
Meesea Muelleri	364, 373
Meeseaceæ	373
Megachile chrysopyga	599
leucopyga	599
ordinaria	599
Megalatractus aruanus,	67, 69, 70, 78
maximus	78
Megastigmus	210
Mehlisia	727, 732
acuminata,	733, 737, 739, 740
ornithorhynchi	737, 739, 740
Mehlisiinæ	738
Melaleuca bracteata	645, 650, 651
genistifolia	589
Huegelii	589
Irbyiana	587, 589
lasiandra	589
leucadendron	589
linariifolia	226
styphelioides	588, 589
thymifolia	226
Melampsalta convergens	601
cylindrica	601
incepta	654
Melhania incana	644, 648
Melichrus urceolatus	630, 646
Melilotus parviflorus	233, 644
Melobesia	162, 163

	Page
Melosira	520, 536
granulata	512, 513, 515, 536
var. circinalis	536
Menispermaceæ	153, 618
Menoideum pellucidum var. inflatum	547
Mentha australis	229
Mesaulus grandis	734, 735, 738
Mesocœla	339
Mesocœlium,	290, 296, 329, 336, 337, 338, 339, 340, 341, 349, 350
megaloon,	291, 296, 334, 336, 352, 359
mesembrinum,	296, 330, 336, 337, 352, 359, 362
oligoon	291, 296, 335, 336, 352, 359, 362
sociale	336, 349, 350
Mesodina croites	237
Mesostenini	175
Mesostenoideus stirocephalus	177
Mesostenus pomonellæ	178
Victoriæ	179
Metagoniolithon	163
Metathemis	573, 574, 575
brevistyla brevistyla	584
subjuncta	572, 574, 584
guttata aurolineata	572, 575
nigra	574
subjuncta	574
virgula	575
Michelinia tenuisepta	706
Microcystina	260
Microcystis Clarencensis	261
incensa	262, 269, 270
ductilis	261
kreffti	260
marmorata	262
moretonensis	261
pudibunda	261
responsivus	262, 269
rustica	260, 261, 262, 270
subrugata	261
Microdictyon	167
Microgasterinæ	196
Microglossus aterrimus	493
Micromyrtus microphylla	629
Microscaphidium	304
Microseris Forsteri	619
Mielichhoferia australis,	371, 382
Miletus euclides	698
hecalmus	200
meleagris	698
Mimulus gracilis	646

	PAGE
Mirbelia grandiflora	224
Mitrasacme polymorpha,	228, 620
serpyllifolia	620
Mixophyes fasciolatus	289
Mniobryum tasmanicum	371
Modiola multifida	626, 628
Mola (Molacanthus) sp.	553
Molacanthus sp.	553, 555
Monimia rotundifolia	152, 156
Monimiaceæ, 139, 146, 151, 152,155,	229, 620
Monophlœbus crawfordi	496
Monostoma bombynae	286
ellipticum	286
Monostomum orbiculare	356
Monotoca scoparia	630
Morgania glabra	646
Mougeotia sp.	513
Muhlenbeckia rhyticarpa	630
Murex tribulus	68
Muscidæ	64
Myoporineæ	229, 630, 646
Myoporum acuminatum	229, 630
platycarpum	646
Myotrotus	106
Myrtaceæ, 226, 617, 618, 619, 626,	629, 645
Myxophyceæ	514, 532
Nacaduba palmyra	700
palmyra	700
tasmanica	700
Naiadeæ	648
Nanina marmorata	262
orbiculum	261
Nannophlebia	712, 719, 720, 721, 722, 725
cludens, 712, 713, 714, 715, 716,	718, 726
imitans	712
lorquini	712
cludens	712
imitans	712
lorquini	712
risi, 713, 715, 716, 718, 719, 726	
Nascio	485
carissima	485
chydæa	485
costata	482, 485
Enysi	485
lunaris	486
multesima	483, 485
munda	484, 485
Parryi	485

	PAGE
Nascio pulchra	484, 485
quadrinotata	485
simillima	485
Tillyardi	483, 485
vetusta	485, 486
var. lunaris	485, 486
viridis	484, 485
Xanthura	485
Nassa	63
Navicula	535
gracilis var. *neglecta*	534
Hitchcockii	535
incurva	535
Neckeraceæ	375, 382
Nehallenia	447
Nemastoma	161
Nemastomaceæ	161
Neocuris cuprilatera	510
discoflava	509
Guerinii	509
Mastersi	509
ornata	509, 511
pilosa	510
pubescens	510
Neosticta	408, 435, 442
canescens	408, 435, 442, 476
r. dorrigoensis	437
Neotheronia antheræ	184
teiæ	183
Nephelium leiocarpum	224
subdentatum	644
Nephrocytium	518, 519
Aghardianum	519
var. allantoideum	518
var. lunatum	519
Nephrolepis cordifolia	397
Neptunia gracilis	644
Neritina	55
Nicotiana glauca	646
suaveolens	229
Nitor	260
Nitraria Schoberi	283
Nitzschia franconia	535
Nososticta	431, 438, 442
solida, 408, 429,440,442,475,476	
Notelæa linearis	646
longifolia	228
microcarpa	630, 646, 648
Notholæna distans	233, 395
Notoneura	408, 430, 442
cœlestina	408, 432, 475
solitaria, 408, 431, 432, 475,476	
Notonophes	84, 85
cichlodes	87

	PAGE.
Notonophes dumosus	87, 90
hystricosus	90
lemmus	87, 90
pupa	87, 90
spinosus	86, 87, 90
tenuipes	90
Notothixos cornifolius	137
Nuytsia floribunda	137
Nyctagineæ	229, 647
Odonata	404, 405, 407, 423, 425
Oedogonium sp.	513, 520
Oestrus ovis	560
sp.	560
Olacineæ	224, 618
Olax stricta	224, 618
Olearia elliptica	629, 645
ramulosa	227
rosmarinifolia	619
viscidula	619
Omphacomeria acerba	231
Onagrarieæ	618, 619, 645
Onchidium	55, 61
Oncinocalyx Betchei	630, 641, 646
Onithochiton	271, 272
discrepans	280, 281
quercinus	280
Oocystis	518
ciliata	522
parva	518
solitaria	524
Ophioglossum vulgatum	396
Ophioninæ	187
Ophthalamycterus laticeps	90
Opiinæ	197
Opisthioglyphe	315, 318, 320
endoloba	286, 315, 349
Opius euthyrrhinii	197
Orchideæ	231, 617, 620, 630, 647
Oristicta	409, 438, 442
filicicola	409, 420, 438, 442, 476
Ornithorhynchus anatinus	727, 737
Orthetrum	725, 726
Orthis australis	706
resupinata	706
Orthoceras sp.	706
Orthognathella	172, 173
longiceps	172
superba	173
Orthotrichaceæ	370, 382
Orthotrichum acroblepharis	370, 381
laterale	370
Sullivani	368, 369, 370

	PAGE.
Oscillatoria	533, 534
amphibia *var.* bigranulata	534
nigroviridis	513, 533
var. australis	533
var. crassa	514, 515
Ostracion boops	555
Ostrea cucullata	557
virginiana	50
Owenia acidula	137
Oxalis corniculata	223, 618, 628, 644
Oxylobium ellipticum *var.* alpinum	619
var. minor	628
trilobatum	224
Oxyrhynchium austrinum	380
Pachymenia	160
Pagrosomus auratus	390
Palæmonetes	66
varians	65, 68, 80, 82
Palmeria	151
Paludina	55, 70
Panax Murrayi	227
sambucifolius	629
Panda	253, 254
atomata	254
falconeri	254
larreyi	254, 255
whitei	254, 269
Panicum	710
crus-galli	558
decompositum	496
glabrum	48
helopus	710
marginatum *var.* strictum	710
pauciflorum *var.* fastigiatum	383
rarum	393
sanguinale	495, 710
sp.	209, 210, 213
tenuiflorum	495
Paniscini	181
Paniscus productus	181, 182
testaceinervis	181
Pantala flavescens	719
Papaver horridum	643
Papaveraceæ	643
Papilio ægeus ormenus	559
sarpedon choredon	558
Paracolletes carinatus	597, 599
chalybeatus	599
hobartensis	599
leai	597, 599

	PAGE.
Paracolletes melbournensis,	597, 599
melbournensis	597, 599
obscuripennis	599
obscurus	599
spatulatus	598
versicolor	598
viridicinctus	599
Paramphistomidæ	296, 302
Parasphecodes altichus	599
excultus	596, 599
lacthius	597
lithusca	597, 599
stuchila	599
talchius	599
taluchis	599
tilachus	597, 599
tuchilas	597
Paspalum	710
ambiguum	48
brevifolium	495
galmarra	394
setaceum	494
Passiflora amabilis	234
brachystephanea	226
cinnabarina	226
filamentosa	234
Herbertiana	226
lutea	234
suberosa	234
vespertilio	234
Passifloreæ	226, 234
Patella	50, 55
Patersonia glabrata	620
sericea	232, 620, 631
Pavonia hastata	626
Pediastrum	516, 517
duplex *rar.* reticulatum	515
tetras	517
rar. australe	516
rar. Crux Michæli	518
rar. Ehrenbergei	516
rar. integrum	518
rar. longicornutum	516
rar. quadratum	517
rar. tetrapedia	516, 517
rar. triangulare	517
rar. unicellulare	517
Pellæa falcata	395, 631, 648
Pelomyxa palustris *rar.* echinulata	548
Penicillus	170
Penium	527
minutissimum	527

	PAGE.
Penium *Mooreanum*	527
polymorphum	528
rar. cylindraceum	527, 549
rar. minutissimum,	527, 549
rar. Mooreanum	527, 549
rar. Turneri	527, 549
Perameles obesula	731, 739
Peridinieæ	512, 513, 514, 539
Peridinium	540, 541
bipes	541
cinctum	541
inconspicuum	541, 542, 545
javanicum	545
minimum	545
Orrei	542, 545
pusillum	541, 545
quadridens	541
tabulatum	515, 541, 542, 543
rar. africanum	544
rar. caudatum	544
rar. granulosum,	542, 543, 544, 545
rar. hieroglyphicum	543
rar. inconspicuum	545
rar. intermedium	544
rar. ovatum	544
rar. pusillum	544
rar. Westii	542, 543
rar. zonatum	543
umbonatum	541
Peritalaurinus macrocephalus	135
Peronospora trifoliorum	592
Personella septemdentata	79
Persoonia ferruginea	230
pinifolia	230
salicina	230
sp.	630
Petalura	723
gigantea	583
ingentissima	583, 584
pulcherrima	572, 582, 584
Petalurinæ	582
Petrophila pulchella	230
Peumus boldus	152, 156
Peyssonnella	162
Phæophyceæ	515
Phaleria Neumanni	249
Phaneropsolus	336
Phebalium dentatum	223
squamulosum	223
Philiris	699
innotatus	699
Philogalleria	190
sextuberculata	191

	PAGE.
Philonotis dicranellacea,	373, 382
falcata	373
fontana	374
remotifolia	374
scabrifolia	374, 382
sp.	373, 374
tenuis	374
Philonotis (Euphilonotis) austro-falcata	373, 374
fontanoides	374
Philopsyche	186, 187
annulipes	186, 187
pilosella	187
Phœnix dactylifera	592
Phragmidium subcorticium	591
Phyllanthus sp.	231
suberenulatus	647
thesioides	647
Phyllodistomum americanum	356
Phyllota phylicoides	224
Phyllox croxenus	202
Phylloxera vastatrix	13
Phytheliæ	512, 513, 514, 520
Phytolaccaceæ	647
Pimelea curviflora	627, 647
glauca	620, 627, 630, 647
hæmatostachya	558
linifolia	630
pauciflora	630, 647
sp.	630, 642
spicata	558
Pimpla excavata	185
Pimplinæ	183, 185, 218
Pimplini	183
Pipa americana	53
Piptocalyx	151
Moorei	152, 155
Pittosporeæ	222, 619, 628, 644
Pittosporum phillyræoides,	222, 644
revolutum	222
undulatum	222, 628
Plagianthus pulchellus	619
Plagiorchinæ	296, 308, 316
Planaeschna forcipata	581
Planaria cylindrica	285
subclavata	286
Planispira	253
delessertiana	258
delicata	258, 259, 269
leucocheila *var.* pusilla	259, 269
rudis	258, 269
Plantagineæ	630, 646
Plantago varia	630, 646
Platycerium alcicorne	395

	PAGE.
Platycola decumbens	548
Platylobium formosum	225
Plaxiphora	272
Pleiophysa	168
Pleuridium gracilentum	381
Pleurogenes, 291, 295, 296, 341, 345,	349
freycineti 296, 341, 344, 345, 346,	349, 350, 353, 359, 362
gastroporus	344, 349, 350
solus	296, 345, 346, 349, 350, 353, 359
sphæricus	344, 349, 350
Pleurogenetinæ	296, 349
Pleurosorus rutæfolius	648
Pleurotoma casearia	67
Pneumonœces, 289, 290, 291, 292,	296, 320, 349
australis	296, 320, 325, 349, 350, 352, 361
breviplexus	349
capyristes	325, 349, 350
complexus	349, 357
longiplexus	349
medioplexus	349
similiplexus	349
variegatus	286, 325
varioplexus	349
Poa bulbosa	654
cæspitosa	631, 648
nodosa	654
pubescens	392
Podagrion	408, 410, 474
Podolepis acuminata	629
canescens	618, 619, 629
Podopteryx	406, 407
roseo-notata	473
Pohlia cruda	371
nutans	364, 371
Polyænus	177
spiniferus	177
Polycyrtus curvilineatus	175
Polyedrium decussatum	519
enorme	519
gracile	519
Polygala Sibirica	222
Polygaleæ	222, 618, 619, 628
Polygonaceæ	617, 630, 647
Polygonum minus	647
Polyommatus cyanites	699
Polyopes	160
Polyphysa	168

	PAGE.
Polypodium australe	397
Hookeri	397
punctatum	402
pustulatum	395
serpens	620
tenellum	395
Polysiphonia	158
Polystichum aculeatum,	400,402,631
var. *Moorei*	401
Kingii	401, 402
Mohrioides	400
Moorei .. 397, 400,	401, 403
Polystoma integerrimum,	285, 286
ranae	285
Polystomidæ	296, 297
Polystominæ	296, 297
Polystomum .. 290, 291,	296, 350
bulliense,.. 296, 297, 352,	353, 359, 360
coronatum	349
hassalli	350
integerrimum, 297,298,299,301,	349, 354, 357, 358
oblongum	350
Polytrichaceæ	375
Polytrichum commune	375
juniperinum	375
Pomaderris cinerea	224
elliptica	224
lanigera	224
phillyreoides	224
Pomax umbellata	227
Porana sericea	249
Poranthera corymbosa	617, 620
microphylla .. 617,	618,620,630
Potamogeton crispus	648
Pottiaceæ	367
Prasia ritticollis	601
Prasophyllum patens	630
Primulaceæ	620, 646
Prionitis	160
Probolus albocinctus..	174, 175
varilineatus	174
Proctotrypidæ	214
Productus longispinus	706
Murchisoni	706
semireticulatus	706
undatus	706
Prosagrion	449
pruinescens	453
Prosopis alcyonea	599
hobartiana	599
honesta	599

	PAGE.
Prosopis vicina	599
Prosotocus	349
Prostanthera lasianthos	630
nivea	630
rotundifolia	646, 648
Sieberi	229
Proteaceæ 230, 620,	630, 647
Protoneura, 406, 407, 408,	428, 429, 431, 475, 476
Prunella vulgaris	620
Psalidura, 83, 84, 85, 88, 90, 99,	101, 106, 120
forficulata	87, 90
Psepholax	612
Pseudagrion 423, 424, 445,	446, 448, 449, 462, 465, 467, 468, 469, 472
aureofrons, 409, 470, 477,	478, 479
australasiæ, 409, 469, 472,	473, 477, 479
billinghursti	409, 468
coeruleum	466, 467
cyane	409, 466
furcigerum	469
ignifer.. .. 449, 468,	469, 477
microcephalum	472
Pseudalmenus chlorinda	701
Pseudodipsas cephenes ..	670, 699
fumidus	699
Pseudolesken calochlora,	376, 381
Pseudophryne bibronii ..	289, 290
Pseudorissoina	71
Psilostominæ	738
Psoralea adscendens *var*.parva	644
parva	644
Psyche sp.	187
Pteridium aquilinum	396, 631
Pteris *aquilina*	631
comans	395
falcata	631
incisa	402
tremula	396
Pteromalinæ	213
Pteromalus stironotus	213
Pterygophyllum nigellum	376
Ptilotus exaltatus	647
Ptychodera australis	673
Puccinia sp.	592
Puffinus assimilis	48
carneipes	48
Pultenæa daphnoides	224
Deanei	225

	PAGE
Pultenaea elliptica	224
polifolia	224
pycnocephala	619
scabra	628
setulosa	628, 636
stipularis	224
Pupina bilinguis	268
nitida	268
robusta	269
strangei	268, 269, 270
tenuis	268, 270
Purpura	63
lapillus	63, 70
sertata	69
tritoniformis	81
Pycnoporus	336
Pyramidellidæ	71
Pyrrhosoma	447
Quercus pedunculata	492
Quintinia Sieberi	225, 621
Rana halecina	358
hexadactyla	350, 355
Ranunculaceæ, 153, 222, 619, 626, 628, 643, 690	
Ranunculus lappaceus	619, 626, 628, 643
var. subsericeus	619
plebius	628
rivularis	619
sp.	626
Reinschiella obesa	545
Siamensis	545
Restiaceæ	232, 620
Restio australis	620
Rhabditis monohysteria	65
Rhacomitrium pseudo-patens	370
symphyodon	381
Rhacopilaceæ	376
Rhacopilum convolutaceum	376, 381
Rhacopteris sp.	708
Rhagodia hastata	647, 648
linifolia	647
nutans	647
Rhamneæ	224, 628, 644
Rhaphidostegium callidioides	380
Rhinocypha fenestrella	464
Rhipiliopsis	170
Rhizogoniaceæ	372
Rhizogonium mnioides	372, 375
Rhizophyllidaceæ	161

	PAGE
Rhizopoda	514, 548
Rhizosolenia	512, 513, 538, 539
eriensis	514, 515, 538
var. gracilis	539
var. morsa	513, 515, 538
var. Zachariasi	538, 539
Rhodomelaceæ	157
Rhodomyrtus psidiodes	226
Rhodopeltis	161
Rhodymenineæ	157
Rhogadinæ	195
Rhynchostegiella convolutifolia	381
subconvolutifolia	363, 381
Rhynchostegium collatum	381
tenuifolium	380, 381
Rhyssa semipunctata	185
Rhyssa tuberculicollis	183
Ricinus communis	233
Risella	71, 72
Rissoina	71
Rosa rubiginosa	137, 591
turbinata	137
Rosaceæ, 225, 618, 619, 626, 629, 645, 690	
Rotatoria	514, 546
Rubiaceæ	227, 627, 629, 645
Rubus moluccanus	225
parvifolius, 225, 619, 626, 629, 645	
rosæfolius	225
Rumex Brownii	617, 647
Rutaceæ	223, 619, 628, 644
Salamandrina perspicillata	357
Sambucus Gaudichaudiana	227
xanthocarpa	227
Santalaceæ	231, 618, 630, 647
Santalum lanceolatum	645, 647, 648, 649
Sapindaceæ	224, 628, 644
Sarcostemma australe	228
Sassafras officinale	139, 146, 151
Sauloma tenella	367, 376
Saxifrageæ	225, 246
Scævola hispida	227, 618, 619
microcarpa	618
suaveolens	227
Scaphella (Voluta) mamilla	67, 69
Sceleocantha	489, 490
gigas	488, 491
glabricollis	489, 490
pilosicollis	489, 490

	PAGE
Scenedesmus	518
obliquus *var.* acuminatus	518
var. inermis	518
Schismus fasciculatus	250
marginatus	250
Schizea rupestris	233
Schizonema neglecta	515, 534
Schizymenia	160
Schœnus Brownii	620
turbinatus	620
Sciaromium (Aloma) climbatum	377
flavidulum	378
Forsythii	378
Scirpus inundatus	619
setaceus	496, 620
sp.	631
Sclerorrhinella	84, 85
geniculata	87, 90
granuliceps	135
Manglesi	85, 90
melanopsis	87, 90
Sclerorrhinus	83, 84, 112
convexus	88, 90
echinops	87
meliceps	132
molossus	87, 90
multigranulatus	89, 91, 112
Sclerotinia sclerotiorum	592
Scolopia Brownii	222
Scrophularineæ	618, 620, 630, 646
Scutellaria humilis	620, 630, 646
Scytonema	532
ambiguum	533
amplum	533
figuratum	532
mirabile	513, 514, 515, 532
var. ambiguum	533
var. amplum	533
Selaginella uliginosa	232
Selysioneura	407
Sematophyllaceæ	380
Senebiera didyma	643
Senecio capillifolius	629, 646
crassiflorus	652, 653
dryadeus	227, 619
lautus *var.* capillifolius	629
velleioides	619
Sepioteuthis sp.	493
Septa	73, 76, 77, 78, 79
rubicunda	78
tritonis	78
Septoria tritici	592

	PAGE
Sida corrugata	644
var. angustifolia	644
var. orbicularis	644
var. pedunculata	644
Siebera Billardieri	227
linearifolia	227
Siegesbeckia orientalis	645
Simarubeæ	244
Sipho gracilis	68
Sitala pudica	264
turriculata	263, 270
Smilax glyciphylla	232
Solandra	5
lævis	233
Solaneæ	229, 233, 646
Solanum armatum	229
campanulatum	229
cinereum	646
esuriale	646
nigrum	229
parvifolium	646
petrophilum	283
stelligerum	229
vescum	229, 646
Solarium	72
Sollya heterophylla	222
Sorosporium eriachnes	653
Sowerbæa juncea	620
Sphærocystis	548
Sphagnaceæ	366, 384
Sphagnum	366, 384
antarcticum	384
var. australe	384
var. fluctuans	384
var. macrocephalum	384
australe	384
Brotherusii	385, 389
var. plumulosum	385
Campbellianum	384
centrale	389
commutatum	383, 386
comosum	387
compactum var. *ovatum*	384
confertum	384
cristatum	384
cuspidatum	385
var.	385
cymbifolioides	388
cymbifolium	388
cymbophyllum	388
decipiens	389
var. obovatum	389
var. rotundatum	389

	PAGE.
Sphagnum drepanocladum,	385, 389
dubiosum	386
crosum	384
falciramcum	384
grandifolium	389
rar. brachycladum	389
rar. densum	389
rar. laxifolium	389
lancifolium	385
laticoma	386
Irionotum	389
macrocephalum	384
macro-rigidum	384
maximum	388
rar. squarrosulum	388
medium	389
molliculum	387
Moorei	387
rar. macrophyllum	387
Mossmannianum	387
Naumannii	385
novo-zealandicum	383, 386
rar. commutatum	386
rar. laxifolium	386
rar. molle	386
rar. pauciporosum	386
rar. pulvinatum	386
orthocladium	384
pachycladum	389
pseudo-rufescens	383, 387
rar. flavescens	387
rar. fusco-rufescens	387
rar. pallens	387
rar. virescens	387
Scortechinii	385
serratifolium	385, 389
serratum	385
rar. serrulatum	385
serrulatum	385
sp.	283
subbicolor	364, 366, 384, 389
subcontortum	387
submolliculum	386
Sullivani	383, 388
trichophyllum	385
Wardellense	389
Wattsii	385, 389
rar. leptocladum	386
rar. macrophyllum	385
Whiteleggei	384, 389
Wilcoxii	388
Sphenophorus obscurus	13
Spirifer pinguis	706

	PAGE.
Spirifer striata	706
Spirifera	706
Spirogyra porticalis	513
sp.	520
Spirotænia	526
acuta	520
bispiralis *rar.* fusiformis,	526, 549
minuta	526, 549
tenerrima	520
Spirula	66, 67
Sprengelia incarnata	228
Squamariaceæ	162
Stachys arvensis	646
Stackhousia linarifolia	619, 628
muricata	644
spathulata	644
viminea	618, 619, 628, 644
Stackhousieæ	618, 619, 628, 644
Staurastrum	530
approximatum	515
connatum *rar.* muticum,	530, 549
rar. Spencerianum,	515, 530
corniculatum β variabile	515
corralloideum	531
leptacanthum	550
margaritaceum *rar.* cruciatum	530, 549
muticum	532
orbiculare	532
rar. germinosum	515
rar. muticum	532
rar. planktonicum	515, 532
rar. protractum	532, 549
paradoxum *rar.* cingulum	531
rar. perornatum	531, 549
pseudosebaldi	531
rar. corralloideum	531, 549
rar. planktonicum	549
sagittarium	515
sexangulare *rar.* platycerum	515
volans *rar.* elegans,	515, 531, 549
rar. trigonum,	515, 531, 550
Staurogenia tetrapedia	517
triangularis	517
Stauroneis	535
Staurophanum cruciatum	519
pusillum	519
Stellaria flaccida	628, 644
glauca	644
pungens	628

	PAGE
Stenobasis	449, 462, 472
mimetes	409, 472, 473, 476
Stenocarpus salignus	230
sinuatus	230
Stenopteris sp.	706
Stenopterobia	535
anceps	535
anceps	535
var. detrita	536
var. Heribaudii	535, 536
var. intermedia	535
Stephania hernandiæfolia	618
Sterculia diversifolia, 137, 223, 628, 644	
quadrifida	223
rupestris	223
Sterculiaceæ	223, 628, 644
Stereodon cupressiformis	379
Mossmannianus	379
Walterianus	380
Stigmodera	497
anchoralis	505
aureola	499, 511
biguttata	506
Burchelli	507
campestris	508
caudata	484
caudata	484
cinnamomea	500
convexa	506, 511
cruenta	504
cupricollis	501, 502
cyanipes	497
decemmaculata	505
distincta	497
Doddi	505, 511
flaviceps	504, 511
fulviventris	497
gentilis	508
gracilis	508, 511
Hackeri	484
ignota	500
insignis	508
iospilota	503, 505
longula	497
nigriventris	501
ochreiventris	497
octospilota	503
pallidiventris	504
producta	508, 509
rubrocincta	504
sancta	501, 511
seminigra	500, 511

	PAGE
Stigmodera septemguttata	504
septemmaculata	504
septemspilota	503, 511
sternalis	497
suavis	507, 511
Tillyardi	502, 511
tricolor	505
varicollis	497, 498, 499
Yarrelli	497, 498, 499
Stipa aristiglumis	648, 653
Lachmanni	653
pubescens	620
scabra	648, 649
verticillata	391, 648, 649
Stizolobium	393
Struvea	167
Stylideæ	227, 619
Stylidium graminifolium, 227, 619, 630	
Stypandra cæspitosa	620
glauca	232, 631, 647
umbellata	620
Styphelia longifolia	228
triflora	228
tubiflora	228
Suvalta	177
transversa	217
Swainsona Cadelli	225
coronillifolia	225, 644
luteola	644
tephrotricha	626
Symphyonema montanum	230
Synedra subtilis	515
Syngaster	195
annulicornis	195
lepidus	195
Synlestes	406, 407, 424
weyseri	424, 473
Synthemis	573, 724
eustalacta	575
leachi	574
macrostigma orientalis	575
spiniger	572, 573, 584
Syrnola macrocephala	67, 69
Tab. flocculosa	515
Tænia marginata	493
Talaurinus, 83, 84, 85, 87, 88, 99, 122	
aberrans	86, 90
acromialis	92, 122, 124, 135
acutipennis	94, 135
æqualis	88, 95
alternans	84, 93
alternatus	94

INDEX.

Talaurinus ambiguus 87, 97
    var. 87, 89
    amycteroides 86, 89
    angularis.. .. .. 92, 125, 135
    angustatus 85, 97
    apicihirtus 91, 105
    var. hæmorrhoidalis, 91, 106
    bucephalus .. 85, 86, 89, 94, 99
    Camdenensis 86, 89
    capito.. 97
    carbonarius.. 87
    cariosus 87, 90
    Carpentariæ 91, 108, 135
    Carteri 96, 135
    catenulatus 86, 89, 94
    caviceps 87, 89, 93, 97
    cavirostris 88, 89, 90
    clavicornis, 91, 97, 114, 116,135
    convexus 88, 90
    costatus 85, 90
    costipennis 96, 135
    crassiceps 88
    crenulatus 96
    Dameli 87, 89
    dubius.. .. .. 87, 89, 97
    dumosus 87, 90
    encaustus.. .. .. .. 86, 87, 89
    euomoides.. .. .. 92, 122, 126
    exasperatus, 86, 87, 91, 99, 100
    excavatus 85, 90, 96
    fossulatus 96, 135
    foveatus 96
    var. montanus 135
    foveipennis 96, 135
    foveogranulatus 94, 135
    funereus 94, 113
    Gayndahensis, 93, 131, 133, 135
    geniculatus 87, 90
    granosus.. 85
    griseus.. .. .. .. 92, 126, 127
    Helmsi.. .. .. 88, 95
    hiscipennis 86, 89
    Howitti, 86, 89, 91, 99, 100, 106
    humeralis, 86, 89, 92, 121, 122,
                   123, 125, 126
    hystricosus 85, 86, 90
    Illidgei 93, 127, 128, 135
    imitator 88, 93
    impressicollis 86, 89, 96
    inæqualis.. 88
    incanescens, 85, 86, 87, 89, 95
    var. muricatus .. 86, 89, 95
    incertus 87, 90
    inconspicuus, 92, 111, 118, 135,

Talaurinus insignis.. 88
    irroratus.. .. .. 94, 135
    Kirbyi 85, 86, 90, 96
    lacunosus.. 96
    lævicollis 96
    laticeps 87, 90
    lemnus 87, 90
    longipes 93, 135
    Macleayi 86, 89
    var. 87
    maculatus 86, 90, 98
    maculipennis 88, 89, 91
    Manglesi 85, 90
    Mastersi 85, 86, 90
    Megalongensis, 92, 117, 119,135
    melancholicus, 88, 89, 95, 104
    melanopsis 87, 90
    M-elevatus, 84, 88, 89, 95, 99
    miliaris 94, 135
    Mitchelli 93
    molossus 87, 90
    morbillosus.. .. 85, 87, 89, 95
    morbillosus, 86, 87, 90, 100, 101
    multigranulatus .. 89, 91, 112
    muricatus.. .. .. .. 86, 89
    Murrumbidgensis 86, 89
    mythitoides.. .. .. .. 96, 135
    niveovittatus 96, 135
    noctis 88
    nodulosus 86, 89, 121
    obscurus 88
    orthodoxus.. .. 88, 89, 95, 101
    pallidus, 93, 130, 131, 132, 133,
                   134
    panduriformis, 91,103, 105, 135
    papulosus .. 93, 121, 127, 128
    parallelus.. .. .. .. 93, 133
    parvus .. 91, 97, 110, 114, 135
    pastillarius 89, 94, 97
    penicillatus, 86, 90, 91, 99, 101,
                   102, 103
    phrynos 87
    prypnoides 97, 135
    pulverulentus, 91, 109, 111,114,
                   119
    pupa 87, 90
    pustulatus 86, 94, 113
    Rayneri.. .. .. 87, 97
    regularis 88, 95
    Riverinæ, 86, 88, 89, 90, 91, 98,
             99, 100, 104, 112
    Roei 85, 86, 92, 112, 113
    rudis 86, 89
    rufipes 88, 95

	PAGE.		PAGE.
Talaurinus rugiceps	87, 90	Tetraedron	519
rugicollis	94	lobulatum	519
rugifer	85, 90, 96, 99	var. decussatum	519
rugosus	86, 89	var. Sydneyense	519
sulebrosus	86, 89	var. triangulare	519
scaber	85, 86, 87, 90, 95	minimum	519
scaber	87, 90	Tetragoneuria	719
scabricollis	87, 90, 96	Tetrapedia Crux Michaeli	518
scabrosus	94	emarginata	517
scapularis	92, 122, 123	Tetratheca ericifolia, 618, 619,	628
semispinosus	85, 94, 97	Tetrathemis	722, 725
septentrionalis	91, 104, 107, 108, 135	Thalassia cyrtocheila	261
		subrugata	260
simillimus	96	Thamnoclonium	160, 161
simplicipes	88, 89, 91, 107	Thaumasura	209
simulator	87, 94	Thaumatoneura	405
sobrinus	94, 135	Thecla chlorinda	701
solidus	88, 95	myrsilus	701
sphærulatus	86, 93, 132, 134	Theclinesthes miskini	700
spinosus	87, 90	onycha	700
squamosus	92, 116, 118	var. atrosuffusa	701
strangulatus	88	Thelymitra ixioides	630
subvittatus	94, 135	Themeda	393
sulciventris	91, 114, 115, 135	Forskalii	393, 618, 631, 648
tenebricosus, 87, 90, 91, 99, 100		var. imberbis	393, 653
tenuipes	87, 90	var. vulgaris	393
tessellatus	91, 111, 112	Thersites bipartita	255
tomentosus,85, 91, 99, 102, 103, 134		dunkiensis	255, 256, 269
		webbi	256
tuberculatus	87, 94	Thetidos morsura	67
tuberculatus	85, 87, 90	Thopha interclusa	600
tumulosus	94, 135	sp.	600
typicus	84, 93	Thophia colorata	394
variegatus	92, 119	Thuidium furfurosum	376, 381
var. Darlingensis, 92,120,135		hastatum	376
vermicollis	93, 128	suberectum	377
verrucosus	84, 85, 87, 90, 94	unguiculatum	377
victor	87, 89	Thuretia	157
Victoriae	86, 89, 106, 107	Thymeleæ	249, 620, 627, 630, 647
Westwoodi	85	Thysanotus tuberosus	619
Tarrietia argyrodendron	223	Tillæa verticillaris	226, 629, 645
Tecoma australis,229, 630, 646, 648		Tillineæ	223
Teia anartoides	184, 185	Tillyardia	489
Telebasis, 445, 446, 448, 449, 462, 472, 473		mirabilis	489, 491
		Todea barbara	233
rufithorax	409, 473, 478	Tolyposporium anthistiriæ	653
Telephlebia Macleayi	584	bursum	653
Macleayi	584	Tortella Knightii	368
Telopea speciosissima	230	Tortula panduræfolia	369
Tephritidæ	37	princeps	369
Tepperella maculiscutis	204	Tortula (Syntrichia) brunnea, 368, 369
trilineata	204	subbrunnea	369
Terebra lauretanæ	67, 69	Toryminæ	209

INDEX.

	Page
Torymus	210
Trachelomonas	515, 547
acuminata	547
caudata	547
var. elegantissima	546, 547
Trachymene Billardieri	247
var. cuneata	247
Clelandi	246
ericoides	618
Stephensoni	247
Trachypterus jacksonensis	492
Tranes	614
Trema cannabina	647
Tremandreæ	618, 619, 628
Tribulus terrestris	558
Trichoglenes	215
braconophagus	214
Trichomanes apiifolium	397
Bauerianum	397
javanicum	402
Tridontium tasmanicum	368
Triforis	71
Triphora	56
labiata	67
Triquetrella albicuspes	368
papillata	368
Tristania neriifolia	226
Triticum vulgare	653
Triton quoyi	79
radialis	62, 63
woodsi	67
Trocharpa pumila	228
Troides priamus pronomous	559
Trophon paiva	557
Trypetidæ	14
Tryphoninæ	190
Tryphonini	190
Turricula pilsbryi	67
Tylocolax	159
Ubius	673, 684, 685, 686
hilli	673, 674, 685
Udotea	170
Ulva	165
Ulvaceæ	165
Umbelliferæ	227, 246, 617, 618, 619, 627, 629, 645
Urocystis occulta	653
stipæ	653
tritici	653
Uromyces orchidearum	592
Uropetala carooei	584
Urtica incisa	627, 630, 647, 648

	Page
Urticeæ	231, 627, 630, 647
Ustilago bullata	653
Utica onycha	700
Utricularia dichotoma	620
Valonia	167
Vanheurckia	534, 535
rhomboides	534
var. Hitchcockii	534
var. neglecta	515, 534
var. saxonica	534
Velleya montana	619
paradoxa	627, 646
Verbascum blattaria	646, 648
Verbena officinalis	627, 646
Verbenaceæ	229, 233, 627, 646
Vermes	514, 546
Vermetus	55, 70
Veronica calycina	618, 630
Derwentia	630
Viniferæ	224
Viola betonicæfolia	628
hederacea	628, 644
Violarieæ	618, 628, 644
Vitis hypoglauca	224
Voluta mamilla	67
Wahlenbergia gracilis	619, 627, 630, 646, 648
Woollsia pungens	228
Wurmbea dioica	631
X. pachystyla	255
Xan. hastiferum	528
Xanthagrion	448, 465, 466, 467
antipodum	465
erythroneurum	409, 465, 466, 467, 478
sobrinum	465
zelandicum	409, 465, 466
Xanthium strumarium	233
Xanthocnemis	409, 447, 449, 465, 466
zelandica	409, 465, 471, 478
Xanthorrhœa arborea	631
australis	232
quadrangulata	642
sp.	631, 642, 647
Xanthosia dissecta	619
pilosa *var.* glabra	619
Xerotes filiformis	620
longifolia	232, 627, 631, 647, 649
multiflora	627

	Page.
Xylomelum pyriforme	230
Xyrideae	620
Xyris gracilis	620
Zaphrentis sp.	706
Zieria laevigata	223
pilosa	223
Smithii	223
Zizeeria alsulus	700
karsandra	700
Zizera	700

	Page.
Zizina labradus	700
delospila	700
Zizula gaika	700
Zoogonus mirus	354
Zornia diphylla	618
Zygnema sp.	513
Zygodon Brownii	370
Hookeri	370
intermedius	370
Zygopides	602
Zygoptera, 404, 405, 406, 407, 423, 429, 725	

Note.—The names on pp. 550-552 were inadvertently omitted.

[Printed off July 10th, 1913.

EUCALYPTUS PARRAMATTENSIS, SP. NOV.

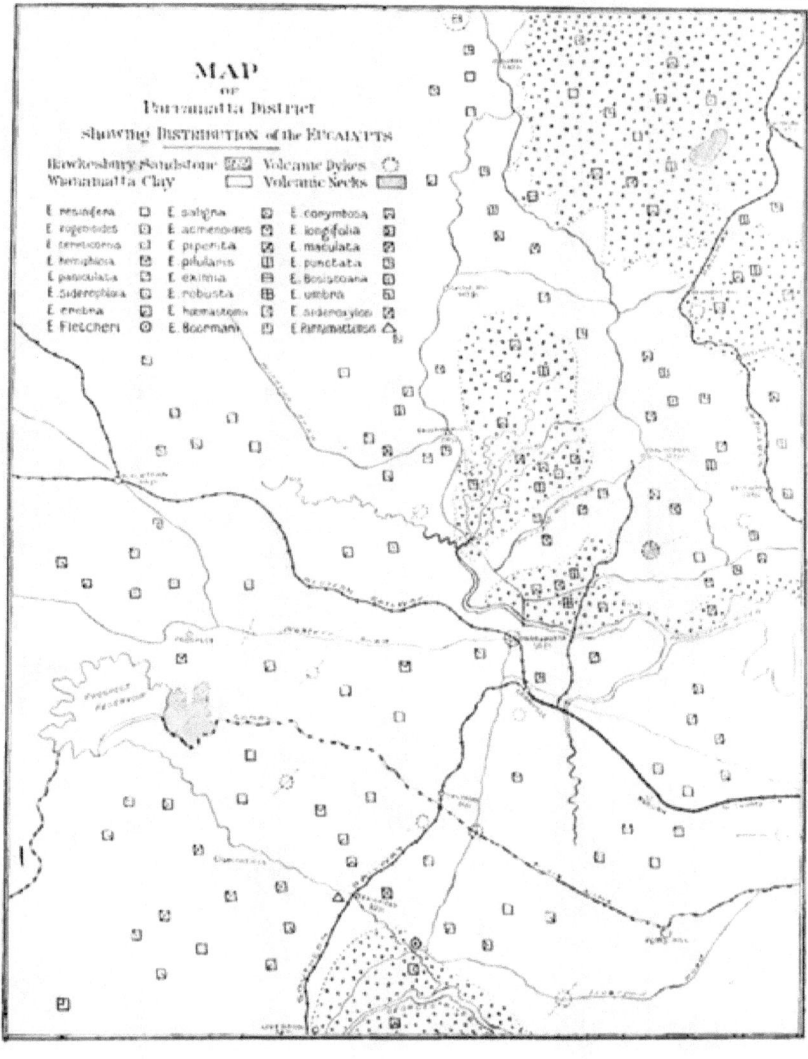

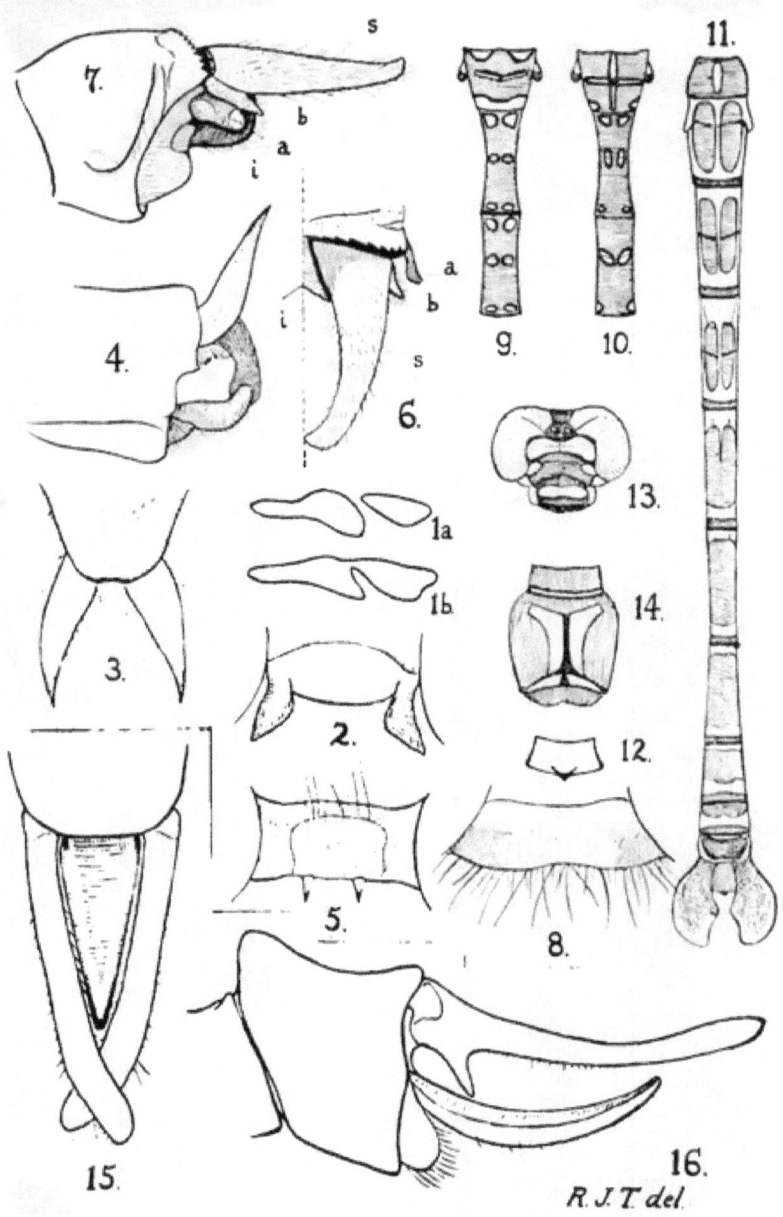

Australian Anisoptera

EUCALYPTUS LASERONI, SP. NOV.

R.T.B. DEL. AD NAT.

Quintinia Sieberi (on the right) from a seed which germinated on a Tree-fern (leaning to the left).

Tumbla or Barber's Peak, Boggabri, N.S.W.

Melaleuca bracteata in the foreground, sandstone cliffs, Maude's Creek, in the background.

Ubius hilli, sp.n.

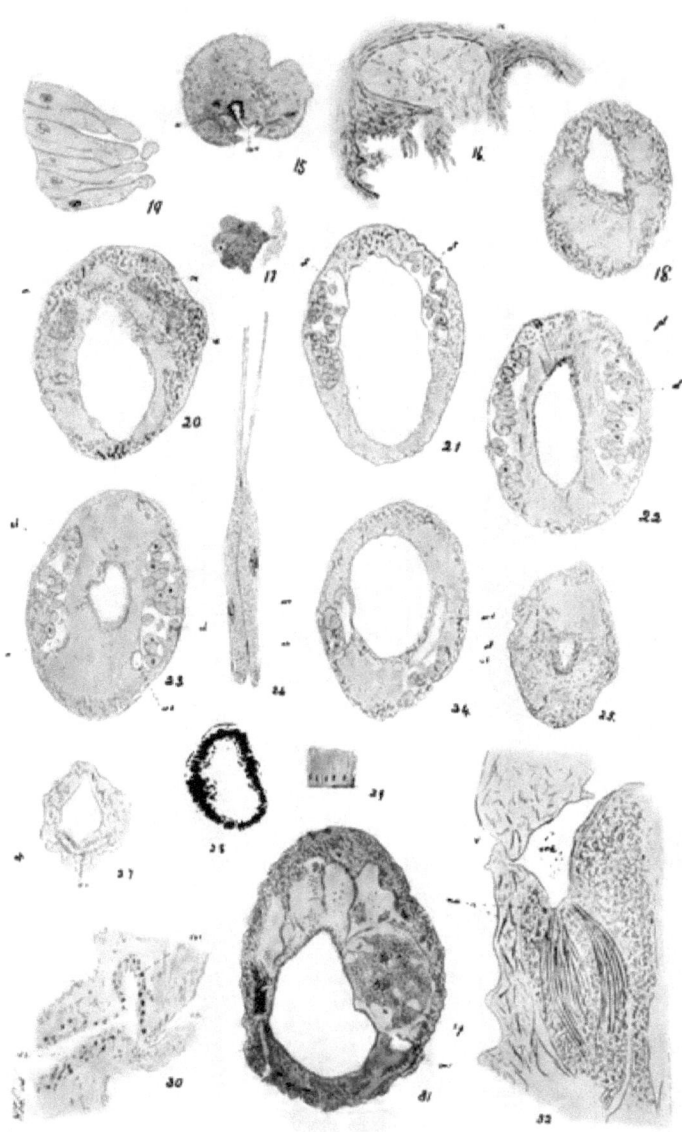

Urius hilli, sp.n.

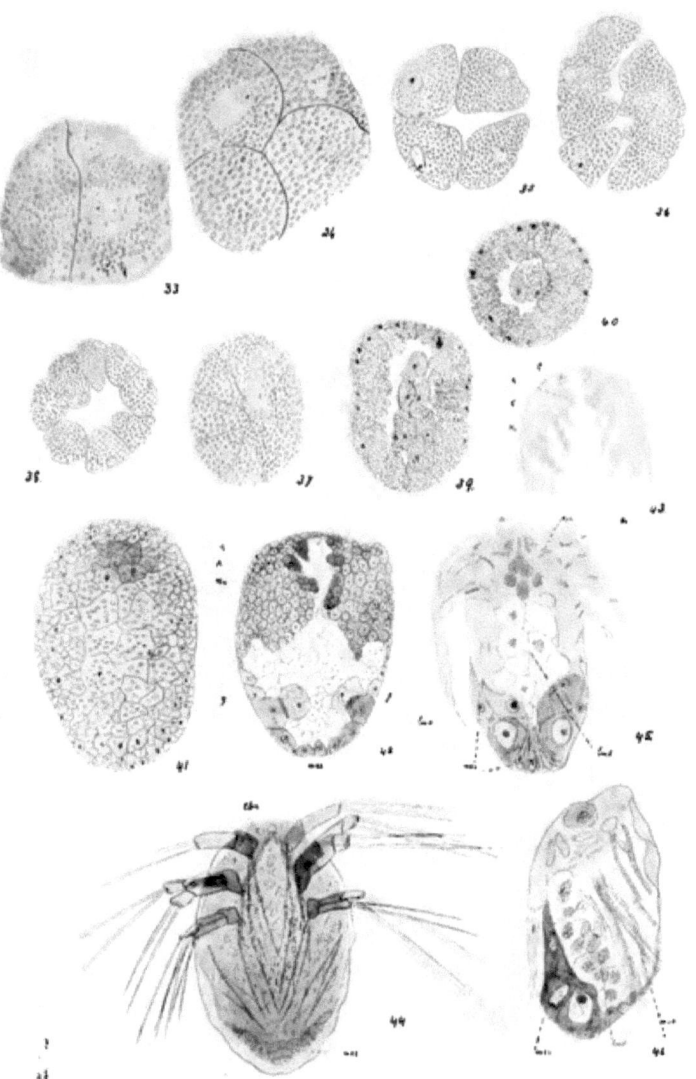

Urnius hilli, sp.n.

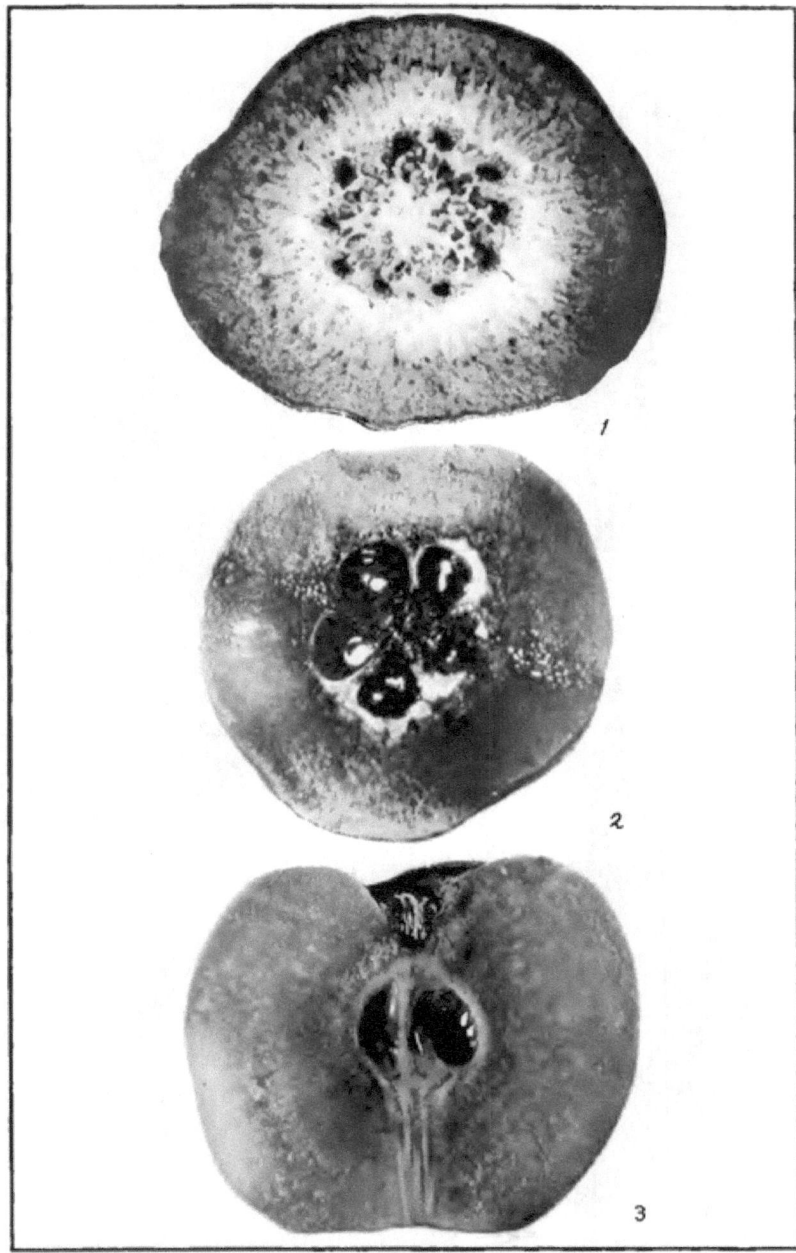

Section of fruit-stalk, and Transverse and Longitudinal Sections of fruit of Quince.

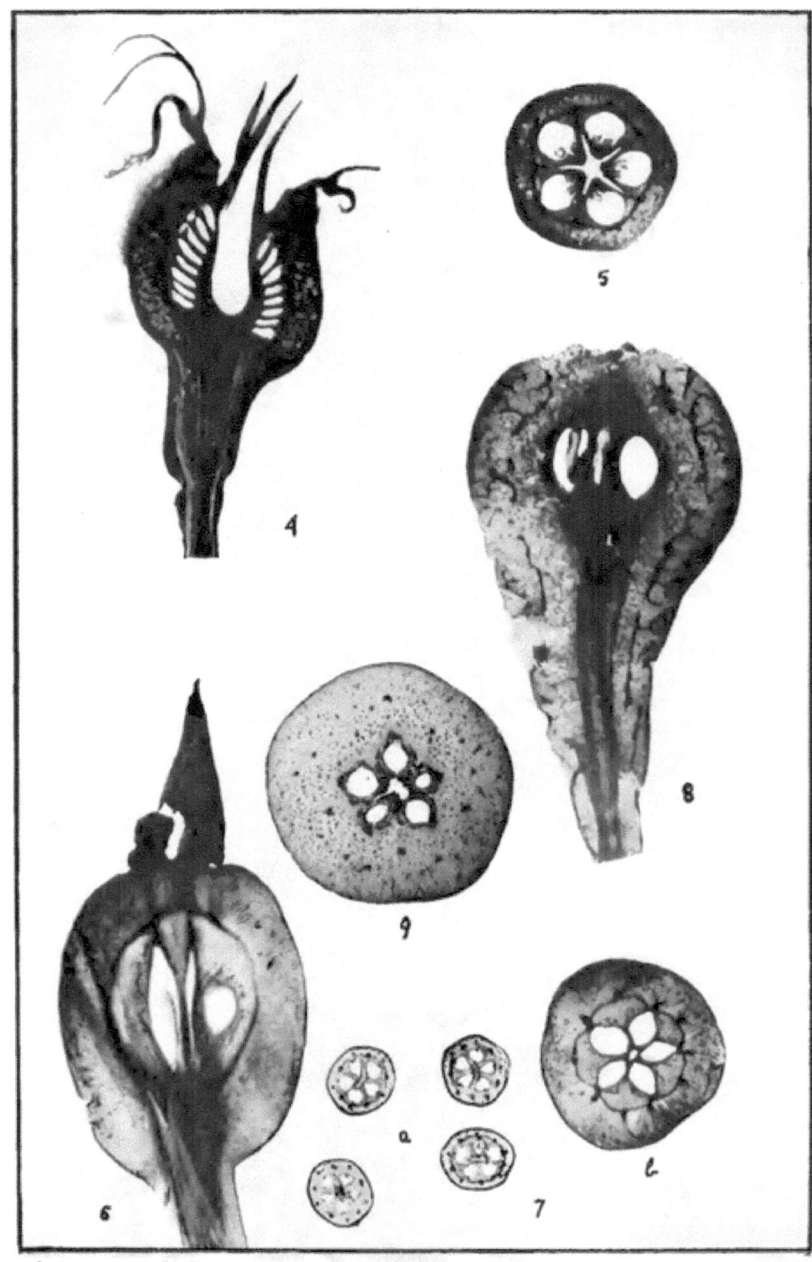

Sections of young fruits of Quince, Apple, and Pear.

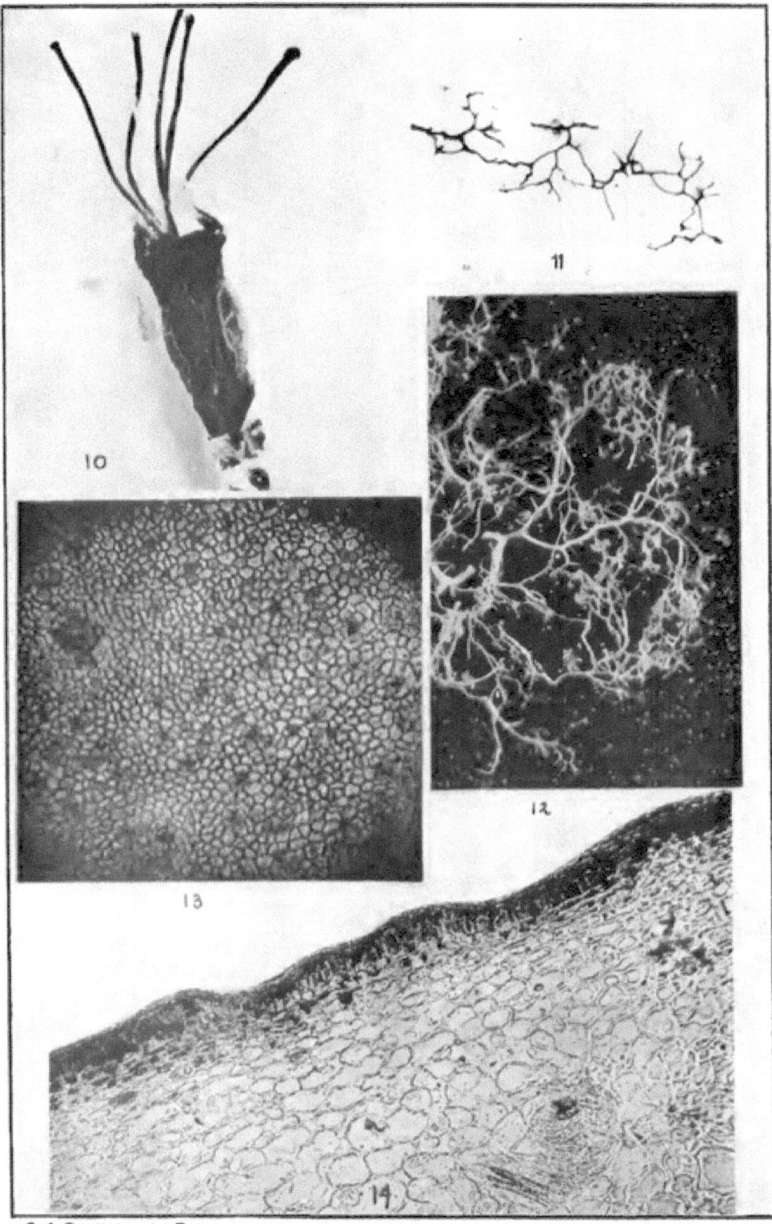

Very young Apple with vascular Net; Skin, Section, and Network of Quince.

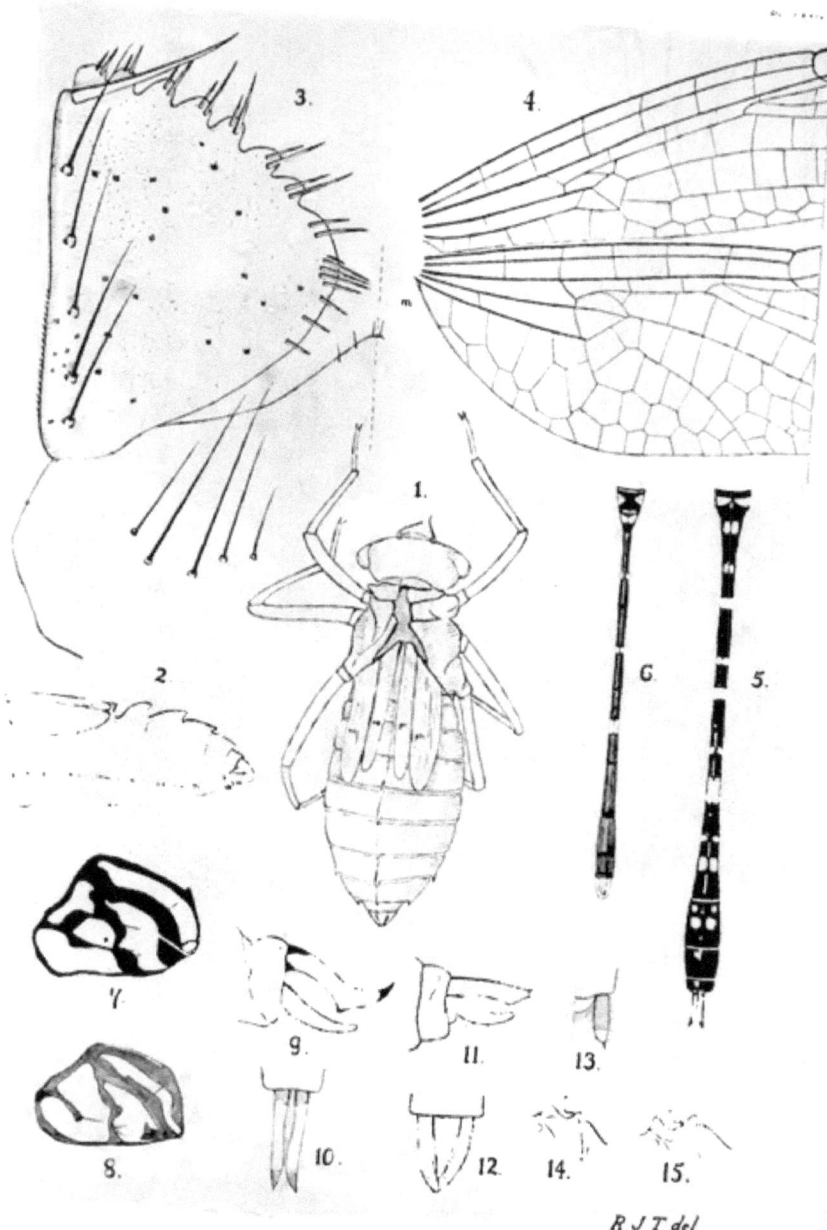

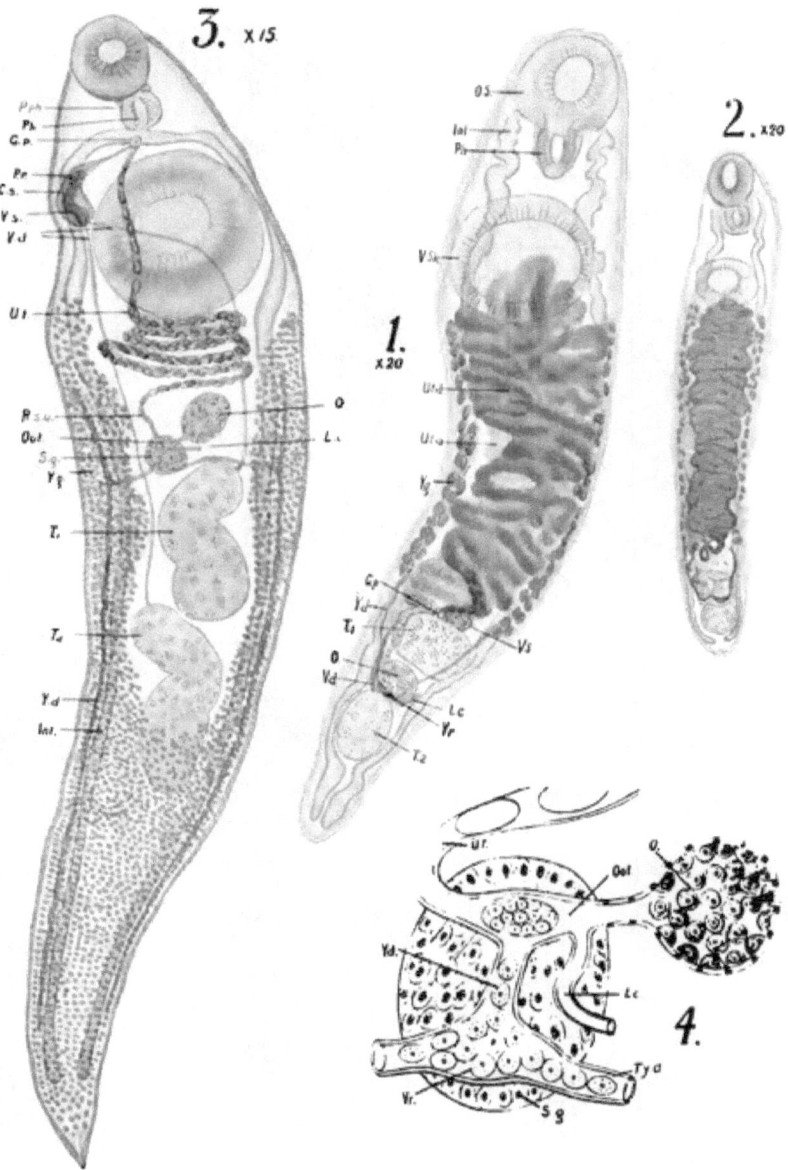

Trematodes from Marsupials and the Platypus.

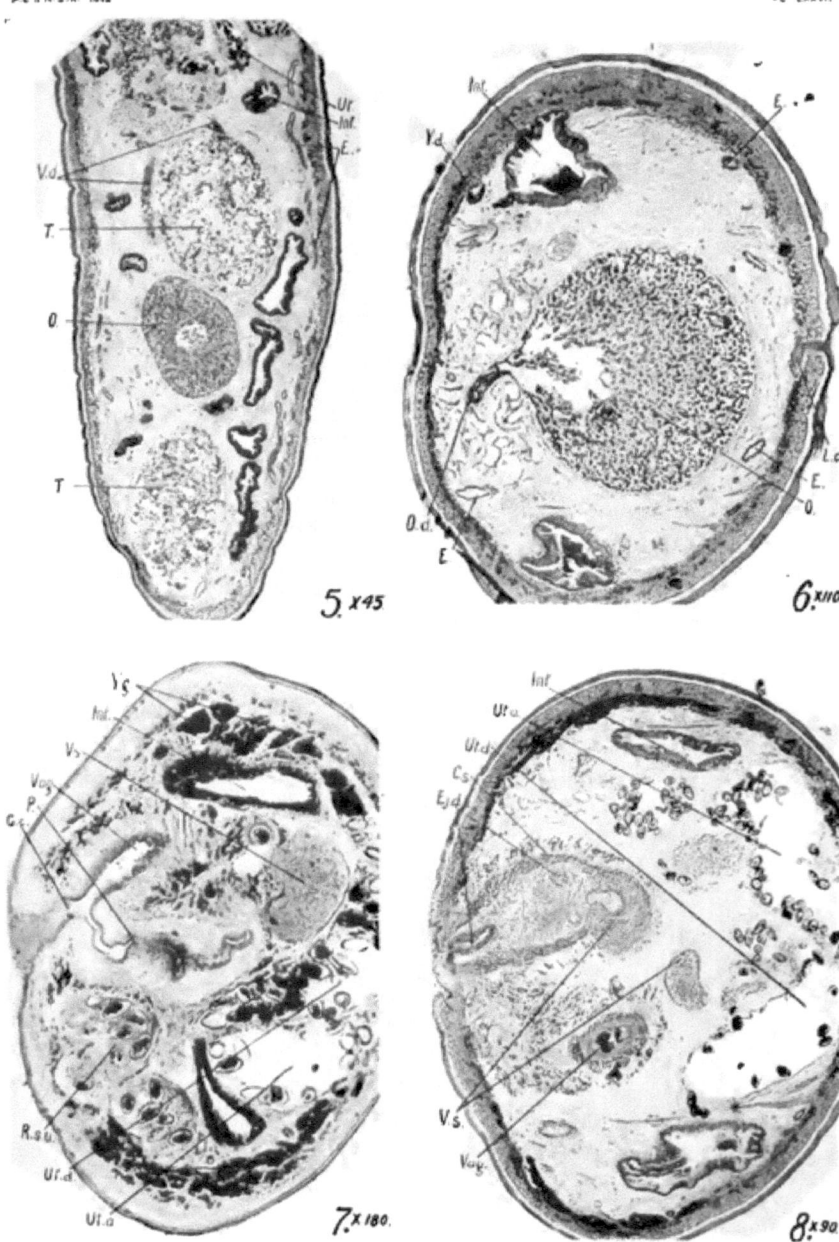

Harmostomum dasyuri, sp.n.

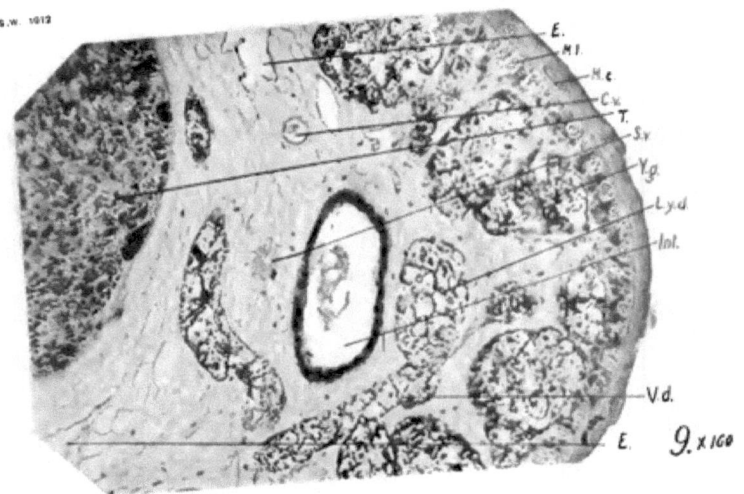
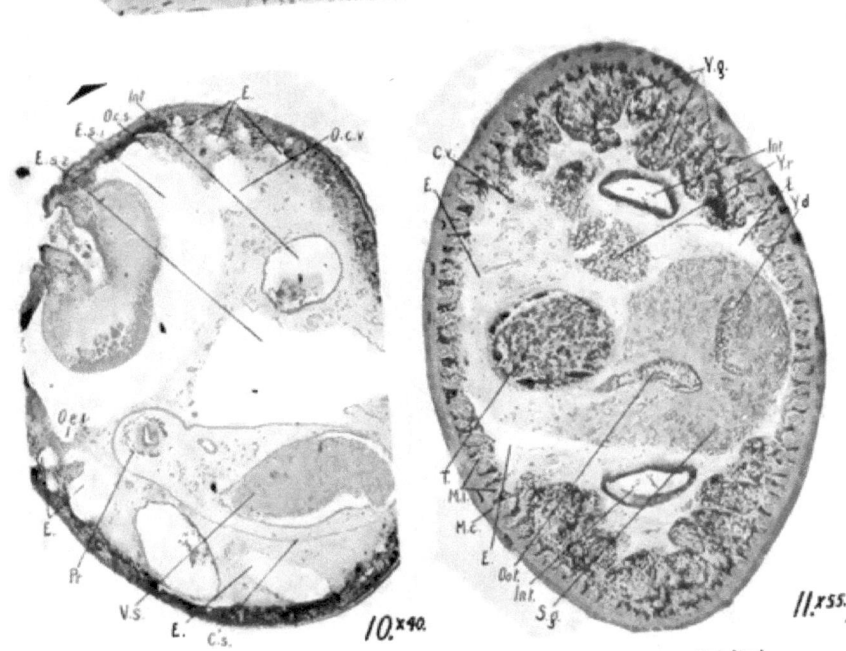

Figs. 9-10, Mehlisia acuminata, sp.n.

Fig. 11, M. acanthochymchi n.sp.

www.ingramcontent.com/pod-product-compliance
Lightning Source LLC
Chambersburg PA
CBHW031342230426
43670CB00006B/419